D1397213

LOBO

GREENS!

TIPS AND TECHNIQUES FOR GROWING YOUR OWN VEGETABLES

KARIN ELIASSON

PHOTOGRAPHY BY CHARLOTTE GAWELL

TRANSLATION BY STINE SKARPNES ØSTTVEIT

SKYHORSE PUBLISHING

Thank you!

Multiple people have helped make this book possible by contributing in various ways to its success.

I would like to give a warm thank you to Mona Wikstrom and the other cultivators in Pungpinans Cultivation Organization in Skarpnack, the cultivators in my neighboring town Villamartin, Johan Nilsson at Skillebyholm, Katharina Angstrom+Isacsson at Wiksund's Garden, Eva Halfworson and Sweden Green House, Rosendal's Garden, as well as Hanna Hofman-Bang for allowing me to dig in their vegetable gardens. It has been fantastic to take part in your gardens and to play around in your plots.

I want to give a special thanks to Elenore Bendel Zahn who took care of my vegetable garden when my own time was not enough, and to Hanna Zetterberg-Struwe who was acting potato harvester. Thanks to you there was harvest.

The birth of a book is the result of an intensive group effort. Thank you Charlotte Gawell and Pernilla Qvist for the beautiful photos and the fine layout that makes the text shine. Eva Marie Westberg—Thank you for your patience and persistent meticulousness. And, naturally, a big thank you to my publisher Susanna Trygve at Norstedts publishing house that accepted the book.

Last, but not least, thank you Lasse, for always being there.

First published by Norstedts Sweden, in 2012 as GRÖNT! ODLA EGNA GRÖNSAKER by Karen Eliasson and Charlotte Gawell. Published by agreement with Norstedts Agency.

10 9 8 7 6 5 4 3 2 1

Library of Congress Cataloging-in-Publication Data
Eliasson, Karin, 1974-
[Grönt! English]
Greens! : tips and techniques for growing your own vegetables / Karin Eliasson ; photography by Charlotte Gawell ; translation by Stine Skarpnes Osttveit.
p. cm.
Includes bibliographical references and index.
ISBN 978-1-62087-729-6 (alk. paper)
1. Vegetable gardening. 2. Organic gardening. I. Gawell, Charlotte. II. Title.
SB324.3.E4313 2013
635--dc23

2013001617

Printed in China

CONTENTS

GROW YOUR OWN VEGETABLES

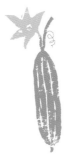

I WAS STANDING ON the brink of a new growing season where everything for the first time was relying on me. I stood there on the edge of the little plot. It was early spring; the clay soil was still cold and wet, grey-brown, and full of promises and challenges. I had an elderly man visiting, one that had done this before. So I asked bluntly, "When do you think I can sow the plot?" He answered that I could start sowing when the soil had settled. "Great," I said. "And when do you think it will settle?" "Well, it shouldn't take too much time. You'll know." "Hmm, exactly how will I know?" I asked stubbornly. "When the heels of your boots no longer sink when you walk on it," he answered in his casual, confident way.

I was hoping for a more specific answer, something along the lines of "The fifth of May." But I was not so lucky. Ultimately, I had to decide when the soil was ready to be worked and sowed. Just me and my boots.

If you're holding this book in your hand, no matter if you're a balcony grower or you own a garden, you are also probably hoping for answers about "when" and "how". You've come to the right place, and you will receive plenty of answers.

It is unavoidable that you will raise your eyebrow from time to time and think that the answers are too vague. This is a natural part of growing vegetables. It is a practice that you first and foremost learn through doing. And this is, at least for me, part of the charm.

A warm wind of newfound farming interest is sweeping Sweden and many other parts of the world. You see the signs everywhere. Flowerbeds are transformed into vegetable gardens, spice pots are on every other kitchen step, balconies are filled with tomato and chili plants, and seed distributors are selling vegetable seeds like never before. Growers meet at conventions, through blogs, and in organizations to exchange ideas and experiences.

This book is part of all this. It was born out of a desire to share all of my knowledge, conclusions, and the joy of harvesting one's own crop. My hope is that it will become a basis for anyone who wants to try growing themselves as well as an inspiration for all of those who've been at it for a while.

There is no such thing as a fully trained farmer. You become a real farmer through growing. But not just growing. You also become a real farmer by being open, curious, and studious. Therefore, conversation and the written word are indispensable. By doing so, you'll advance quickly. You will learn more and more each year that you have a vegetable garden. And for every conversation with a farmer, you'll gather the knowledge of generations. And still there are oceans of tips, ideas, experiences, and new observations to take part in out there. With this book, I wish to be your company, a support, and hopefully a source of inspiration.

Today, my garden grows in the South of Spain. My vegetable garden is part of the small farm I moved to a couple of years back and that is operated today as a bed & breakfast and olive garden. With the Swedish croft and clay soil behind me, I've moved on to a Spanish river bank with warmer soil and a different climate. I have gotten to know *El Levante*—the burning wind from the East and *El Poniente*—the cooling, rain-bearing wind from the West. So far from Sweden, the land has such great differences, and still so many similarities. The beauty of farming experiences is that they don't know national boundaries. You have them with you forever, and they can be utilized almost anywhere in the world.

In this book you are invited into my vegetable garden in Andalusia, this hybrid community of Nordics and Spaniards. However, many images were also taken in Sweden in different farming situations that I still have a part in, or in the gardens of my friends. The book is written with Swedish climate conditions in mind, but many of these techniques can be adapted to suit any climate.

Today, very few Swedes need to grow their own vegetables for survival reasons. We are granted the luxury of cultivating because we want to. So let it be a happy affair! Experiment and play. Browse seeds online, try new varieties, try cultivating Asian seeds, try and see if the small stubby carrots might grow in a large pot on your steps this year, let the lettuce blossom and sow its own seeds, sow radishes in your balcony flower bed, build a bumblebee nest and ask the butterflies to dance in a hedge of verbena among the potatoes.

Grow and Enjoy!

Karin

PLAN YOUR CROP

ALMOST ALL THE VEGETABLES I write about in this book are annuals. Growing annuals is very special. A vegetable garden in a backyard that is otherwise filled with perennial growths becomes much like a stage where new things are constantly happening. There is a creative and somewhat cyclical process in working with vegetables that I enjoy. Each year you have to think how you want it to look; plan, create, maintain, harvest, and then finally turn the soil and rest. This provides room for experimentation and new ideas. You are forgiven if something doesn't succeed. There is always a new season with new possibilities.

Tasting home-grown vegetables often becomes something special. Allowing a vegetable to fully mature on its plant, and then eating it immediately after the harvest gives it a totally different quality from the ones you buy at the store. And when you grow vegetables yourself, you can decide how large you want the vegetable to be before you harvest it. We rarely find baby vegetables in the shops. But in our own gardens we can pick small, fine summer squash; 3-inch long pencil-thin carrots; asparagus tips; mild scallions; or mini cucumbers that you can pickle whole. It is up to us to decide when and how the vegetables should be harvested, creating a customizable bounty to our liking. A true luxury.

Another luxury is the option to choose which vegetables we want to eat. The selection of seeds in Sweden is much greater than the selection of vegetables at the grocery store. This allows the cultivator to have a greater variety on his or her plate—varieties that you may otherwise never have tasted.

Planning is a wonderful part of the cultivation process. When winter is just starting to loosen its grip on nature outside our windows and our tables are filled with seed catalogs, books on cultivation, papers, pens, and rulers, and you sit down with a large cup of tea—that moment is one of the finest. It is the sense of order and control that I most enjoy. But also the knowledge that good planning will save me a lot of work, money, and—most of all—the uncomfortable feeling of never having enough time that you may get during the chaos of high season.

The images on the left: You can easily harvest seeds from certain vegetables. Keep the seeds dry and cool.
Shovel, grip, rake, hoe—not much more needed. Malva (left) and Purple Cranesbill (right).

VEGETABLE GARDEN, CASE, OR POT?

The first question you should ask yourself is how ambitious you wish to be. Cultivation takes time. It's best to face facts and make a realistic estimation of how much time you have to spend on your vegetables. This varies throughout life and across the years, but if you are completely honest with yourself, you can find a compromise between ambitions and reality. If you feel unsure, then start small with a few of your favorite vegetables and let the vegetable garden grow as you go.

It is a good idea to begin the season with the vegetables that need a little more time to develop, or that you can reap over time, such as squash, cucumbers, tomatoes, beans, and lettuces. If you wish, you may expand the selection during summer and sow the vegetables that are best suited for growing in July and August, such as pak choi, celeriac, radishes, red beets, and scallions.

A QUIET PLACE IN THE SUN

The kitchen garden should be in a place that you enjoy spending time and can easily keep an eye on. It may be tempting to use a hidden corner of your garden, but it is rarely practical. If you want to water the vegetables while drinking your morning coffee, it should be close and easy to access. If you need to clean your garden while keeping an eye on the kids, it can't be hidden away. And it's nice to be able to hop outside in the middle of cooking and easily break off a cucumber. In other words, choose a central place for your garden.

Vegetables need both warmth and sun in order to ripen and develop a nice flavor. The vegetable garden should therefore be placed in a sunny spot. With the option of morning sun or evening sun, evening sun is preferable. The soil will then keep warm better overnight.

A wall, a plank, a trellis, a hedge, or a dense set of bushes can protect against harsh winds. If there is no protection against wind in your garden already, you could always grow something that will shield against the worst of the winds. Artichoke, garden cosmos, and corn are examples of growths that are high and dense. Just remember to set up support sticks so they don't fall.

No vegetable wants to grow dry. Makes sure that the patch is well hydrated. Avoid corners that collect puddles from winter snow and ice.

CULTIVATING FOR EVERY ENVIRONMENT

If you grow in the open, this means that you are cultivating an open patch of land. This is safe, as most country kitchens look out over the garden or yard. You can give the garden a sense of space and structure by dividing the patch into squares, rounds, or beds with paths in between. The advantage of this is that it helps show you where you can safely walk to avoid trampling your plants. While it's fine to spread your vegetables around your garden, you can also simply add a separate space reserved only for vegetables—a true vegetable garden. There are many cultivation benefits to growing vegetables in the bed system.

CULTIVATING IN A RAISED BED

Growing in a raised bed means that the growing surface is higher than the surrounding soil. Ever since I first started cultivating, I have used raised beds and I can't think of one single argument against it. The advantages are many: a bed provides an increased depth of loose soil for plant roots; it is easy to work with the plants in the bed without stomping around and disturbing the soil; it is easy to keep the surface free from weeds; the soil can easily drain; and the bed warms up in early spring.

The beds can have any shape you please, but you should be able to easily reach all the plants. This is how you make a raised bed in your garden:

• Measure a patch that you would like to raise and mark it with string.

• Dig out the whole area, deeply (see p. 26 for trenching).

• Then shovel a layer of dirt from the surrounding ground on top of the bed. This way you create a passageway around the entire bed and it automatically heightens a few centimeters.

I am arranging a raised bed with my friend Hanna in her yard.

• If you want, you can later place a frame around the raised bed so that the soil will stay in place. The frame could be made out of wood, stone, metal, brick, or braided willow.

CASE

Cultivating in cases, such as large balcony cases or homemade tree cases, is not a bad idea. A case can have chassis so that it ends up at bench height. The chassis can be a wooden bench, a wall, or a metal stand. Growing in cases is a good alternative for anyone that has difficulty bending down and working on the ground. Furthermore, cases, such as on top of a low stonewall, can be a very beautiful way of framing an outside space. There are no rules as to how a case should look and they often need to be uniquely built. The most important thing is that the chassis is stable, the case well drained, and that the soil is deep enough that the plant will grow.

CULTIVATING IN A POT

If you have a balcony or a terrace it is usually easier to cultivate in pots, which can be a fun challenge.

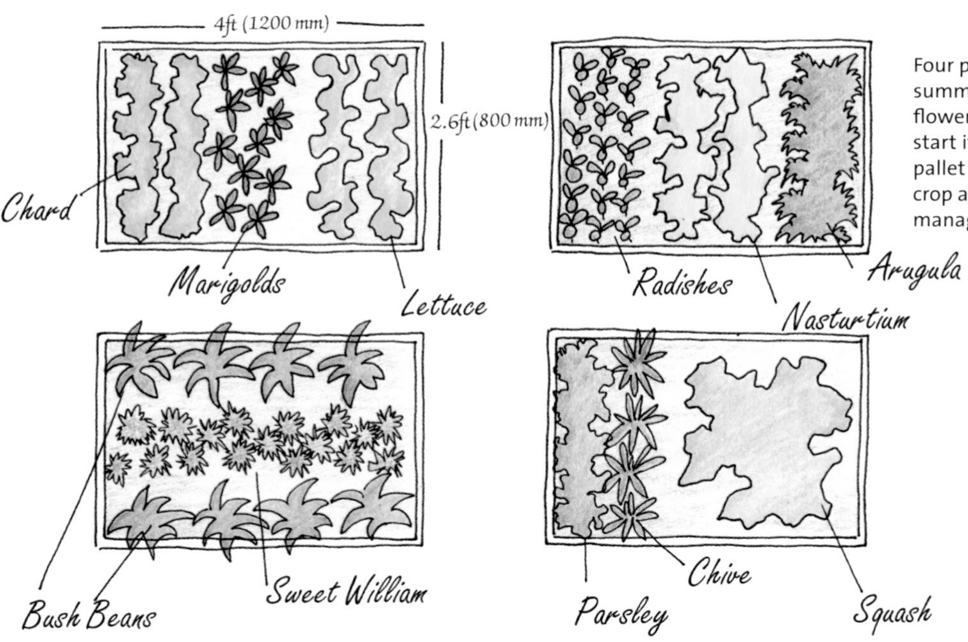

Four pallet frames with summery vegetables and flowers—a simple and good start if you're a beginner. The pallet frames make the small crop attractive and easy to manage.

> *Tip!* *If you're growing vegetables from your balcony, you should choose vegetables that you can harvest continuously, this way you can maximize your use of your growing space. Examples are winter lettuce, chives, mizuna, chard, tomatoes, lettuces, green beans, or squash.*

If you use not only the floor space, but also the walls and railings to hang pots, you can create an impressive vegetable crop on your balcony. It is important to remember that different vegetables need different soil depths. Many leafy vegetables will grow in shallow containers, such as a balcony box, while other plants, like tomatoes, potatoes, squash, and eggplant, will need 15–19 inches (40–50 cm) of soil depth to be comfortable. Always pick good quality soil; it will pay off.

COLD FRAME

Cold frames are part of the Swedish cultivating culture. Cold frames are wooden boxes with a glass lid that can be opened or closed as needed, like a mini greenhouse. They are also called hotbeds because they are used for plants in spring, as the lid protects against the cold. In the summer you can remove the glass, fill the box with manure and soil and use it as a vegetable garden. Box gardens are great tools in cultivating.

WARM FRAME

A warm frame looks like a cold frame, but it has a heating source in the form of fresh manure in the bottom. The frame makes it possible to start cultivating outside in early spring. In the fall, you dig a rectangular pit that is 20 inches (50 cm) deep and close the top of the box. By March, it is usually time to lift the lid and fill the pit with fresh horse manure, straw, and a few thin twigs, and top it with 8 inches (20 cm) of soil. Let it rest so the composting process can begin. Afterwards, you may sow both seedlings and plants that you may plant in the garden later on. The heat from the manure will lessen over time and when summer comes the effect will be gone, but by then you don't need it.

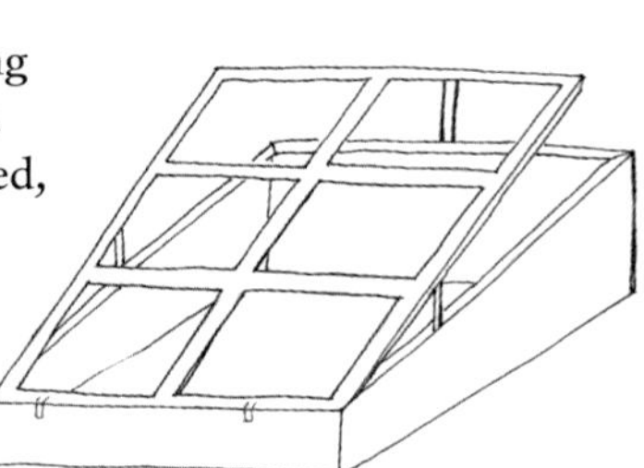

The window should be opened on warm days and should be closed during the nighttime and on cooler days. Some have soil in the bottom of the square and grow plants directly in the soil, while others use a ground cloth in the bottom and use the space for small pots and trays.

A vegetable garden with classical shapes. The center point creates a roomy feel, even though the crop is small.

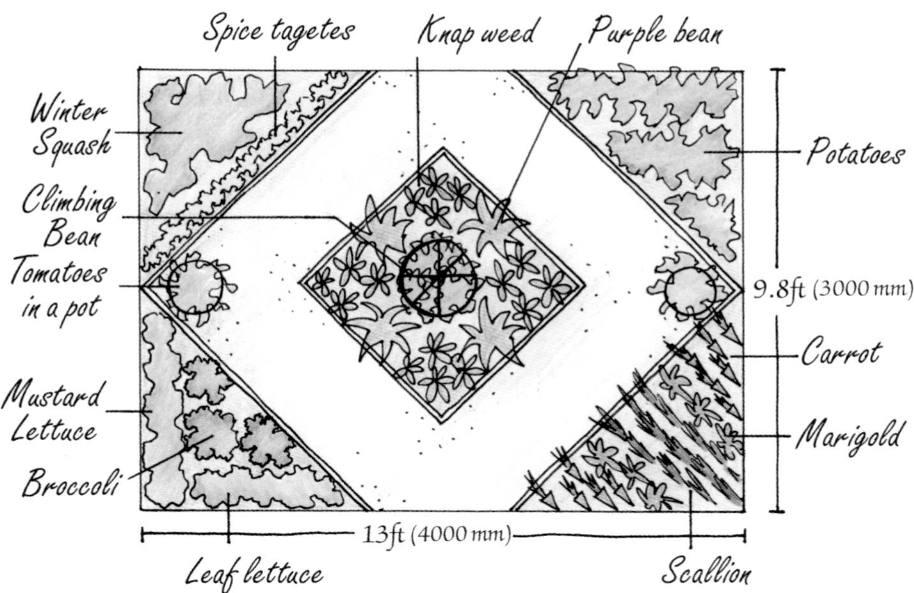

GIVE THE VEGETABLES COMPANY

PERENNIAL GROWTHS GIVE STRUCTURE

Perennial growths create stability and make the framework of a garden, and the vegetable garden in particular. They make the vegetable garden interesting throughout the year and the blossoming season is elongated. Maybe you don't have time to fill your vegetable garden with new vegetables every year. In that case, it might be nice to have a few berry bushes, some flowers, and spices to enjoy and leave the rest of the area with green manure. This way, you keep the whole surface healthy while still looking good.

Suitable perennial growths for the vegetable garden:
currants
gooseberries
blueberries
Blackberries
Aronia
Buckthorn
Roses
Japonica
Raspberries
Rhubarb
Strawberries
Wild Strawberries
Eskimo Raspberries

Perennial nectar-rich flowers:
Aubretia
Poppies
Odor Violet
Birdfoot Deervetch
Pion
Lavender
Oregano
Astrantia
Calamintha
Thyme
Aquilegia
Lyre-flower
Pattys Plum
Kidney-root
Bergamot
Purple Coneflower
New York Aster
Japanese Anemone
Orpine Geranium

OCEANS, LE POTAGER, AND THE VEGETABLE GARDEN—BE INSPIRED

One way of gaining inspiration and ideas for your vegetable garden is travel. You may travel within Sweden, to other countries, and to other times. If you look back in history you can see how the Swedish vegetable gardens have been very structured, multifaceted, and filled with all kinds of vegetables and flowers for hundred of years. Marigold, Cress, and Tagetes have been a standard part of kitchen gardens not only for their beauty, but also because flowers with a strong scent are assumed to deter vermin.

Farther south in Europe, gardeners have been even more consistent with their combination of vegetables and flowers. In France, the renaissance ideal is still followed with growing squares with beautiful straight lines of boxwood, apples on trellis, or Teucrium. They mix fruit trees, ornamental plants, berry bushes, and vegetables in what they call potager.

In English vegetable gardens—inspired by the Arts and Crafts movement—the vegetables are also mixed with ornamental plants. The beds are allowed to deviate from the strict renaissance squares and have a more organic, soft shape, bordered by braided willow or flexible planks.

You can also look to Denmark to get plenty of ideas. The Danish garden bears elements of the French tradition, but it is more rampant.

Spice growths, buxbom, boxwood, Morus, and potato patches are intermingled with meadows of annual and perennial flowers. These

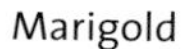
Marigold

Strawberries make fine frames for the vegetable garden.

Japanese Rose

pieces of art are great sources of inspiration for your vegetable garden.

Favorite annual flowers for the vegetable garden:
Nasturtium
Wadding
Cornflower
Marigold
Flossflower
Verbena
Garden Cosmos
Rudbeckia
Malva
Sweet William
Spice Tagetes
Sunflower

CHOOSING VEGETABLES

Now it's time to start thinking about which vegetables to choose. This depends mostly on taste and preference. You should obviously start out with the vegetables you like and look beautiful.

Many travel a lot during summer and in that case it may be practical to choose vegetables that grow quickly so you can harvest them before you leave for vacation or sow them after you come back. If you have small children, it can be good to choose vegetables that are easily maintained and robust enough to keep for a long time, or that may be fun for the kids to help with.

Quick-growing vegetables
Leaf Lettuce
Arugula
Brown Mustard
Scallion
Mangold
Spinach
Summer-carrots
Radishes
Sweet Peas

Cultivating with kids is fun. Children can be just as happy to find a ladybug among the beans as they will when they find an actual bean, this is a refreshing perspective. When you let go of the strict boundaries and typical notions of how a vegetable garden should look or what it should contain, a world opens where flowers go on parade, and where birdbaths and beetles reside among the carrots. The vegetable garden could become the most beautiful and exciting part of your garden.

Fun to grow for children:
Pumpkin
Squash
Corn
Tomatoes
Mouse Melon
Radishes
Red Beet
Potatoes

CLIMATE

Other factors that influence the choice of vegetables is, of course, the kind of soil you sow in and the climate where you live. From Southern to Northern Sweden, the cultivating season varies by multiple months. In the North and inland, it's colder for a longer period of time, while the never-ending sunlight during the summer in the north of Sweden compensates, to some degree, for the slow start. There are therefore no set answers to what you may grow and what you can't.

In the garden world we often speak of cultivation zones. Sweden is divided into eight zones, where zone 1 has the mildest climate and zone 8

Some planning makes the garden easy to maintain.

the coldest. When it comes to growing trees, bushes, and perennials, the zone divisions are very helpful. But for annual vegetables, these zones don't apply. The option to create microclimates in an otherwise unfriendly terrain makes it possible to sow vegetables where you least expect it.

In the vegetable section on page 51 you can find the most recommended sowing times between certain dates. The earliest date refers to the warmer climates and the latest for colder climates. In certain instances I am very particular about how dates relate to certain geographical areas. It is difficult to give advice that applies to the entire country, but here are a few general rules for cultivating in Northern Sweden, and other colder climates:

- Choose vegetable varieties with a short development time. The different varieties may vary with multiple weeks—it is usually specified on the seed packets.
- For vegetables that need heat like tomatoes, eggplants, and bell peppers, you need a greenhouse, glass veranda or plastic protection.
- Daylight gives many vegetables an extra kick, while others, such as Asian cabbage and leafy greens will get stressed and grow too fast.
- Create as much warmth as possible during cultivation through, for instance, warming stonewalls, heightened beds, warming benches, and greenhouses.
- Never be afraid to try the things that "don't work." Someone has to be the first to make it work.

A RICH SELECTION OF SEEDS

The selection of seeds is a jungle. Still, this is nothing compared to the seed catalogues during the 1800s. During the 1900s, the seed selection decreased radically. In order to maintain the diversity we still have today and not let it diminish even more, we need to keep as much variety in our cultivating as possible. We all need to contribute—professional cultivators as well as vegetable consumers—and of course, all hobby-cultivators.

Vary your seed purchases and don't be afraid to try varieties you haven't tried before. Welcome both new and old culture varieties.

Nasturtium
Pak Choi
Kale
French Marigold
Red Cabbage
Cauliflower
Dill
Cosmos
Mangold Beetroot
Common Bean
Parsley
Corn
Brown Daisy
Cucumber
Broad Bean
Lettuce
18ft (5500 mm)
Calamintha
Low pea
Leaf Salad
Tall Sugar Pea
23ft (7000 mm)

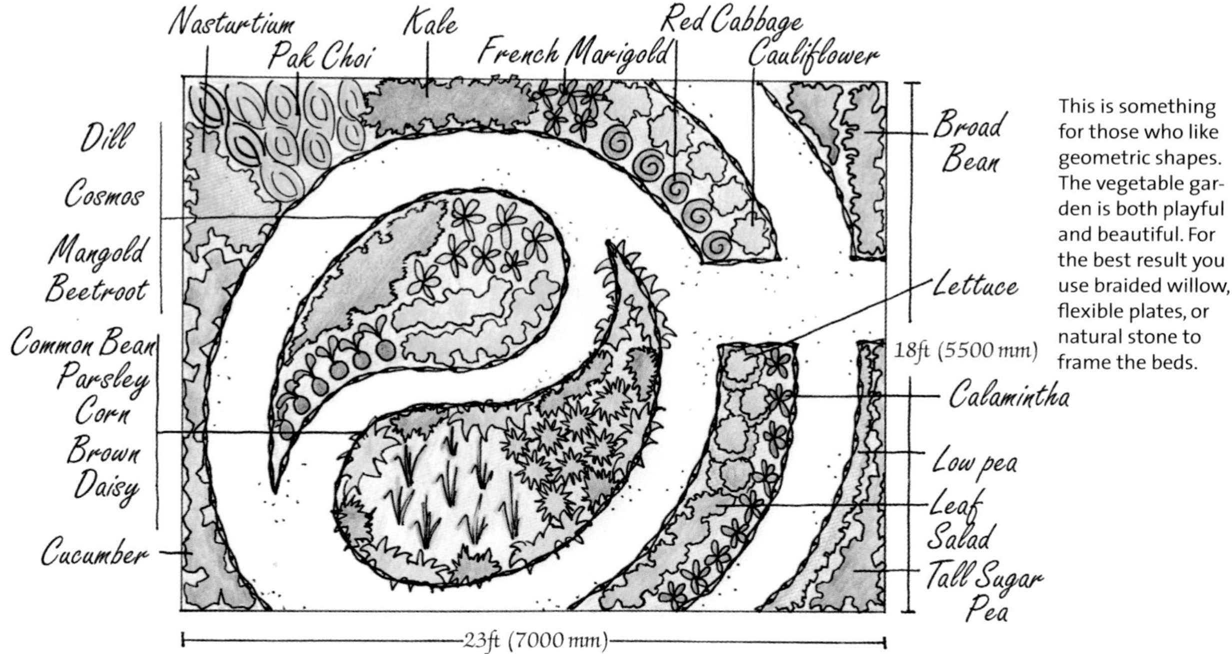

This is something for those who like geometric shapes. The vegetable garden is both playful and beautiful. For the best result you use braided willow, flexible plates, or natural stone to frame the beds.

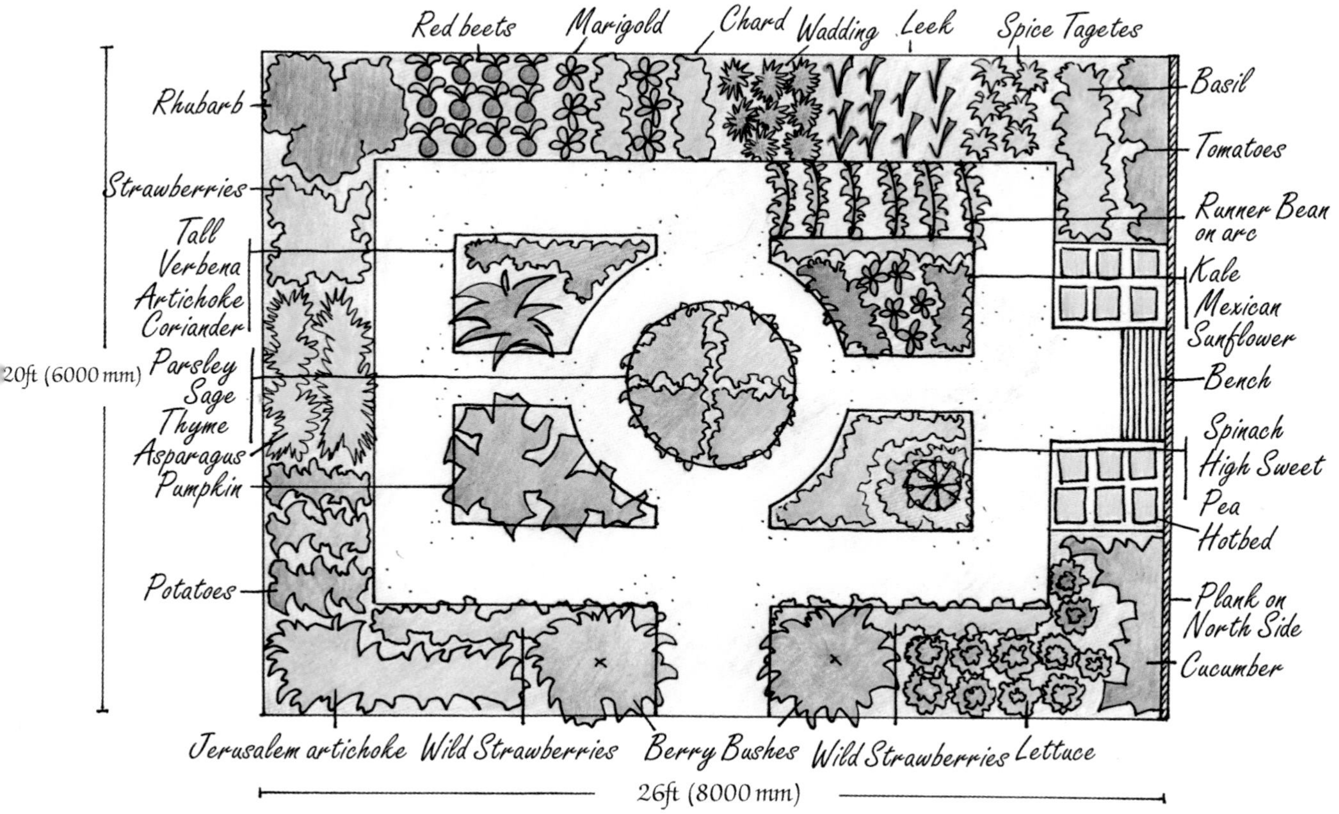

Red beets
Marigold
Chard
Wadding
Leek
Spice Tagetes
Rhubarb
Strawberries
Tall Verbena
Artichoke
Coriander
20ft (6000 mm)
Parsley
Sage
Thyme
Asparagus
Pumpkin
Potatoes
Basil
Tomatoes
Runner Bean on arc
Kale
Mexican Sunflower
Bench
Spinach
High Sweet Pea
Hotbed
Plank on North Side
Cucumber
Jerusalem artichoke
Wild Strawberries
Berry Bushes
Wild Strawberries
Lettuce
26ft (8000 mm)

A rich garden with an elegant, organized layout. A luxurious kitchen garden with a beautiful entrance, a patio, hotbeds, and sufficient space for sowing.

A LIVING VEGETABLE GARDEN

Today, growing organic is a given for most hobby-cultivators. When we stay away from chemicals and artificial fertilizer, we are gentler with nature and spare it from substances that are poisonous and hard to break down. That is a good thing.

But avoiding pesticides does not automatically make our gardens well-balanced and fresh. We will have to keep dealing with attacks and vermin. No matter how much we wish for it to be different, it is a fact that sickness and vermin is part of cultivating. That doesn't mean, however, that we are just supposed to stand by and watch this happen. Vermin and disease must and can be tackled in organic cultivation as well. The difference is that we do it with products that protect the ecological system. Eco-friendly cultivation is all about understanding the ecological balance, giving it space, and knowing how to utilize it during the growing process.

At the far back of the book there is a chapter about problems that may occur during cultivation. There you will find advice as to how you can deal with various attacks when they arise.

Much of the work that goes into having a vegetable garden with fresh growths is about preventing problems and making sure that the soil and cultivation is flush with life and nurtured. The next section is about prevention.

CROP ROTATION

Crop rotation is the practice of growing different types of crops in the same area in sequential seasons. All growths have different deep-root systems that affect the soil in different ways. In other words, they get their nutrients from different layers in the soil and loosen the soil at different depths. Not all growths soak up as much nutrition from the soil or the same amount of various nutrients. When you allow the vegetables to rotate, it helps replenish nutrients in the soil and will keep your crops healthy over the years.

Another upside of crop rotation is that it reduces the risk of infections lingering in the soil. Plants that belong to the same species are often vulnerable to the same diseases. Through keeping species together in your garden, and then changing the place for the entire group each year, you reduce the risk that infections will continue to live in the soil because without host plants, the infections will fade and eventually die.

If you cultivate a lot it may be helpful to create a crop rotation chart—a plan for how the various vegetable groups will move around the vegetable garden through the years. It's ideal to let four years pass before a vegetable group is back in the same spot. If you have a small vegetable garden, it might be helpful to stick to such a rule. My advice is first and foremost to consider three things:

- Be especially meticulous with the potato family and kale family as they are host plants for diseases that can live for a long time in the soil. Make sure that those crops change places every year, or skip them in certain years.
- Use pots, boxes, or sacks for cultivation some seasons, to let the soil in the ground rest from certain growths now and then. Potatoes and tomatoes, for instance, will grow just fine in a hackensack.
- Even if you do not follow an exact schedule, keep rotation and variety in mind. Vary what you grow and where you grow it. If you only make that a routine, much is already done.

The vegetable family divisions in this book:

The cucumber family:
Pumpkin
Squash
Cucumber

Sunflower family:
Mizuna
Arugula
Mustard Greens
Komatsuna
Pak Choi
Choy Sum
Broccoletti
Broccoli
Cauliflower
Turnip
Black Radish
Garden Radish
Chinese Cabbage

Pea growths:
Peas
Beans

Chenopodioideae:
Spinach
Red Beet
Chard

Potato family:
Potato
Tomato
Bell Pepper
Eggplant
Chili

Parsley family:
Carrot
Parsnip
Fennel
Celeriac
Celery
Dill
Parsley
Coriander

Sunflower family:
Artichoke
Cardoon
Lettuces

Onion growths:
Red Onion
Yellow Onion
Shallots
Garlic
Leeks
Scallion
Chives

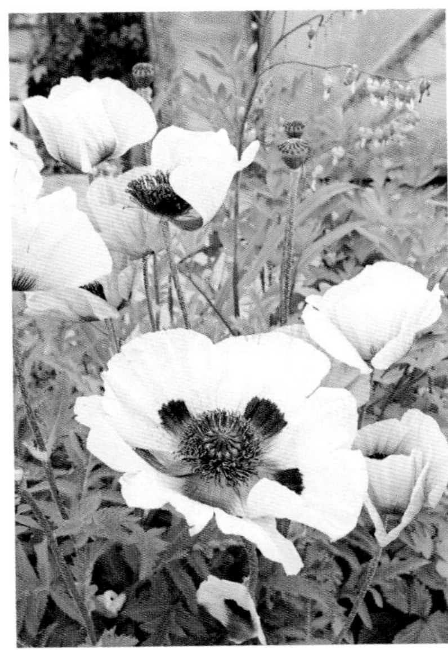

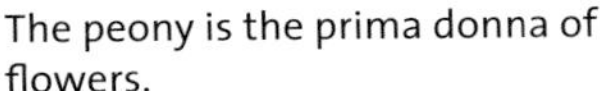
The peony is the prima donna of flowers.

My fertilizer station

The perennial giant poppy has seed heads as beautiful as its flowers.

FRIENDS IN THE VEGETABLE GARDEN

Even though we may not always realize, when we work with our vegetable garden, we work with various insects, soil organisms, and small animals that aid us in different ways. There are multiple things we can do to make these helpers comfortable and they will be even more useful.

Soil life

The soil inhabits everything from earthworms to beetles, woodlice, fungi, and bacteria. They air the soil, transform dead material into nutritious material, balance pH, and transport minerals from the deeper soil layers to the surface. Furthermore, they fight damaging fungi and bacteria. In other words, they are both grunt workers and soldiers for the well being of the growths and they are completely irreplaceable. Here are a few simple things you can do to protect soil life:

• Use organic fertilizer. It increases the amount of nutrients in the soil and provides food for many soil organisms.

• Add compost to the soil regularly. The compost brings many important organisms, fungi, and bacteria that help the soil.

• Cover cultivate with fresh growth material like grass and green fertilizer. This keeps the soil moist and rich and it feeds, among others, worms and woodlice.

• Cover open soil with straw, leafs, or green fertilizer over winter. This makes a protective cover and ensures that the spring organisms will have access to food.

On p. 23 you can read more about soil improvement, compost, and cover cultivation.

Small animals

There are also many small animals that may help keep the garden clean.

Small birds are great at picking larvae and snails, as well as capturing all kinds of insects. To make the birds comfortable, you should keep some thorny bushes nearby, perhaps hawthorn or sloes. Your garden will also grow quite popular if you feed the birds during winter and set up birdhouses.

Tip! *If the ladybugs have difficulty finding your vegetable garden you can order a gang of them online. Search for businesses that provide products for biological pest control.*

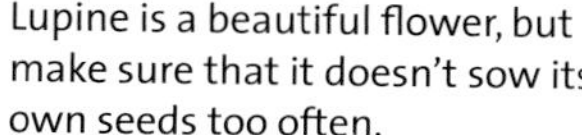

Lupine is a beautiful flower, but make sure that it doesn't sow its own seeds too often.

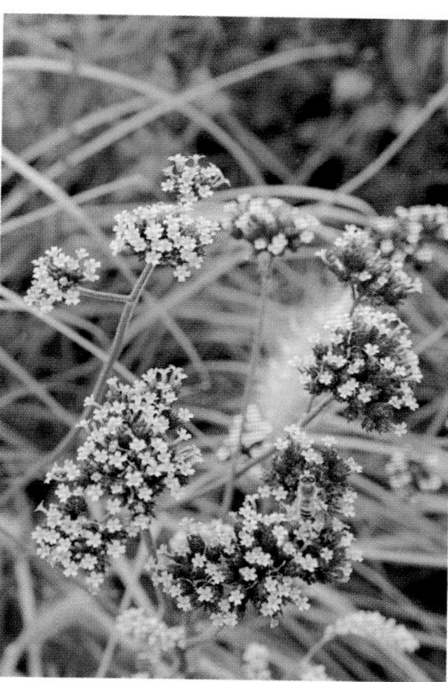

Large Verbena stands firm through heavy winds and it blossoms far into the fall months.

I cover the beds with straw as part of the soil covering.

Hedgehogs like snails of all kinds. However, they can be quite shy and they need unkempt terrain in the garden like piles of leaves and hidden log stacks where they can live. But if you manage to get a hedgehog family to feel comfortable on your land, be careful with them, they are excellent hunters.

If you have a pond in your garden, frogs and toads will usually show up. They belong to the snail patrol as well and definitely lend a service to the vegetable garden.

Hunting insects

Ladybugs are diligent aphid hunters. Both the larvae and the grown ladybug lives off of aphids. This is effective enough that ladybugs are actually used as biological pest control on larger crops.

Green lacewings, true bugs, vespidae, and earwigs are other insects that keeps the amount of, among others, thrips, aphid, and larvae down.

Hoverflies are always welcome. They are completely harmless and they help keep the garden clean. The larvae of hoverflies eat aphid. The fully grown hoverfly sucks nectar and pollen from flowers.

Bumblebees, bees, and butterflies

Many plants in the vegetable garden need help with pollination in order for them to develop their fruit. Therefore, all kinds of flying insects looking for pollen and nectar are indispensable when cultivating. Aside from the hoverfly, bees and bumblebees are the most diligent out of all the insects. Including islands or rows of flowers in your vegetable garden is therefore not just visually appealing, but also functional as it attracts pollen-seeking insects.

The flowers should have a strong scent, be colorful, preferably in red-yellow or violet, and of course contain nectar. In choosing flowers for your vegetable garden, the rule of thumb is that the old-fashioned varieties are better than the modern and refined. This is related to scent and nectar content, which is not always emphasized in modern flower refinement.

Butterflies will show up as an extra bonus once you fill your vegetable garden with fragrant and colorful flowers. They spread joy, and, to a certain extent, they can also contribute to pollination.

TIP!

Plan your garden so that there are spring- and fall-blossoming herbs, bushes, and trees near the vegetable garden. This way you lengthen the season and the animals thrive and will be in place once the aphid and larvae attack the vegetable garden.

GET STARTED!

HARVESTING VEGETABLES REQUIRES a variety of preparations and effort, from digging and fertilizing to tying it all together. In this section, I will go through all the practicalities of cultivating, step by step, as well as why we need to do it and the easiest way to attack the tasks at hand. It is intended to be used as a guide and is a blend of science, tried experiences from generations of cultivators, and my own personal advice and tips. And where should this practical journey begin if not in the soil?

SOIL

Working with soil is a rewarding part of gardening work, as every minute you invest will be repaid. It can be heavy, tiring, and unbelievable bothersome—but also unbelievably meaningful. This is where you lay the groundwork for all the nice things to come.

Good soil is a basic requirement for a successful harvest. How much energy you put into buying seeds, sowing, and other preparations won't matter if you ultimately do not have well-functioning and healthy soil to set the plants in. When a plant is allowed to develop fine roots, not only will it give a nice crop, it will also manage stress better, including drought, diseases, and hard weather. Good soil makes strong plants.

SOIL GOOD FOR CULTIVATION

Underneath the surface of the ground there is a whole world, a mini-universe, of various materials, elements, and organisms that we gardeners need to make use of and work with. The first step is to understand that dirt is more than the strip of grime left under your fingernails after a days work.

All dirt consists of minerals and humus, in various proportions. Minerals are nothing but broken-down stone and we usually see it in the form of clay, sand, or gravel. Humus is broken-down organic material like animal waste, bones, hair, leaves, grass, and branches. Minerals and humus make a framework in the ground that becomes the home of many microorganisms and fungi that contributes to a constant decomposition of organic material and transport of nutritious elements.

Good soil can vary in appearance, it may contain much or little sand and clay, be reddish-brown or greyish-brown, have a compost fragrance or a more metallic one. However, all good soil has certain characteristics in common: they are airy and permeable, nutrient-rich, moist, and rich in microlife.

To create soil with these characteristics, you need to put in hard work. Few earth patches are perfect to begin with. But they can all become good. It just demands patience and the knowledge of how to proceed.

How to make the perfect cultivation soil depends on what you have to work with. The following is a description of the three most common earth-types that you find in a typical Swedish garden, how you recognize them, and how you go about improving them.

MUDDY SOILS

Muddy soil is usually heavy and wet, dense, and hard to work with. If you roll a moist piece of soil in your hand you will get a sticky ball that is smooth and even. The clay particles are tiny and hold together tightly. They give lots and lots of nourishment and they have a great ability to hold water, which are good traits. But if the soil consists only of clay, the water-containing trait will soon become a problem for the plants, as they also need acid for their root systems.

Muddy soils need to be aired out. If you imagine the clay soil as a dough—compact, sticky, and heavy, we need to add something that has the function of yeast, something that forces air particles in between the clay particles and makes the earth rise and dry a little. Humus serves this purpose. The humus will push clay particles apart and create pockets of air in the soil, and as a result, the soil will also heat up and the root systems will establish more easily. I give examples of various humus materials below.

SANDY SOILS

Sandy soil is in many ways the opposite of muddy soil. The sand grains are too large to stick together, the soil feels gritty, and when you attempt to roll a ball it will fall apart. This kind of soil has trouble holding water and nutriments. Everything just runs off of the sand grains. There is, however, a lot of air, which makes the soil light and easy to work with. You will need to add something that will help bind the sand grains together and that will work as putty in the soil.

Humus is best for this soil as well. The humus has a spongy way of holding water and can also store nutriments. In sandy soil the humus will fill the large air pockets between the grains, and make sure that the pockets are filled with nutrients and water.

Finely ground stone dust may also be added to sandy soils to contribute with smaller mineral particles with the traits of clay. The easiest way is to blend the stone dust and humus together and then add it to the soil.

HUMUS SOILS

Certain soils contain more humus than minerals, although they are not as common. This is often old peat land that has been plowed up and used. They can be good growth soils, nutritious and humectant, but they will often have an excessive capacity to hold water. You should therefore be very meticulous about draining so that extra water will seep out of the crop. If you experience that the Humus soil is too spongy, you can add stone dust or rough sand to the soil to create a better texture. Soils that are rich in peat should be kept medium moist at all times; if it dries out it may be hard to make it humid all the way through again. You therefore need to be meticulous about watering the soil during dry periods if you are dealing with this kind of soil.

SOIL IMPROVEMENT

Once you know what kind of soil you have in your garden or in your allotment and you know which traits you need to improve, it is time to choose the improvement material. Here I describe the most common materials that are the easiest to find and that I like to work with. They are all completely natural and are either humus-based or rich in minerals.

HUMUS

Humus is magical! Something you may have realized by now. Humus provides soil with many beneficial traits, such as the ability to hold moisture, elasticity, airiness, nutrients, and food for microorganisms. If you have muddy or sandy soil to begin with, you can never really add too much humus. But it can be a good idea to vary the kind of humus you use, just to make the soil as healthy as possible.

Certain soil-improvement agents are very nutritious, whereas others will only give structure. You need to take this into consideration to make sure that the soil is not overly fertilized. Feel free to blend nutrient-rich humus with something else to create balance, such as manure and bark humus.

Bark humus
Is composted bark. Dark brown humus works well in all kinds of soil, but is especially good for muddy soil.

Peat humus
Is clean peat from bogs. It is a finite natural resource that should be used with care. It has a natural low pH level and holds moisture well, although it will reject water if it is completely dry. It is important to work it deep in with the soil so that it doesn't end up on the surface and dries out. It works best with sandy soils.

Compost
Is blended decomposed organic material. It may be the best soil enhancer there is and definitely the least expensive. It adds microorganisms and balances out the pH level in the soil. Compost also works as a light fertilizer.

Leaf compost
Is leaves that are decomposed into humus. A cheap and great soil enhancer for all kinds of soils.

Manure
Usually consists of cow and horse manure. It has to be composted at least a year before you use it. Burnt manure is the same as composted. It is great for the soil, but very rich in nutriments and should be used with this in mind.

Straw
First and foremost, decomposed straw makes a fine and nutritious soil enhancer. It is very good for muddy soils and great for the bugs in the soil.

MINERALS

Minerals of various kinds may be from a stone-crusher. You can also request the exact size (fraction) you wish to receive. You may also buy stone dust in bags at specialty trade farms.

Rough sand
Is a good addition to muddy soil in order to make it airier and increase its elasticity and firmness. Use size 0–8 mm or larger. When you add sand to muddy soil, you need to mix the sand with a soil enhancer, such as bark humus, before you add it to the soil. This makes it easier to work it in with the soil.

Stone dust
Adds minerals to the soil, creates airiness and increases its ability to bind water. It works well to enhance the structure of all kinds of soils. If you wish to improve muddy soil, you should use a stone dust with fraction 0–11 mm, or bigger. If you are working with sandy soil you should instead add a finely grained stone dust. Humus soils benefit from both.

SOIL IN A BAG

We are often advised to buy soil. This may be for the purposes of planting in large pots or balcony cases. There is a wealth of various soil brands on the market, as well as many specialty soils. I recognize that in certain situations there is indeed reason to buy a specialty soil. This is first and foremost true for sowing, and for soil that is meant for larger growing cases.

A sowing soil should be clean, lean, and airy. These are the basics in order for the seeds to grow and for the roots to establish. If you don't have the option of blending a good soil, then buying might be a good choice.

If you grow in large pots or other kinds of cases, the demands of the soil are especially high. It should be able to maintain an airy and fine structure all through summer, as well as hold nutrients and water efficiently. Cheap planting soils, which are mostly a combination of chopped peat and sand, do not have any of these qualities and they will collapse after just a few weeks. A successful potted crop is worth investing in soil that is well-made and suited for growing in larger cases. Ask at the market-garden what they offer.

WORKING THE SOIL—DIGGING, TILLING, AIRING, FORKING, OR JUST LET IT BE

Mechanically working with the soil is another way to give it structure. With a shovel, garden fork, hoe, and rake we can open the soil surface, finely spread lumps, turn layers of soil, and blend in soil enhancers. The choice of tools and various techniques will yield different results depending on the soil.

DIGGING

Digging is a powerful way of breaking the soil up. The goal is to create air pockets, which will make it easier to add soil enhancers. Digging has no value in itself; it is rather something we do if the soil is unable to stay loose and airy on its own.

Heavier soils with a lot of clay are usually in need of digging. It is best to dig these in the fall. The winter frost will later break the clay particles so that they collapse and create a lovely crumbly loam when they thaw, which makes it easy to mull manure in with the soil.

You should always keep in mind that digging is a rather brutal way of treating soil, you turn the soil-life upside down. This is no great concern in spring or summer, but in the fall, you should remember that many of the organisms move to the lower layers of the soil to stay away from the cold. Dig your vegetable garden before the cold sets in so that the sensitive soil life doesn't freeze to death.

There is usually no need to dig sandy soils; it might be better to use a garden fork.

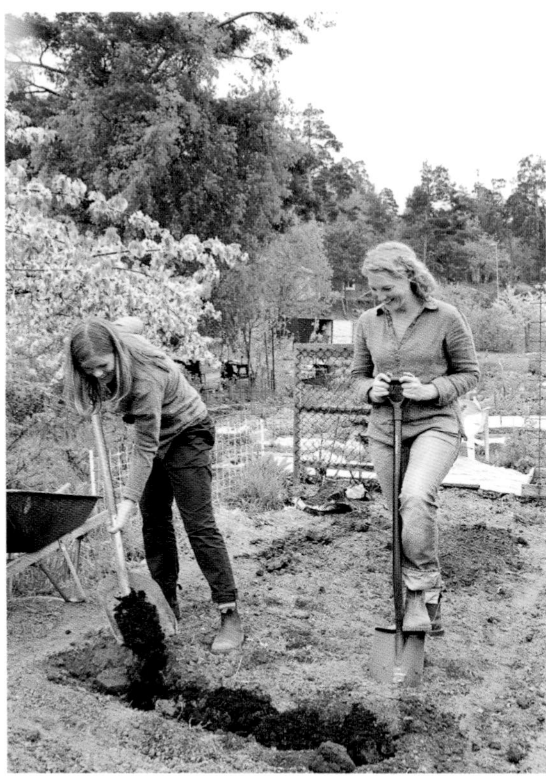

Deep digging at Hanna's new garden to give the crop a great head start.

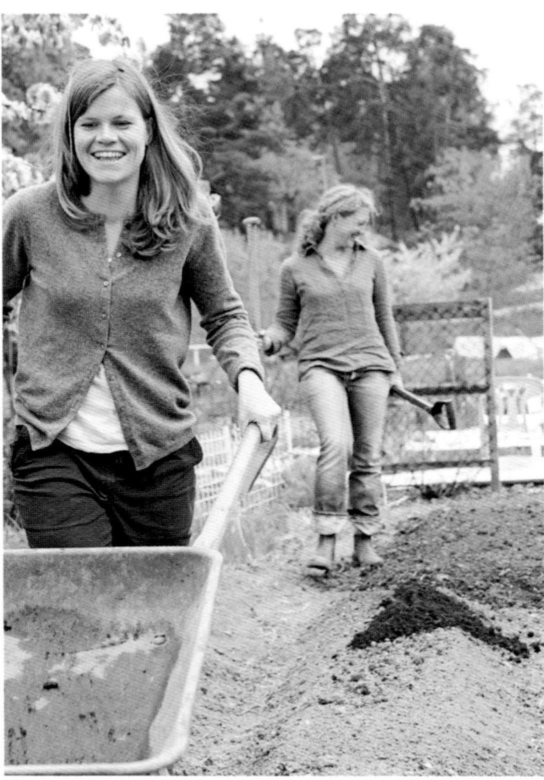

Tough jobs are more fun and easier when there are two of you.

DEEP DIGGING

Deep digging is a technique used to loosen and improve the soil down deep. This is a good way to take care of a new patch of earth where you wish to establish a crop. You give your crop the best possible start. But you may also use this technique when you wish to revitalize your vegetable garden and give it a detox. This is what you do:

• Mark the area you wish to dig. Start in one end and dig a rut along one edge. The soil you remove is placed aside on tarp.

• Fork the soil at the bottom of the rut to loosen it up.

Tip! When you are digging you should always work sideways and backwards. This is practical, as you should not walk where you have been digging. First and foremost it is psychologically better to see what you have accomplished and not what you still have left.

• Place a layer of well-composted horse manure or compost in the rut. You may also use a blend of bark humus, cow manure from a bag, leaf compost . . . whatever soil enhancers you have. A fourth of a wheel barrel is usually enough for a 6½ foot (2 meter) long rut.

• Then you work your way backwards throughout the whole patch. You dig a new rut next to the last and use the earth you've dug up as a top layer on the previous rut over the compost/ manure. Fork through the top layer a couple of times so that the soil and compost blend.

• When you are finished digging, forking, fertilizing, and refilling the entire marked area, the deep digging is complete and you have a perfectly aerated and soil enhanced cultivation surface.

FORKING

I really enjoy forking. It is basically sticking a garden fork in the soil and pulling it back and forth, twisting it around, or even digging with the fork. Forking is somewhat more gentle on the soil life than digging with a shovel. Not to mention the fact that it is not as heavy. Sometimes you will want to air or loosen the soil a little without having to turn everything inside out, for instance, if you want to use sandy soil in springtime. In such instances you can thrust the fork into the soil, pull the handle towards you and then pull the fork back up. You continue by sticking it down right next to the soil you just lifted and so on. If you work your way through an entire patch this way, it will be nicely aired at about 10 inches (25 cm) deep.

Using a garden fork is always great for removing larger weeds. The garden fork gets around the roots and therefore is able to get a better hold of the weeds than a shovel would.

HARROWING

The best way to loosen the soil is to use a harrow. This is a shaft with three or five claws attached that you pull through the soil. It is unbelievably practical when you are folding in manure in springtime or harrowing between vegetables. But it is important to be careful. The more the vegetables grow, the more important it becomes to be careful so that you don't pull the root systems.

MILLING

Milling means using a machine to efficiently chop the soil so that it falls apart. Right after milling you will have the most fantastic soil structure and sowing surface; fine and smooth. But milling is ruthless on worms and other animals and it may also be too hard on muddy soil. You won't be able to notice this before it rains and the clay will pack together even tighter than before.

My advice is to shy away from milling if you are working with small surfaces and could just as well work by hand. If you, on the other hand, are working with surfaces that are large enough that a machine is necessary, the milling can be of help in preparing the soil during spring. The result is always best if you add fine manure or compost so that the crushed soil is blended with humus.

CULTIVATING WITHOUT WORKING ON THE SOIL

Many cultivating-enthusiasts are engaged in cultivating without digging. The theory is basically that you should allow microorganisms to do the job instead of going out there and digging yourself. This way, the organisms may do this at their own pace and natural rhythm. Instead of disrupting the soil life through mechanic influences, you stimulate it by adding soil enhancers and fertilizer over the surface. And then, little by little, the bugs will pull it down to the deeper layers and the soil will automatically become looser and well worked. This is not a new method or theory; on the contrary, it has been practiced by cultivators throughout history. It is definitely worth a try. My personal experience is that it works best if you have a healthy soil to begin with, that contains rich microlife and a decent soil structure. If so, you may save a lot of time and effort through using this method and you will still end up with a good result.

FERTILIZER

Vegetables use a lot of energy during a growth season. And if the energy is used, it will also need to be replaced with, in this case, water and nutrients. Nutrition is important for plants for a variety of reasons. Certain nutrients helps build the plant itself, while others are needed to keep the life of the plant going, like oxygen, liquid uptake, and photosynthesis.

Through fertilizing regularly with natural fertilizers like manure, stone dust, bone meal, or nettle water, you can make sure that the soil is always packed with the nutrients the plants will need. All of these fertilizers also help build soil structure and a rich microlife, while they contribute nutrition. If you use store-bought manure, which is sometimes called artificial manure or NPK, you'll add some nutrients, but nothing else. It is like giving the plants injections with nutrients instead of food. Furthermore, organic fertilizers are a cheap form of nutrition. You can make compost and organic liquid fertilizers on your own, and you can often get horse manure for free from stables that wish to get rid of some of theirs.

Tip! *Consider how nature prefers to fertilize: some weathered minerals, some decomposed plants, and some old animal waste. Use stone meal, compost, and horse manure. It doesn't have to be harder than that.*

BASE FERTILIZATION

In order to give the plants a good beginning, or solid breakfast, you need to do a base fertilization. This is the fertilizer you add, usually in springtime, when you are preparing your soil. The base fertilizer should fill the soil with a wide spectrum of nutrients and minerals.

Manure and compost are irreplaceable as base fertilizers. They are rich in humus and have a well-balanced nutrient content, as well as fungi and bugs. If you choose only to use compost then add a little extra, as it is not as rich in nutrients as manure. Furthermore, it could be good to add a type of fertilizer that is rich in minerals like stone meal, crushed seashells, or Algomin.

How much you should add depends on how much you have available and how strong the fertilizer is. But as a general rule of thumb, a 1–2 inch (2–5 cm) thick layer over the soil surface is about right. Mull the fertilizer in with the top 4 inches (10 cm) of soil, and worm organisms and other bugs will blend it in the deeper layers as it goes.

SUPPORTING FERTILIZATION

In addition to the base fertilization, there is a need for multiple snacks, suppers, and late-night sandwiches before the plant ultimately falls asleep in the fall. These additional meals are called supporting fertilization or continuous fertilization and here you may vary between different kinds of fertilizers.

If you are working with a very light and sandy soil, supporting fertilization is crucial as the soil has little ability to hold nutrients on its own.

How much you should fertilize depends on the type of growth and the type of fertilizer. There will often be directions on the package. Do not overdose, as it doesn't help with anything. Some growths do not need support fertilization while others will need a couple of rounds to keep up the strength to continue carrying crops all through summer. I will write more detailed advice in the vegetable chapters.

All fertilizer added during the growth season should just be lightly mulled in the top layer of the soil, so that the roots of the plants are not damaged. It will eventually leak down to the roots with the help of small transporters in the form of worms and bugs.

The garden becomes popular when you have just fertilized with bone meal.

GREEN FERTILIZATION

Green fertilization is the process of growing plants just for the benefit of the soil; a detox for the soil. All green plants produce a lot of plant mass, leaves, and stems that will be turned in with the soil as a soil enhancer after the growth season. In certain instances you can even cut the plant multiple times and use the green mass as a cover fertilizer on the rest of the crop.

Some green fertilizer growths, such as clover and legumes, have the ability to fixate nitrogen by cooperating with nitrogen-fixating bacteria in the soil. The ability to fixate nitrogen is at its strongest right before they blossom. At this point, you cut the plants, which are packed with nutrients, and fold them in with the soil. Common peas are terrific to grow as a green fertilizer, but it may be hard to combine the fertilization with a crop. In order for the peas to be effective as a fertilizer, they need to be harvested before they develop pea pods.

Other green fertilizer growths, such as broad beans and sweet clover, are first and foremost effective because their sturdy root systems process and loosen the soil down deep, as well as pull nutrients and minerals upwards to the surface layer where other plants may reach them.

Some of my favorites of the green fertilizers, such as crimson clover and Phacelia, have beautiful flowers that attract many bugs and butterflies. If you let them blossom, just remember to cut them before they develop seeds to avoid having them multiply.

There are many varieties of green fertilizers to choose from and they all have their own specific advantages. Start trying a few and you will soon find your favorites.

THE FERTILIZER PANTRY

Horse Manure
Powerful fertilizer with a broad spectrum of nutrients. It needs to be composted for at least one year before you use it. It's great as a base fertilizer.
There is nothing wrong with manure that is multiple years old. The humus improves as the years go by, but the nutrients decrease, so you may use more.
I would like to warn against manure from racing horse stables, as they are often full of antibiotics and anthelmintic. Rather you should find manure from a private stable and ask them what they use to treat their horses.

Cow Manure
A powerful fertilizer similar to horse manure, but it may be more difficult to get a hold of in bulk. Most often you may buy this in bags, but it is often composted and heated and consequently contains less nutrients. Good as a base fertilizer.

Poultry Manure
A nitrogen kick for the plants. Works well as a support fertilizer for growths that need only one support fertilization. Buy pelleted poultry manure for a long-lasting effect. It has a rather strong smell and is not recommended for porch growths-the neighbors won't be all that happy.

Bone Meal
Good support fertilizer that contain a lot of nitrogen and phosphorus. Shy away from this if you have a dog and don't want you garden excavated.

Blood Meal
Another nitrogen-rich fertilizer. It can have a certain repelling effect on wild animals.

Seaweed
A mineral-rich and powerful fertilizer. The weed is chopped and blended with the soil, or used as a cover fertilizer during the growth season. It can also be composted. Be careful though, not all growths respond well to the salt from the seaweed. Good base fertilizer.

Algomin
A product of algae and crushed seashells. It is rich in calcium and minerals. A good supplement to base fertilizers, as well as a good support fertilizer during the season.

Stone Meal
Is rich in minerals and soil enhancers. It increases the nutrient uptake of plants, counters soil acidity, and helps to prevent soil erosion. Good as a supplemental base fertilizer.

Liquid Nutrient Blends
These can sometimes be very practical. Choose an organic variety that is approved for organic farming. They are good for microlife in the soil as well. Do not overdose. Good as a support fertilizer, especially when you grow in pots.

FERTILIZERS YOU CAN MAKE ON YOUR OWN

Compost
Is very versatile in nutrients and naturally has a good pH. It does not have a very strong fertilizer effect, but it is great as a soil enhancer. Good base fertilizer.

Wood Ash
It is, among other things, rich in potassium and calcium. It is perfect as a support fertilizer and should be powdered over the soil and carefully mulled in with the upper layer. One handful per 10 square feet (one square meter) should be sufficient.

Grass Clippings
Add one inch (a couple of centimeters) on top of the soil. First and foremost to add nitrogen to the soil.

Nettle Water
Nettles actually contain a lot and make an excellent source of nutrients. Harvest them and empty them in a bucket. Pour water on top and cover with a lid. Let it sit for three to four days before you remove the nettle and throw them in the compost. Pour the liquid in a container. Dilute the smelly liquid with water until it has a light tea-color and then use it to water your plants. If you dilute it even more, you may even spray it on the leaves to give the plants an extra kick.

Comfrey Water
The principle is the same as with the nettles, but comfrey contains more water and so you only need to juice them. Cut the comfrey in large pieces and place them in a bucket. Place a chicken wire and a stone on top so that the leaves are pressed down. Cover with a lid and let it rot for a couple of days. Scoop up the liquid and dilute it with ten parts water before you use it.

Field Horsetail
This growth is a great source of valuable silicone. The field horsetail needs to be heated so that the silicone is released. Boil water with chopped leaves. Let it boil for 20 minutes and let it stew for 24 hours. Sift the tea. Dilute with water until the proportions are 1–10 for instance,
1 cup field horsetail to 10 cups of water. Can be poured directly on the soil or sprayed on the leaves.

Tip! Stable manure with peat or straw is ideal. Sawdust may take very long to decompose and it steals nutrients as it decomposes.

A SMALL GUIDE TO NUTRIENTS

Nutrients are usually divided into groups of macronutrients and micronutrients depending on how much of it a growing plant needs. It can be helpful to have a basic understanding of what the various nutrients do for the plant and how to recognize excess or deficiencies. First the six macronutrients:

Nitrogen (N)
Is primarily important for the growth of shots and leaf mass. Nitrogen deficiency will give small, yellowing leaves. Excess nitrogen gives large, limp, and dark green leaves. Susceptibility to disease increases with nitrogen fertilization.

Phosphorus (P)
Is important for the metabolism of the plant, as well as growth and budding. Phosphorus deficiency is rare, but may occur in low soil temperatures where the phosphorus may be hard to absorb.

Potassium (K)
Is important for the balance of liquids and metabolism of the plants. Access to potassium is therefore crucial for plants, but it also provides certain qualities to fruits and vegetables, such as a longer shelf life and a richer taste. Potassium deficiency will often have diffuse symptoms like dry and crisp leaf edges and a dull color.

Calcium (Ca)
Is important during the building of the plant's cellular walls or skeleton, so to speak. Calcium also has an important function in the growths' immune system. Calcium defiance is evident through curling of the leaves and sometimes, deformed leaves.

Magnesium (Mg)
Is, among other things, significant for the seed maturation. Magnesium deficiency is rare, but will be very visible as it shows through bright green leaf nerves against a yellow-brown color of the rest of the leaf. Is most often a result of uneven fertilization.

Sulfur (S)
Can be found in certain proteins with important functions for the growth. Influences growth. Deficiency is apparent through weak growth.

In addition, we have some micronutrients that are needed in very low dosages, but that are still vital for the plants. Most often they are important for photosynthesis. These are: iron (Fe), zinc (Z), manganese (Mn), copper (Cu), chlorine (Cl), boron (B), sodium (Na), cobalt (Co), aluminum (Al), and molybdenum (Mo).

THE PH THING . . .

Besides from the actual nutrients in the soil there are other factors that may affect the growths' possibility of absorbing nurture. These are for instance, soil temperature, soil water, and acid in the ground. But it is also pH values that provide a measurement of how acidic or alkaline a soil is. The pH value is given on a scale from 1–14 where 7 is neutral. Soil for cultivating should be between 5.5 and 7.5, to suit most growths. Values above or below this will give effects, such as nutrients being bound up so tight in the soil that the growths can't absorb them. Magnesium, Calcium, and Potassium, for instance, will bind together tight in acidic soils, while alkaline soils binds manganese and iron too tight.

Most soils have a good pH value and it will be even more balanced if you add compost and manure regularly. If you for some reason suspect that the pH value in your soil is too high or too low, you can buy a test stick and measure the soil. If the soil is too acidic, you can add lime as instructed on the package to heighten the pH value. If the soil is too alkaline, you can add peat to help balance the soil pH. You should always avoid adding anything before you have made sure that the pH value is out of balance, such as adding lime "to be safe." Changing the pH value in the soil may have consequences for the plants' nutrient uptake, and you should therefore be careful.

Tip! The best way to maintain a healthy pH balance in the soil is by keeping a strong colony of earthworms in the vegetable garden. Their digestive systems continuously produce calcium carbonate that exits the worm and is mixed with humus and soil. This creates perfect soil grains with a neutral pH.

COMPOST

Composting is good for the garden, the environment, and the economy. Soil enhancement can get pretty expensive—unless you have compost. It is just as wonderful every time you realize that what would otherwise just be garbage will now be used in the vegetable garden and actually be beneficial. All composting is about breaking down organic materials to humus, but depending on what kind of material we want to decompose, there are various composts you may use. The sensitive kind is food waste. It attracts pests like rats and mice, and is therefore regulated in every municipality as to what you need to do in order to compost your food waste. Find out which rules apply to your municipality before you invest time and money in hot compost equipment.

HOT COMPOST

Hot compost is also called worm compost. It is a closed compost container with ventilation holes. It is made out of plastic or wood and can be kept both inside and outside. The composting process is completed by compost worms, and many of them. For a hot compost to work and not smell too bad, it is crucial that the food materials in the compost are quickly processed; thus, the high amount of worms. You may buy compost worms over the Internet or in a store where they sell compost containers.

In kitchen compost, you first and foremost place food waste, preferably torn in smaller pieces so that they decompose easily. Nothing that may harm the worms should be included, like chili, lemon juice, or other strong foodstuffs.

It is important to always maintain a good environment for the worms so that the compost works. They prefer a temperature of 60–70°F (15–20°C). If the compost becomes too wet you may add a little paper, straw, or compost seeds to dry it up. If it gets too dry you may moisten it with water. To keep the balance it is important to avoid adding too much of one kind of waste at the same time.

To start a worm compost you need an appropriate compost container, a few kilos of compost worms and a blend of dirt, peat, wet newspaper, straw bedding, or similar to line the container so that the worms can rest in it.

GARDEN COMPOST

The garden compost is compost out in the fresh air. Here you may place anything biodegradable, EXCEPT food waste. Everything from the garden is fine: twigs, leaves, flowers, wilted plants, and clippings. Various materials will decompose at different speeds, and to even out the differences you may, for instance, evenly distribute the twigs or chop the leaves before you add them to the compost.

Compost can be organized in different ways. How you organize it depends on your space

> *Tip!* *You can make a simple compost heap by using an old box with a plastic grid in the bottom. Place compost in the box and shake it over a wheelbarrow. Whatever is left in the box is later placed on the compost again.*

restraints and preference. I think it is easiest to build the compost like a loaf and add material as you go. I add all of the materials as they come instead of gathering materials in various piles and then later combining them in the large compost loaf, which is another option. I have a water hose and a straw pile next to my compost. If there's a lot of nitrogen-rich materials during a period, I add some straw to balance the materials. This way, I build a compost loaf till it's about 6½ feet (two meters) long, 3 feet (one meter) wide, and 3 feet (one meter) tall. I cover it with straw and let it rest over winter. In early summer I remove the straw and use the top layer of the compost loaf as a base for another loaf, then I sift the entire compost. I let all the compost filter through a fine net, such as mink netting. The compost that passes trough the net is fine and ready to be used in the vegetable garden. The rest is added to the new compost and is decomposed for another year's time. This is an easy and good way to compost your garden waste.

The decomposing process in garden compost is handled by a range of organisms. There are woodlice, millipedes, springtails, ground beetles, pseudoscorpions, worms, ants, predatory mites, nematodes, fungi, bacteria . . . a whole brigade of various workers and officials. And for the work to proceed smoothly, the circumstances need to be ideal. In other words, the compost should be well balanced with just enough moisture and moderate heat.

Even though you, in principle, may add anything biodegradable to the compost, you always have to make sure that there is a balance between dry and wet materials, or between carbon-rich and nitrogen-rich materials, for the decomposing to work as it should. Straw, twigs, sawdust, and cartons are examples of carbon-rich materials. This dries up the compost. Leftover fruit, clippings, and green leaves are examples of nitrogen-rich materials that make the compost moist.

The compost is constantly changing and you have to keep an eye on it to make sure that it is functioning. Something may easily go awry, such as it suddenly becoming too warm or cold, too dry or too wet. If you keep an eye out it will be easier to determine if adjustments are needed. You can control the temperature by sticking a stick in the compost and then feeling with your hand how warm the stick is. When the stick is really warm, 140–160°F (60–70°C), you know that the decomposing process has begun. The temperature will later decrease as the decomposing process finishes.

COMPOST CONTROL

If the compost is too warm, you may decrease acid by stomping on it.

If it is too cold, the decomposing process has halted, usually because of a nitrogen deficiency. Rearrange the compost and add some old compost or some manure. Make sure that you have a nice balance of carbon and nitrogen.

If it smells rotten, it is too wet. Use a garden fork to lift the layers slightly and create air pockets. Add straw or bedding.

If it has a bitter smell, like ammoniac, the nitrogen level is too high. Rearrange the compost and add straw, paper, or bedding.

This should not be placed on the compost:
- Diseased growths
- Weeds
- Waste from dogs or cats
- Large amounts of ash
- Rough branches

Tip! *To help the compost reach a temperature of 140–160°F (60–70°C) there must be a draft. Add a good layer of rice at the bottom of the compost loaf so that air can pass underneath. This way the acidic content of the compost will increase and the temperature rises. You do the same as when you light a fire.*

LEAF COMPOST

Leaf compost is a third variety of compost. Leaves often take longer to break down than other materials, but during fall we often end up with so many leaves that they engulf our entire garden. It can be nice to get the leaves off of the lawn and place them in a pile where they can decompose.

If you simply gather the leaves and let them lie in a pile it may take multiple years before they decompose. If you treat your leaf pile more as active compost, one year can be sufficient, but this demands that you chop the leaves with a lawn mower, arrange a compost loaf, and are diligent with the temperature and moisture—just as you would with regular compost. If it is too dry you water it and if it is too wet you air it out with a garden fork.

The whole point of pure leaf compost is the mull it creates: a dark-brown, fungi-scented leaf humus with a structure reminiscent of a cross between bark and peat humus. It is a fantastic soil enhancer for all kinds of soils.

SOW

SOW YOUR OWN OR BUY FINISHED PLANTS? To many, sowing their own vegetables is an adventure in itself, an introduction to the growing season and a time you don't want to miss. The large advantage of sowing yourself is that there is a greater variety of seeds compared to what you can find as plants. Sowing yourself is also cheaper in the long run. A bag of seeds will usually contain more seeds that what you need for one summer, but if you save the seeds that you don't need or share your seeds with friends and acquaintances, you may save a lot of money on growing your own. If you store the seeds in a dry and cool place, they will keep longer than you might think.

However, sowing and pre-cultivating takes time and involvement. It is just not always possible to do everything on your own, and in those cases, buying ready plants is a great option. If it is your first vegetable garden and your first time growing vegetables, it could be a nice relief to buy a few plants and just sow a couple on your own.

Vegetable plants are sold in plugs or in pots depending on the size. Well-stocked trade farms will usually have much to choose from in springtime, but not all garden stores sell vegetable plants. It is most practical to search online. Many enthusiasts pull up plants and sell them by mail order, and here you may also find varieties that you can't find in stores.

Small plants should not sit too long in the plug so it is important to buy fresh plants. You can recognize if they are fresh by the root system. If the entire plug is covered in roots, they are too old. There should be a smooth lump of dirt with an even network of roots. If you see plants of vegetables that you want, but it is still a few weeks too early to plant them, then buy them anyway and place them in larger pots while they wait to be planted. The seedlings you buy are almost never weathered. Make sure that you let them get used to the outside climate by placing them outside during the day and bringing them inside overnight for at least a week before you plant them.

TO SOW AND GROW YOUR OWN PLANTS

Seeds are growths just waiting to be brought to life and begin growing. You'll need to know when and how you should begin coaxing the life out of them. The wrong method or the wrong time can be fatal. They can rot, dirt, freeze, or simply just continue sleeping quietly.

Some seeds you may sow directly into the garden. Others demand a pre-cultivation in small pots and in most instances, you may choose which you prefer. Sowing can seem so trivial, but there are many things that can go wrong. To succeed, it is best to follow the instructions and good advice that comes with the bag of seeds. If you are meticulous and make sowing an art, you will save time, money, and frustration.

SOWING DIRECTLY INTO THE VEGETABLE GARDEN

The advantage of sowing directly into the vegetable garden is that you avoid harming the roots during moving. The plant is placed where it is supposed to be and you save the time and work of replanting it.

Tip! Seeds with hard shells, like peas, beans, and cress, will grow more easily if you soak them in water 24 hours before you sow them. Other seeds, like chili and bell pepper, can either be placed in a moist paper towel or you may lightly rub them against a stone before you sow them, to wake them up more easily.

The largest risk of sowing on free land is that you may sow too early and the seeds may rot in the cold and dampness before they have time to start growing. To avoid this you need to check the temperature of the soil. If you are experienced, you'll only need to stick a finger in the soil. If you feel uncertain you simply use a soil thermometer—one of my favorite tools. A good rule of thumb is 46°F (8°C). There are varieties that grow on lower temperatures, but to make it simple: do not sow unless the soil has reached 46°F (8°C).

If the spring is unusually cold and wet and you are getting impatient, you can always cover the soil where you wish to sow with some transparent plastic; this way the soil will heat up faster. After a couple of weeks it will have dried up and the temperature will have increased. You may also use a fiber cloth, which warms, but liquid passes through, which is why I prefer plastic.

Prepare the patch so that the sprout can easily find its footing and the fine root threads can penetrate the soil without trouble. If the soil was dug during fall so that it is already loose down deep, you only need to soften the surface with a cultivator and fold in some compost to make the soil humus-rich and even. Remove large stones and rough pebbles, but you don't need to be too meticulous. If there are lumps of clay soil on the surface that you have trouble crushing, remove them and throw them on the compost so that the worms can do the work for you.

Later you mark where you want the rows. A row marker with a line can be very helpful if you want straight, pretty rows. Make a rut with the right sowing depth, depending on what you are

SOWING IN THE VEGETABLE GARDEN

1. Prepare the sowing rut; a row marker will help you make it straight

2. Water the rut

3. Place the seeds with adequate distance in between

4. Cover the seeds

5. Finish by watering the whole area

TIP!

Sowing vegetables in small patches instead of in rows could be a good trick if you struggle with snails. They usually keep to the outer edges of the patch and leave the plants in the middle alone. It looks pretty as well—like a quilt of various vegetables.

sowing. Always follow the instructions on the bag of seeds, or read the vegetable chapter for the respective vegetable to see what will be the right depth, but a thumb rule is that the depth should be 3–5 times the diameter of the seed.

Water the rut before you sow the seeds. If you are sowing small seeds this is especially important, so that you don't have to water on top of the seeds and risk them floating away. Larger seeds are more stable and can be watered from the top as well.

Arrange the seeds in the rut. If the seeds are large you may either arrange them in pairs or somewhat closer than how tight you imagine the plants to become. Later you can remove the plants that become excessive. If the seeds are smaller you can sprinkle them or you may hold then in your palm and let them "run" out in an even stream through your fingers. Making this even may take some practice.

Cover the seeds with soil. Make sure that the row is marked with sticks and mark what you sowed. This makes it easier when you are removing weeds later on.

Finish by moistening the whole surface with a spray bottle for small seeds and a watering can with a fine spray for larger seeds.

You can sow vegetables in patches instead on in rows. They will still want their own room to grow, so you won't avoid culling, but they don't care if they grow in circles, squares, or rows. Sowing in squares is called broadcasting. You spread the seeds evenly over an even surface and cover them with light soil. How much you need to add on top depends on the size of the seeds. If the seeds are small, you water the surface before you sow and only gently spray water on top afterwards. If the seeds are slightly larger you'll need to cover with about one inch (2 cm) of soil and water with a watering can.

Most seeds needs darkness to grow and should be sowed as described. But there are also seeds that need to be exposed to light to grow. The seed bag usually describes how the seeds grow. Light-growing seeds should not be covered with soil, but rather be sprinkled on a moist surface, that later must be kept moist until the

Tip! If you know that there are a lot of weed seeds in the soil where you want to sow—cover with transparent plastic one month before sowing. As soon as the weeds starts growing, take them out and loosen the soil down deep. Cover the soil again and wait for the next round of weeds. Carefully pull it up, then only loosen the surface and sow your seeds.

When you broadcast seeds in a case, first water the soil properly.

seeds are growing and the plants have come up properly. Enlist the help of a fiber-cloth to keep the surface moist.

PRE-CULTIVATING

The advantage of pre-cultivating—sowing in cases, pots, or root trainers—is that you have control over warmth, moisture, and attackers. There are many small bugs in nature that enjoy gnawing on small plants and sprouts. I have personally witnessed how bug parades have greedily worked their way through my entire chard crop right in front of my eyes. Upon seeing this, it's hard not to laugh, but despite the humor of it, it is a given that it's preferable to avoid having to sow the whole patch again.

When you're approaching mid-season, pre-cultivating becomes a way of staying one step ahead. It is an advantage to have small plants ready that may be planted and fill small openings as you harvest.

When you pre-cultivate, it may happen that you sow too much. Try to plan according to how much room you have and how much you want of each kind. Sow a couple of extra plants, but nothing more. If you still end up with too much, then give it to a nice neighbor. Everyone appreciates a pot of vegetable plants.

BROADCAST IN A CASE

Sowing in cases first and foremost saves space. The seeds don't need much room to grow, but once they start stretching, you need to be quick to move them into larger pots so that they don't end up long and wobbly.

You can definitely buy sowing cases, but you may just as well use old glass bowls, wooden boxes, plastic buckets—anything, just as long as they have holes in the bottom so that the seeds are well-drained. Use soil for sowing. The seeds don't need nutritious fat soil, but rather they like it best in lean and airy soil. You can buy soil or make your own: three parts ready compost or plant soil and one part vermiculite or sand is usually good.

Fill your case with 2 inches (5 cm) soil. Moisten the soil all the way through. Sprinkle the seeds evenly. If they are very small you can blend them with sand and sprinkle them with a sugar dispenser to spread them out more easily. If they

BROADCAST IN A CASE

Larger seeds are sprinkled over the moist soil.

Smaller seeds with a sugar dispenser.

Always finish by moistening the seeds.

TIP!

To regulate the moisture more easily when you water the root trainers or cases from underneath, you can place a washcloth underneath the trays. This will absorb surplus water and release it again when the soil needs it.

need light to grow, cover them with perlite that lets light through, or don't cover at all. With other seeds, cover them with a thin layer of soil. If you are meticulous about marking what you have sown, the replanting will be more fun later on.

The whole garden should be moist and kept that way. However, it should not be wet. The best way to achieve this is to water the seeds from underneath by keeping the case on a tray or a dish. This way the soil will absorb the water slowly and you can be certain that the seeds will get the moisture they need. Feel free to cover with plastic or a piece of fiber cloth, which helps keep the surface moist, but make plenty of holes in the plastic so that acid leaks through. If the surface dries out, just carefully moisten it with a spray bottle.

As soon as the character leaves appear, it is time to move the plants to larger pots.

SOWING IN ROOT TRAINERS AND POTS

If you sow directly in root trainers or pots you don't need to move the plants, but rather they can stay put until they are going out in the vegetable garden. With heavily expanding vegetables such as squash, pumpkin, cucumber, and melon, you might as well plant them with loads of room from the start, in 3½ inch (9 cm) pots. In these instances you can also use soil with more nutrients, so that they have loads of nutrients from the start.

Fill the root trainers or pots half full of soil and carefully press it into place with a brush or shake it lightly. Distribute the seeds. It is best to sow two or three seeds in each plug so that you are certain that one seed will grow. Cover with soil and water generously with a watering can so that the whole bed is moist. Place pots or root trainers on trays and then water from underneath. You may cover with perforated plastic if it is difficult to keep the surface moist.

If multiple seeds grow, just cut off the weakest plants with small scissors and leave a strong plant in each plug to continue growing. Do not let the small plants stand too long, because if the roots sense resistance or lack space, the plant will stop growing and it can be hard to get it to grow again.

Tip! When you've mixed up the tomato and squash plant enough times you find that it might be a good idea to mark each pot. Nowadays, I use masking tape and black markers and write the name and date on each pot—foolproof.

SOWING INSIDE

Most of us are unbearable in springtime. Our fingers itch to sow and we long to get started. Certain plants, such as chili and artichoke, demand that we begin between February and March if we want a good crop. But warmth and light is still a while away so if we want to get a head start on the season we have to cheat a little in order to get strong and plump plants.

Warm and light have to be proportional when we sow. The warmth makes them grow and the sprout will seek light. If there is a lack of light and too much warmth, the plant will stretch very quickly as it is searching for light. This is how we end up with long, meager, and weak plants. If you have a greenhouse or a glass veranda where you can regulate the temperature and where the flow of light is larger than inside, that is perfect. That way the plant will develop at a slower pace and you will end up with fine, sturdy plants.

You can still succeed if you have to use a regular inside environment, but you will need to add light to compensate for the high inside temperature. Regular cold white light rods work perfectly. If you are a frequent hobby cultivator, it could be worth investing in a growth lamp that will provide the very best light for the plants.

Most often the seeds prefer a warmer environment when they are growing. When you see the plant emerging, you may lower the temperature, but keep just as much light.

My inside crops have failed many times because of a lack of light and lack of patience. It is hard to stay calm in spring, but if you don't have a good light substitute, you are better off saving the seeds for another month and then sow them. Failed crops are a waste of time and money. And most often, seeds that are planted slightly later will grow faster once the sun and warmth is out and you will eventually end up with a beautiful vegetable garden.

Growing chives

Tip! Long, shaky tomato plants are very common . . . this can actually be reversed. Save three-four leaf-pairs in the top, remove the rest; plant the entire plant in a pot so that only the small part with the leaf is above the dirt. Roots will develop along the entire trunk and the plant will become thick and fine.

EDUCATION

The first leaves that develop from the seed are called heartleaves and can look quite similar on many plants. As soon as the heartleaves crack, it will start getting cramped in your cases. Wait until the characteristic leaves, the leaves specific to the plant, develop on the little plant before you start the education, which refers to the move to a bigger pot. It is important that growing plants are not halted in their growth. When the characteristic leaves appear, the plant will also need more nutrients. This is one of the reasons why you need to move them, so that they get a more nutrient-rich soil to grow in. Another reason is that they need their own space to develop.

When you move the plant you have to be very careful so that you don't damage the small plants. Make sure that the soil is watered and that the plants are given time to absorb as much water as possible. They call these turgescent plants. Prepare the pots or root trainers that you are moving the plants into. Do not choose a pot that is too large in comparison to the plant. The root system develops better if the size of the pot is changed as the size of the root system changes. Fill the pot with nutrient-rich soil and lightly shake the pots so that the soil falls into place. Continue by removing the entire dirt lump with little plants, place it on a tray and carefully divide the roots. Use a small wooden stick, the shaft of a fine brush, or a blunt twig. Make a small hole in the

UPBRINGING

1. Crowded box

2. Divide the roots with the help of a stick.

3. Carefully hold onto one of the heart-leaves when you move the small plants.

soil with the stick, lift the small plant and release it into the hole.

When you lift a small plant, you hold on to one leaf while at the same time using the stick to help lift the roots. The stem is too weak to lift by. The best approach is to get a hold of the heartleaf, as that is the strongest part of the leaf at this point. Do not fiddle too much with the roots; they need to be left alone as much as possible. They should not be exposed to sunlight either. Set the plant a little deeper than it was in the tray and fill the hole in with dirt. Then carefully water so that the dirt sinks together and wraps around the roots. A couple of weeks after the move, you can begin watering the plants with a light liquid fertilizer.

RE-EDUCATION

When the root system of the plant has reached the walls of the pot, or the root trainer, and the entire dirt lump is pierced with fine roots, it's time to give the plant even more room to grow. If it is still too early to replant the plants, you simply move them onto a bigger pot while they wait to be replanted. If you leave a plant for too long without enough room to grow, the development will halt and it may be hard to get it started again, even under the best conditions. It is therefore important to follow the growth of the plant and give it all it needs to grow evenly.

PLANTING

HARDENING AND PLANTING

All pre-cultivated plants are more sensitive than the plants that are sown directly in their growth spot. It is like growing up in an incubator, with the perfect amount of moisture, the perfect amount of warmth, and protection against attackers. But the day comes when they need to be planted outside in wind, cold nights, strong sun, and pouring rain. To prepare the plants we harden them. This means placing them outside during the day and moving them inside during the night, alternatively covering them with a fiber cloth or something similar. You can also move them in a cold frame, a box with a window as a lid, and open the lid during the day and close it overnight. If the sun is very strong, you have to cover them with a thin fabric or fiber cloth during the day so that they don't burn. The hardening should take a couple of weeks. Afterwards you can plant them in your outside vegetable garden.

Even if you've been diligent with the hardening process, the new environment will be tough on the plants. They may need a little extra attention in the beginning. By the time you plant them there should no longer be any risk of frost, but cold nights are unpredictable, so have a fiber cloth ready and follow the weather forecast during the first couple of weeks just to be safe. Choose a cloudy day to replant them so that it's even easier for the plants to reacclimate.

Prepare the soil by digging, enhancing the soil, and fertilizing. Follow the directions for distance for each vegetable so that they have room to grow. If you are growing in heightened beds, the plants get a greater chance to develop their roots down deep. In this case you may also decrease the distance between the plants by about an inch (2 cm). If you place the plants in a zigzag pattern they will automatically have more room.

Make sure that the plants are watered well when you set them out and water them directly after you've planted them so that the soil closes tightly around the root system.

NURTURE

CULLING

When you sow directly into the vegetable garden you have to cull (or thin) the rows as the plants grow. The planting distance specified for each vegetable is known as the "final distance" and the row will go through a gradual thinning. Culling is the process of making sure that the plants always have enough air and space around the roots so that they can develop at the optimal pace. If you plant the seeds close together you will indeed get more plants, but they will develop poorly, and your crop will not be very impressive. It's best not to start the culling process right away so that you have a few plants on reserve. You can, for example, be visited by snails, larvae, or grasshoppers that will scarf down half of the seedlings. In those cases it is nice to have a few extra plants. Culling is best achieved by using scissors to cut away the sprouts you don't want. This way you avoid the disruption of the root system of the plants that are left. In the last culling, which may take place when small carrots have already begun to develop and the red beets are like small marbles, you can pull up the whole plant and eat them as preemies. You should then water after the culling so that the soil packs tightly around the roots of the remaining plants.

WEEDING

Weeds are a natural part of a living and healthy garden. But that doesn't mean they should be allowed to roam free. You need to keep the weeds in check so that they don't compete against the plants that we actually want to be growing there. The large weeding should always happen before you sow or put out plants. After this you have to be that much more careful with the cleaning; only weed on the surface and not too close to the roots of the plants. Use a small hand cultivator, a Dutch hoe, or a weeding knife.

If you have made pretty rows and marked them with sticks, it is easy to hold the surface between the rows free from weeds even before the plants are blossoming. If you have broadcasted over a patch in the vegetable garden you have to delay the weeding until the seeds have grown and are somewhat along. If not, there's a risk of pulling up small sprouts or pushing the seeds so that you ruin the crop. Be patient and wait until you see which are weeds and which are vegetables, and then do some weeding.

The secret of weeding is to catch the weed before it shows. This means dragging a Dutch hoe or a cultivator over the soil now and then to disturb whatever is in the process of growing. If there's no time for this, the goal is to get them before you sow. But I know—there's just not always time. To get a step ahead and make it harder for the weeds to establish, you can use tricks other than weeding, such as cover cultivation.

> *Tip!* *Use radishes as row markers. Since radishes grow so quickly you can sprinkle some seeds here and there in the rows of seeds that takes longer to grow, like dill and carrot. When the radishes have appeared you will see where the row is and you can weed around it. It is especially smart if you are planting in waves or spirals as it might be hard to use string as a marker.*

COVER CULTIVATION

Cover cultivation is basically covering the open soil around the plants with organic material, so that the unwanted seeds have more difficulty reaching the soil and growing, and other weeds will have difficulty emerging from the bottom.

In theory, you can cover with any kind of material you want as long as water can seep through. But I prefer using organic materials in a vegetable garden, partly because it is easy to get a hold of, it's cheap, and partly because it provides nutrition for the plants, maintains a nice moisture in the soil, and stimulates a good microlife in the surface layer.

Organic materials can be clippings, straw, chopped weeds, or similar. Make the cover layer thick enough that light does not seep through, about 1–1 ½ inch (3 cm). Make sure that there is space between the roots of the plants and the cover material so that the plants do not suffer from root damage. You should not fold the cover material in with the earth, but rather just let it cover the

Fiber cloth is the savior of any cultivator. Here it protects the plants from the cold night.

Cover cultivation with clippings is easy and effective.

surface. With cover cultivation the need to loosen the soil will lessen as the cover maintains a nice structure on the surface. If you still wish to loosen the surface, maybe to fold in fertilizer or add more soil around the plants, remove the cover material first and move it back when you are finished.

Never place cover material on the vegetable garden before the soil has properly warmed during spring. If you do, the cover will work as an isolating layer that maintains the cold and the roots will freeze.

In my own vegetable garden, I cultivate in heightened beds and the grooves in between are covered with straw. When the straw starts going old, wet, and somewhat decomposed, I move it onto the beds as a cover material, and place new straw in the grooves. This is superb for the soil and the plants!

AIR THE SOIL SURFACE

You loosen the surface during the growth season to ease the breathing and water transport in the soil, but also to speed up all of the microorganisms so that more nutrients are released for the roots to absorb. The surface can stiffen after powerful rain, especially muddy soils. When you loosen the soil you increase the amount of soil that is in contact with the air by making the surface uneven and grainy. More water can then evaporate from the soil. When the water evaporates, the soil warms quicker and the soil climate will be more comfortable for the growths. Loosening is also very important when it rains.

Cover cultivation can, as previously mentioned, decrease the need for loosening, but it is still best to lift the cover now and then to check on the soil underneath. Stick a finger in the soil to make sure that it is porous and just moist enough.

The loosening process in itself should be delicate. It is easy to pull through the soil a little too deep and hard when you get going with your cultivator. Loosening the soil should be like tickling its back. If you get too deep and too close to the root systems, it is more like pulling someone's hair really hard. Loosen lightly, softly, and carefully.

UPWARD CUPPING

Many vegetables need upward cupping. Upward cupping involves pushing soil up around the base of the plant so that it is growing out of a small pile of dirt. Potatoes need upward cupping for the tubers to properly grow in the dark. Beans and Brussels sprouts are other examples of vegetables that should preferably be cupped, but in their case, its purpose is to make them stand more steadily in the ground. If you sense that plants have wobbly stems, are unstable, and wear and tear in the wind, cup a little dirt up around the base of the plant to give it support. Sometimes when water flushes dirt away so that the roots will be exposed, upward cupping is also a good solution.

TETHERING

Sometimes upward cupping is not enough to make the plant stabilize. Depending on how the plant behaves, you may need to adjust the support method. There are ready made support systems—both inexpensive and more costly. You can buy rings, clips, and elastic bands to tie to the plant for support and to aid growth. My suggestion is to buy a large roll of string, that can be used for everything, it is cheap, and it can be composted when you are done using it. Branches or bush twigs may be used as a support cane.

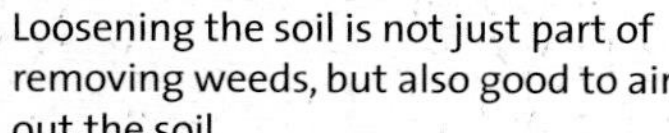

Loosening the soil is not just part of removing weeds, but also good to air out the soil.

An example of stable tethering for tomatoes, for free land or in a greenhouse.

The string is tied around the tomato stem so that the plant gets support.

TRELLIS AND CLIMBING TOWERS

There is no need to do much with the growths that have the ability to latch on to a climbing device on their own, such as peas and certain cucumbers and squash. You just need to guide them in the right direction and make sure that they grow in close proximity to a stable climbing device. If they have difficulty holding on properly, you can help them out by tying a few loose loops around the stem against the trellis.

A climbing device can look like a cylinder, a tent, a tower, or a pergola. The most important thing is that it is stable enough that it can carry a fully-grown plant. Use a skewer to get the rods deep in the soil when you build your climbing devices. Wedge them with a stone so that the sticks are unwavering in their holes. For the construction to work well they must also have sufficient density between the sticks or wires so that the plant can easily grab onto something and swing upwards. A sparse trellis may be made denser by binding threads where there are none.

POLES, STICKS, AND STRINGS

Large beans twist towards the sun of their own free will, but if the plant grows very large and heavy, you can help it out by adding a nail or two below its branches in the construction so that it doesn't glide downwards.

Broad beans, chili, and bell peppers are other examples of plants that may need support, and in the form of a pole next to the stem of the plant. Since these types of growths lack the ability to latch on to the support, you will need to fasten it to the pole with string. Depending on the size of the plant, the amount of fastenings you need may vary. Make sure that the loop of string is loose enough that it will not harm the stem. Bind the stem right above a leaf so that the loop won't glide down even though it is quite loose.

You may support tomato plants with poles as well that you bind together as a tipi over the plant. But I prefer allowing the plant to twist around a string that leads them upwards. The string can be fastened to the ceiling of the green house or in a construction and should be long enough that it can reach the ground and back. Take the string and carefully twist it around the tomato plant. When you reach the base, the lowest pair of leaves, you let the string turn back up. Fasten the string by twisting it around the downward string so that the knot can run up and down. As the plant grows, you twist it around the string so that it always has support. This kind of tethering is good for cucumbers as well.

TIP! *The best way of binding a stem against a support is to make an eight out of soft string. The stem will be fastened to one of the circles and the support will be stuck to the other.*

WATERING

I've always appreciated watering the plants. It has become a habit to see how the plants are doing while I water them, placing the hose in a bed on low pressure while I squeeze some aphids or bind some raspberry plants that are dancing about. This little daily moment in my vegetable garden gives me a sense of closeness to the crop, even if the days are later filled with everything else.

Watering is an art. Too little water can make the plants wither and too much water can make the root system rot as a result of acid deficiency. If you find it difficult to water, make it a habit to stick a hand trowel in the soil after watering to see how deep the water went. After a summer, it will feel natural.

Small growths are completely dependent on being watered from above, the roots system is not developed enough that they can absorb water from below. But the small plants are sensitive. Carefully water with a fine spray so that the plants are not pushed down by the weight of the water. The plants prefer to be watered in the morning so that excess moisture can evaporate during the day and both soil and plants can dry a little before the natural moisture of the night.

Grown plants are best to water along the base. It is the roots and not the leaves that need the water. Most plants will actually be quite happy to avoid water on their leaves. On sunny days the water drops may cause burns and on cold days the water can have trouble evaporating from the leaves, which attracts fungi.

When you are watering, make sure that the water really reaches the deep layers of the ground. Feel free to make a small embankment around each plant so that the water stays around their root system and sinks down. Surface watering only

Tip! Gather water in rain barrels. All plants prefer temperate rainwater instead of ice cold tap water.

All plants need the most water when they are about to blossom and give fruit. If you have a limited amount of water, concentrate the watering around these periods.

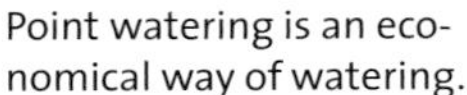

Point watering is an economical way of watering.

Single-drop watering is done with a hose with small holes.

allows the roots to develop on shallow ground since that is where the moisture is, and this makes the plant unsteady. The plants should dig downwards to get nurturing and minerals from the deep soil layers. During drought, they can also absorb water from the reserves further down in the ground.

Growths in pots are more sensitive than growths that are planted in the ground; they have no water reserves if they don't get water. Warm summer days demand watering every night. Watering in the evening is preferably in this instance. The water won't evaporate as quickly, the plant will have time during the cool night to absorb the water and the risk of the roots "boiling apart" in a sunbaked wet soil is not as likely. If the pots are left in the shade, the watering time is not as important.

SPRINKLERS

Using sprinklers can be smart when you have a large surface that needs watering and you don't have the time to water it by hand. The downside is that much of the water is lost through evaporation in the air and moreover the leaves of the plants are watered. If the soil is to get the water it needs, the sprinkler has to water the area for a long while. If you choose to water with sprinklers then do it during the morning so that the water on the leaves evaporates during the day.

DROP WATERING

This is an excellent way of watering vegetable growths, especially if you have limited access to water. The slow drips allow the water to penetrate down to the roots in an ideal way. Drop

NOTE! *Drizzle is not enough to water the plants in a flowering vegetable garden. Grab your umbrella and get out there and water!*

watering is a system of hoses that run through the vegetable garden and by each plant there is a small drop valve. There are valves that release the different amounts of water per hour. This way you can control how much water each plant receives. If the whole system is then attached to a timer, you have saved yourself a lot of work. But it is worth mentioning that this is a technical system and cannot replace the human eye. You have to be there and make sure that the timer works, that the valves don't calcify, and that the hoses are in place.

FAST TEMPORARY SOLUTIONS

If you are going away for a couple of days and some of your plants need watering, you may make your own drop watering system. Cut the bottom off of a plastic bottle. Stick it in the ground next to the plant with the bottom upwards. Fill it up with water. The ground will absorb the water it needs. It is simple but it will only keep for a couple of days and then you'll need to refill the bottle.

There are also strings you can use to automatically water pots. Squeeze one end of the string into the pot and place the other in a container of water. Make sure that the water container is placed above the pot; you should then be able to see how the moisture moves from the container to the soil at a moderate pace.

The easiest trick might still be to ask a neighbor or a friend if they can water your plants for a couple of days.

SUPPORT FERTILIZATION DURING THE GROWTH SEASON

Whether it's a vegetable garden, a pot, or a cultivation case, the soil needs to be fertilized with base fertilization. This will give your growths a good start and they won't need to be fertilized during the first weeks after planting them.

But annual vegetable growths have a very hectic life. The seeds will germinate, and the

My garden memo board in the form of a string with clips—here I keep all of the things I need to remember.

plants will grow, blossom, grow fruit, and ultimately in about 5 months altogether. These plants obviously need more nutrients than the plants that takes multiple years to finish the same process. You should therefore do support fertilizations, or additional fertilizations, on kitchen growths a couple of times during the season. In the vegetable section you may read more about the recommended number of support fertilizations of your vegetables during the season.

Plants in a pot or a balcony case need more fertilization than plants that grow out in the ground. They don't have access to the same pantry of nutrients that they could find out in the free. It is easiest to buy a good organic liquid fertilizer and regularly add it during watering for the entire growth season. A nice trick is to keep a note next to the bottle that describes when you added fertilizer to which plants and when.

My Vegetable Garden

My vegetable garden is a hybrid of Swedish and Spanish. It is situated along a small watering canal that runs through the valley where we live. Access to water is not a given in Spain and therefore that was one of our requirements when we looked for a plot. Along the little hill stands a quince tree and an apple tree someone planted at some point. They form a jungle-like shrub that provides shade for one part of the vegetable garden and a casual green frame for the patch. I believe someone has cultivated here before, because the soil is very good. But the ground was overgrown and hadn't been used for long time when we bought it. Slowly but surely.

This place has become the vegetable garden it is today, one step each year. First we plowed an open patch, then we made flowerbeds, a fence as a windbreaker, a small shadow ceiling for the plants that are sensitive to the sun, some fruit trees, a few more flowerbeds, frames on the beds, and straw in the grooves. The next project will be a hotbed, because even here we get cold spring nights and the small plants need protection. Today, this is one of our favorite spots on our land, not only because it gives us so many delicious vegetables, but also because it has become a serene place we like to take care of, a place where you take the evening sun with you and just enjoy for a while.

RED FIG TOM
Sunflower
Semiens

CHERIE
MARINE

80 VEGETABLES

LETTUCE & CHICORY

No meal is complete without a large and flavorful salad. Especially in summertime when we can freeze freshly harvested leaves. And you can vary a salad an infinite number of ways, add all kinds of vegetables, nuts, seeds, and fruit, but personally I think the most elegant salad is the simple leaf salad that is only leaves of different colors, flavors, and textures. With a good dressing as a flavor enhancer, it can become the absolute highlight of the dinner table.

LETTUCE IS A kitchen growth, and it has always been part of my vegetable garden. It is great because it is so easy to grow— you can grow it in a pot, balcony case, hotbed, or in the vegetable garden. Anyone can grow their own lettuce in summertime! With all of the lettuce varieties you can find today, you can also make a very decorative planting of lettuce and enjoy them for a long time. Multiple lettuces are made to harvest continuously and this way you can enjoy the same plant for a long time. This is especially true for leaf lettuce, but also certain head lettuce varieties.

Even though the selection of salads in the vegetable sections of out country's stores have gotten a lot better over the last years, it is still a huge advantage to harvest your own. As with all vegetables, freshly harvested lettuce is crisper and more flavorful. Directly from the earth to the salad bowl, the shorter the time in between, the better. I always want my lettuce like after a dewy, fresh summer night, chockfull of leaf cells that break when you chew so that it sounds fresh and releases sweet, bitter, and fresh flavors.

In Sweden, we are accustomed to milder lettuce varieties, like the popular "butterhead" and loose-leaf salads, but I highly recommend cultivating a couple plants of the bitter chicory, such as radicchio. Blend in a few leaves and generously drizzle with dressing made with olive oil, lemon, and salt. You will be surprised by the flavors a simple leaf salad can offer.

In order to succeed in having a nice lettuce to harvest for the entirety of summer, it could be a good idea to sow some plants now and then. This way you will continuously keep a small family of lettuce plants on the stairs. Some that are almost done, some teenagers that are now ripening, and a few babies that still need a couple of weeks before their leaves are fully developed. If you end up with too many plants you can always eat the small-plants as well; they generally have a milder flavor, tender and tasty.

Lettuces are not demanding vegetables. Since we only want the leaves and no flower or fruit, everything that stimulates leaf growth is good for the plant. They need a lot of water and nitrogen to obtain a nice color and crispness. The greatest challenge might be managing to keep these plants to yourself. Snails, grasshoppers, woodlice, and all other small bugs love lettuce. But they rarely create enough trouble that it disturbs the joy of growing it.

Rows of romaine, a lettuce that keeps ripe and fine for a long time.

Lettuce in pots is very smart, especially with balcony cultivating. Choose a leaf salad.

Lettuces add both beautiful form and color to the vegetable garden.

CULTIVATING LETTUCE

Under the umbrella lettuce (Lactuca sativa) you find leaf lettuces, iceberg lettuce, head lettuces, and romaine—also called Cos lettuce. What separates leaf lettuce from the rest is that they grow in bouquets instead of heads. This makes it possible to pinch leaves off continually without ruining the plant. You can do this with the head lettuce as well, and first and foremost with romaine. In the beginning of the season you can carefully loosen a couple of the outer leaves, but when the lettuce finishes their heads, you should stop removing leaves and let them shape their heads in peace.

PREPARING THE GROWING SITE

Lettuce should grow in the sun or in half-shade. It is most important that the growth site is warm and sheltered from the wind. It grows in light and humus-rich soil that can hold warmth. Therefore, prepare the soil with rough sand, compost, and/or composted manure if you know that you have a muddy soil. If you grow in pots, use special soil for that purpose. It should contain quality peat that helps the soil keep its structure and airiness and prevents it from falling apart around the roots of the plants.

SOWING

WHEN? You can choose to either directly sow the lettuce or pre-cultivate them inside. Leaf lettuces develop quickly and are great to sow directly while certain head lettuces and iceberg lettuce take a while longer and may therefore benefit from pre-cultivation. The time it takes for the various kinds to develop is listed in the seed catalogues or the seed bag.

Expect to start sowing three to four weeks before you plan to set the plants in the ground.

Romaine lettuce 'Jericho'

PHOTO: KARIN ELIASSON

Plant various lettuces together so that it is more fun to harvest and the salad will look more beautiful.

Lettuce seeds can grow at a temperature as low as 40°F (5°C). In other words, you can sow them early, also in a regular hotbed. Most lettuces endure cold nights, even a couple of nights below 30°F (0°C), so you can safely plant your lettuce early in summer and not harvest until late fall.

It is important to remember that lettuce seeds will not grow in overly high temperatures; 65°F (18°C) is the general limit. Anything under 65°F (18°C) is fine, but over that, the temperature will effect the sprout negatively and it may take much longer before it grows, if it grows at all. This makes it hard to sow lettuce in the middle of summer.

HOW? Sow the lettuce very shallow, only ¼ inch (½ cm) deep, preferably with perlite as a cover material as the seeds need light to grow. If you are pre-cultivating you can sow in root trainers or briquettes. Place a couple of seeds in each plug. If all of the seeds grow, remove the plants so that you end up with one plant in each plug. If you sow directly in the vegetable garden, you should still stay with the same depth.

Water the row before sowing. This way you won't have to water as much afterwards. This is good when you sow shallowly and there is a risk of the seeds floating away with the water. Don't sow the seeds too close to each other—that's just wasting seeds. If you sow with about 2 inches (5 cm) of distance in between each, you won't need to do as much culling. You can wait with the culling until the plants have grown large enough that you can use them, and this way, nothing goes to waste. In the end, the leaf lettuces should have about 8 inches (20 cm) distance between the plants, and the head lettuce about 12 inches (30 cm). Cover with a thin layer of soil after sowing and lightly moisten the soil.

PLANTING THEM OUTSIDE

Make sure that you harden your pre-cultivated plants before you move them outside. Make them accustomed to weather and wind as lettuce has especially sensitive leaves. Plant the little plants shallowly so that the leaves themselves are not covered in dirt, if they are, they will be easily killed by root disease.

NURTURE

Many lettuces are quick cultures. With this I mean that they generally don't take long from sowing to harvesting. This means that there is no need to add support fertilizer. But if you choose to plant new plants to replace the harvested ones, it is a good idea to fold in some bone meal or poultry manure to replenish the soil's nutrient pantry. The same goes for planting lettuces that take longer to develop. They may need a snack after a couple of months. Make sure that the soil is moist, but not wet, and that the surface is loose and fine around the plants. Covering with clippings is great, but don't place the grass next to the root of the plants, as the air needs to be able to circulate.

Tip! Plant leaf or romaine lettuces with small-flowered pansies in a large pot and keep it on your stairs. It makes a beautiful pre-summer plant.

HARVEST

WHEN? The head lettuce gains flavor from being allowed to mature properly, so wait until it has formed its proper head. If you want to use a leaf here and there before it is ready, just take from the outer leaves. The leaf lettuce can either be harvested as a whole plant or you may pick the leaves you need now and then. Don't start picking the leaves until the plant is at least 8 inches (2 decimeters) and there's something to get a hold of.

Lettuces have a tendency to blossom during heat waves, and if that happens it's best to harvest right away.

HOW? You harvest head lettuce with a knife. You make a cut right below the head so that it is separated from the stem. Leaf salad can be harvested a little at the time. Pick the leaves by twisting them off of the plant so that they let go of the base of the plant.

PROBLEMS THAT MAY ARISE

Lettuce and Chicory are relatively problem-free to cultivate, but snails are a common theme. The plants may be kept snail-free by protecting them with electric fencing or copper thread, or by fighting snails with traps or poison. Read more about defeating snails in the section on pests on p. 187.

Another threat is downy mildew. This usually occurs during cold and wet summers when the leaves have difficulty drying. To prevent attacks, you should make sure that the salad crop has plenty of air, and that watering does not happen over the leaves and not more than necessary.

CULTIVATING CHICORY

The chicory umbrella also offers a variety of edible leaf-growths and they all have a bitter taste. Frisée lettuce and escarole lettuce, that both belong to the group *Cichorium endivia*, grow as open lettuce heads with more or less curly, dented, and toothed leaves. The outer leaves are often a clear green while the inner lettuce core is yellow-white and less bitter.

As you harvest lettuce, you can fill the holes with new seedlings.

Chicory (*Cichorium intybus* var. *foliosum*) is a group of growths with various shapes and colors on their leaves. The radicchio develop tightly knotted heads in beautiful red tones. Other varieties grow like leaf lettuce or develop heads in oval shapes late in the season. You can harvest the leaves of all of them continually and eat them while they are still small and crisp.

SOWING

Chicory is sown like lettuces but with the difference that you should sow a little deeper; about ⅓ inch (1 cm) deep is good. The seeds do not like the cold like the lettuce seeds, but rather they need at least 50°F (10°C) to grow. Keep an ending distance, after culling, of about 8–11 inches (20–30 cm) between the plants and 8–11 inches (20–30) cm between the rows.

Preparing the growing site, planting outside, and nutrition requirements are the same as for lettuce.

HARVEST

Chicory's sensitive leaves can be harvested continually during the season by carefully loosening them from their base. Certain varieties, like "Varigata di Castelfranco," form a slight head.

Radicchio is harvested when the small, red heads have knotted properly. This doesn't happen until early fall.

Escarole and Frisée lettuces are harvested like whole heads by cutting them off the root stem by the soil surface. To bleach a larger part of the leaves and make them milder before eating, you can simply tie the whole lettuce head together a couple of weeks before harvesting so that the leaves are protected against sunlight.

MY FAVORITES

PHOTO: KARIN ELIASSON

1.

2.

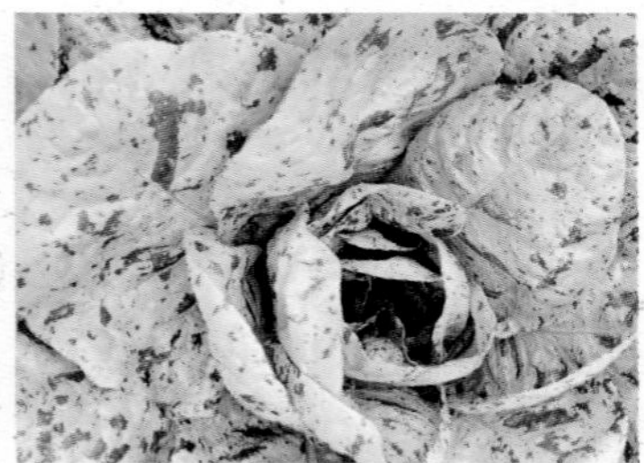

3.

1. 'Butterhead'
A head salad with strong, green, dented leaves. It is crispy and flavorful and doesn't blossom easily.

2. 'Cocarde'
A leaf lettuce with an oak leaf shape in red and green nuances. It has a fresh and slightly bitter taste.

3. 'Freckles'
Romaine lettuce with lime green leaves and wine-red freckles. It has a crisp and sweet flavor and keeps well.

'Grobo'
An escarole lettuce that bleaches itself; in other words you don't have to make the effort to protect it against sunlight in order for it to develop a mild and soft taste. The leaves are a fresh green color, wavy, and can withstand cold. Suitable for late sowing.

4. 'Maravilla de Verano'
A Spanish favorite of Batavia lettuce that works just as well in other areas. It has a green lettuce head with a red edge and white insides. The variety is crispy, sweet, and packed with flavor and vitamins.

5. 'Rossa di Treviso'
Incredibly beautiful small red-white heads of radicchio. The leaves can be picked one at time or you can harvest the entire head. It has a mild, round, bitter flavor and is wonderful oven-roasted or in warm dishes like stews, as the bitterness disappears.

'Spadona'
A Chicory that you can harvest from continuously and it keeps for a long time. The thin, green leaves with their mild bitterness are great in salads.

'Varigata di Castelfranco'
A Chicory that develops a large coiled head, green leaves with wine-red spots and butter-yellow juicy insides.

Tip! If you don't like bitter flavors, use the chicory in prepared meals. Oven-bake or blend the lettuce in vegetable stews or a wok to lessen the bitterness and enhance all of the other delicious flavors.

PHOTO: KARIN ELIASSON

4.

5.

MIXED LEAVES

I spent some of my childhood years in South Asia, more specifically, Vietnam. A region and a country I have later had the joy of returning to. There's so much to like over there—the colors, bamboo, mountain bikes, Mekong, boats loaded with chrysanthemums, rice fields, the people, the soil . . . but what I like best are the vegetable markets and the small street kitchens.

WANDERING INTO A Vietnamese market is like being in an art show. It is beautiful, fresh, lavish, and green. Green, green, green. Leaves, leaves, leaves. Their way of using leaf growths in their food is fantastic. They use leaves to make rolls, leaves in soup, leaves in woks, shredded leaves in the rice, leaves in drinks, leaves in salads, and leaves to package food. Each leaf has its own specific trait and function. The leaves in the food bring a freshness that every chef should aspire to.

I have mimicked them; I like finishing my cooking by folding in a bowl of mixed leaves in the noodle wok, sprinkling them on top of oven-roasted chicken filets, decorating soups and stews with them, setting the table with various bowls of spicy leaves. And, of course, I use them in salads. They enhance the flavor and are beautiful, and healthy.

And I'm sure I'm not the only one. If you look in stores, the selection of leaves and leaf blends in the vegetable section has exploded during the past years. But it is quite expensive. And it is extremely simple to grow these on your own. So if you're a leaf enthusiast, you would benefit from sowing a few pots.

Many of these lettuces are perfect for growing in a pot, on the balcony, terrace, or in the yard, but of course you can grow them in the vegetable garden as well. They grow fast and many are "cut-and-come again-growths," which means that you can harvest multiple times from one single seed. One general fact to keep in mind is that leaf vegetables do not like drought, so water them properly if they are about to dry out. Feel free to support fertilize the growths that you cut often, and they will keep even longer.

On the following pages I will share some simple cultivating advice for growing leaf growths. You can grow some of them year-round inside, and some will hold in the vegetable garden over the winter months as well. Some are cabbage growths, others spice growths—it's a blessed mix. A mix to make you smile.

Chard and small plants of romaine lettuce

CULTIVATING BLENDED LEAVES

I have divided the leaf growths that appear in this chapter into three groups: classics, Asian leaf vegetables, and spicy leaves. We will begin with the classics, a gang of leaf growths that are familiar to many and easy to cultivate: Chard, Spinach, Corn Salad, Purslane, and Arugula.

CHARD

Beta vulgaris var. *cicla*

The chard is a vegetable favorite for many, myself included. It grows in bouquets and both the mild, spinach-flavored leaves and the stalk is used. The leaves can be used raw in salads or replace spinach in stews, lasagna, or soups. The stalks are best if they are parboiled, sautéed in a wok, or prepared in some way. The chard is an ornament in the vegetable garden. The stalks can have various colors—white, yellow, or red. The white chard is the most powerful in its growth, while the colorful varieties are somewhat more graceful. I usually plant the variety "Bright Lights", which is dependable and tasty and has multicolored stalks. But "White Silver 2" and the red "Rhubarb Chard" are fine and tasty.

SOWING AND HARVESTING

Chard may both be pre-cultivated in root trainers and be sown directly, which should be around May-July. The seeds are sown about an inch (a few centimeters) deep, culled, or planted out to a distance of 10 inches (25 cm) between each plant. The distance between the rows should be 12–15 inches. The soil should be fertilized and humus-rich so that it can hold moisture easily. The plants are cold-resistant, but if they are exposed to a lot of cold they might become stressed and start seeding. Otherwise, they will keep till late fall.

Harvest continuously during the season. If you are using them for a salad you should pick the leaves while they are still small. If you want to use them as spinach they should grow properly. The stalks are carefully twisted off down by the root.

SPINACH

Spinacia oleracea

The spinach grows powerful and crisp leaves with a mineral taste. They are a good addition to a salad, but also stewed, in soups, or browned in olive oil, lemon, and salt. A fantastic winter vegetable that can even be harvested in snow. I have tried a couple of varieties and I have ended up with "Medania" and "Blomsdal Long Standing" since they easily blossom and they give a nice crop.

SOWING AND HARVESTING

Sow directly in rounds from April to September, with a small warning against sowing in high summer as warmth and long days makes the spinach blossom very quickly. Sow one inch (2 cm) deep in humus-rich soil. Cull to a plant distance of 8–11 inches (20–30 cm), row distance 16 inches (40 cm). Feel free to cover cultivate with clippings to ensure both nutrients and moisture. The spinach develops quickly and can be harvested one month after sowing. If you want a winter crop you need to sow in August-September to make sure that the plants have time to develop before the cold hits. Afterwards they will keep just fine outside and you may harvest in late fall and winter. Spinach can be both harvested as leaves or as the whole bouquet.

MACHE/CORN SALAD/ FIELD SALAD

Valerianella locusta

A loved child has many names. Corn salad is a leaf growth that forms rosettes of crispy oval leaves with a mild, grassy, and fresh flavor. It is winter-resistant and can be harvested during winter in the warmer climates.

SOWING AND HARVEST

Sow directly in pots or the vegetable garden, outside from June until September or inside year-round with added light. Sow ⅓ inch deep (1 cm) and cull the plants to a distance of 4–6 inches (10–15 cm). Harvest about eight weeks after sowing. Carefully pick the leaves so that new ones can start growing. The plant will continue to grow leaves for multiple months. During high season the corn salad may blossom easily and then grow tired. It works best in early summer and fall.

PURSLANE

Portulaca oleracea
Claytonia perfoliata

Purslane is a leaf growth with meaty small round leaves and stalks. It has a nutty, fresh flavor. Purslane can be both of summer and winter varieties. The latter withstands temperatures as low as 28°F (minus 2°C). The summer variety is often called "Garden Purslane" and has either lime-yellow or green leaves.

SOWING AND HARVEST

Sow directly in a pot or vegetable garden, the summer purslane from May to June and the winter purslane in August-September. You can also grow purslane inside during winter, but you'll need extra light.

Harvest about eight weeks after sowing. The leaf rosettes are pinched off of the top and single leaves can be picked off the stalk. Harvest continuously to keep the plant from blossoming.

This batch of the spinach 'Blomsdale Long Standing' was sown under too high of temperatures and the plants therefore turned out thin and wobbly. But the leaves still tasted good and I used them for sandwiches and salad.

Keeping leaf greens on the steps or the balcony is both decorative and practical. Here you see two varieties of purslane and a leaf lettuce in between.

ARUGULA/SALAD ROCKET

Eruka sativa

Arugula has irregular leaves with a peppery flavor. There are two varieties: one with a narrow leaf that's called Italian arugula or wild arugula, and one with a larger leaf. The narrow variety, which is my favorite, does not blossom as fast as the one with the large leaves, which is a clear advantage.

SOWING AND HARVEST

Sow directly in a pot or the vegetable garden outside from May until September, and inside year-round with access to additional light. The seeds are sown ⅓ inch (½ cm) deep and grow in about 10 days. They can be sowed tightly and then you can carefully cull the plants when the plants are 2 inches (5 cm) tall, as a primary harvest. Leave one inch (a few cm) between each plant.

Best harvested when the leaves are 7–8 inches (a few decimeters) high. Cut right above the bottom leaves so that new leaves may grow. You can harvest from the same plant for two to three months, but feel free to add a liquid fertilizer in between to give the plant a new beginning. Arugula blossoms quickly, so don't wait too long before you start harvesting. If the leaves become too large and the blossoming process begins, the taste of the leaves will change as well. They will become even more peppery, and sometimes a little bitter.

> *Tip! Growths in pots do not have the same access to nutrients as the growths in the vegetable garden. If you want fine pot vegetables for the whole of summer you should water with fertilizer regularly.*

PROBLEMS THAT MAY ARISE

Arugula is easy to grow but it can attract earth fleas. The easiest way to avoid this is to cover the plants with fiber cloth right after sowing. When the plants have grown larger you just make sure that the soil stays moist. You may also use clippings to cover the soil between the rows.

ASIAN LEAF VEGETABLES

Here follows a group of Asian leaf vegetables. Many of them belong to cabbage growths, but not all of them. They are easy to cultivate, grow quickly, and are fun to use in the kitchen.

PAK CHOI

Brassica rapa var. *parachinensis*

An Asian cabbage variety with large leaves and fat stalks. It tastes like both cabbage and spinach and is best prepared in soups or woks. It grows as a gathered lettuce head, more or less open. Pak choi is very dander and fine as a young plant. I especially like the old variety "Prize Choi" for its succulence and excellent color.

SOWING AND HARVEST

Pak choi can be sown directly or pre-cultivated. The plants will be best if you sow them in late summer, but you can sow them from May-August. You sow the seeds an inch (2 cm) deep. The plants need a 10–12 inch (25–30 cm) distance between each plant and 12–16 inches (30–40 cm) between each row. Pak choi prefers even moisture and well-fertilized soil. It tolerates cold well and is, therefore, one of the vegetables we can harvest well into the fall. When you harvest, carefully twist the single leaves or loosen the whole head by cutting it loose from the root stem with a sharp knife.

PROBLEMS THAT MAY ARISE

Pak choi is a cabbage relative and therefore attracts the same diseases as cabbage, (see p. 187). The biggest problem is usually earth fleas and this is easiest to fix by covering the seeds with fiber cloth and cover cultivate with clippings. Make sure that you rotate the place of the cabbage growths each year to avoid diseases and tired soil.

KOMATSUNA/MUSTARD SPINACH

Brassica rapa var. *perviridis*

Anther contribution from Asia, a cabbage with large, crisp, lettuce-like leaves that tastes like spinach and has a mild tone of mustard. Used in salads or quickly heated in a wok. Delicious! It tolerates cold, just like pak choi, and can, if protected with fiber cloth, be harvested long after the frost takes a hold.

SOWING AND HARVEST

Sow, cultivate, and harvest like pak choi, except with less distance between the plants; 6–8 inches (15–20 cm) is usually fine, and 8–12 inches (20–30 cm) between the rows. It grows and develops faster than pak choi. For problems that may arise, see pak choi.

MIZUNA/JAPANESE MUSTARD

Brassica rapa ssp. *nipposinica*

Mizuna is an Asian leaf vegetable that looks a lot like arugula, with its long, narrow dark-green leaves. There are varying kinds, and the most common is kyona, which has narrow serrated leaves, and mibuna with long narrow rounded leaves. They both have a mild cabbage flavor and are year-round favorites in a salad.

SOWING AND HARVEST

Mizuna is sown and harvested like arugula, but it tolerates cold better and can keep even with frost as long as it's covered with fiber cloth. Mizuna is, precisely like arugula, a "cut-and-come-again" growth, which makes it possible to harvest continuously. It is important to use liquid fertilizer between harvests so that the plants don't grow tired. For problems that may arise, see pak choi.

MUSTARD GREENS/INDIAN MUSTARD

Brassica juncea

This is a fun plant for enhancing salads, stews, or soups. The taste is reminiscent of horseradish and the leaves are deep green or red-green. It keeps into fall and tolerates temperatures below 30°F (0°C). The leaf grows similarly to spinach, in a large rosette, and "Yukina Savoy," with its dented and peppery leaves. This is one of my favorites.

SOWING AND HARVEST

Sow directly from May to August. Cull to a distance of about 12 inches (30 cm) between the plants and 12–16 inches (30–40 cm) between the rows. They can be harvested when the rosette has opened and the leaves are at least 2 inches (5 cm) large. It is best when it is harvested young. Pick single leaves to allow room for new ones, or harvest the entire rosette. For problems that may arise, see pak choi.

Mache

Arugula with narrow leaf

Pak Choi

Mizuna/Japanese Mustard

Mustard Greens 'Yukina Savoy'

Basil 'Genovese'

Coriander

Dill

Shiso

CELTUCE

Lactuca sativa var. *angustana*

Celtuce has long, light green, crispy salad leaves that grow along a stem, and the stem is edible as well. The leaves are preferably eaten fresh while the stem is peeled and boiled or marinated and grilled, just like asparagus.

SOW AND HARVEST
Sow directly from May-June. Sow ⅓ inch (1 cm) deep, plant a distance of 8 inches (20 cm), and row a distance of 12 inches (30 cm). Keep the soil even and moist and support-fertilize a couple of times during the season. You can pick the leaves as you go and use them as salad. The stem must be left until late summer or into fall and is harvested before the plant blossoms.

MITSUBA/JAPANESE WILD PARSLEY

A sturdy leaf growth with heart-shaped, irregular leaves, reminiscent of parsley. It has a spicy, slightly mineral taste and is great fresh in salads, sauteed in a wok, and in Asian soups and stews. Grows in gathered clusters, like common parsley.

SOW AND HARVEST
Sow mitsuba inside during April/May or outside from May-June. It is best to sow in a pot or plug and then later plant it outside when the soil has had time to warm at the beginning of June. You can also let it grow in a pot. Keep the soil moist and water with fertilizer regularly. Harvest from the stem continuously so that it can shoot out new sprouts. The leaves taste the best when they are young. Mitsuba biennial can, in favorable conditions, survive the winters of more temperate climates.

SPICY LEAVES

In this little group I have gathered the growths that represents the basic spices in our summer kitchen. They are all annual growths, and they are therefore perfect to combine with annual vegetables in the vegetable garden. Basil and Coriander demand heat and are best grown in a pot.

BASIL

Ocimum basilicum

You can find basil in many different varieties. Most common is "Genovese," the Italian large-leaf basil that's traditionally used in tomato salads, various pasta dishes, and pesto. But other basils, like lemon basil and cinnamon basil, can give a salad a different and welcomed kick. And Asian inspired cooking isn't complete without fresh Thai basil. The Thai basil "Siam Queen" blossoms slowly, which is a good thing, but even when it blossoms, the plant maintains a nice shape and fresh leaves. It works just as well as a decorative plant.

SOW AND HARVEST
Sow very shallow; just sprinkle a little bit of dirt over so that the seeds are barely covered. Keep the soil moist. You can either broadcast sow in a box and later plant five to seven plants together in a pot once the character leaves have formed, or you can sow directly in small pots and cull it out so that you end up with a good amount of small plants left in each pot.

None of the basil plants like cold. Under 50°F (10°C) the leaves start turning yellow. It should therefore be kept in a warm and sheltered place. Take it in when the nights starts getting colder. You harvest the leaves by cutting or pinching the stem right above a new set of leaves. In other words you harvest the entire top of the plant and not just the leaves. After harvest, new leaves will form.

Basil is the best fresh but you can also save it through drying it, preserving it as pesto, or freezing it.

CORIANDER

Coriandrum sativum

Coriander leaves look like parsley, but are slightly thinner and shinier; it grows in bouquets. Most have a strong feeling about this spice—either people love it or they hate it. For me, this takes me straight back to Vietnam and Thailand, and hot noodle soups. I think it has a freshness and aroma unlike any other spice and that it definitely belongs among the basic spices on the stairs.

SOW AND HARVEST
Sow many seeds in the same pot, with about an inch (2 cm) of distance between. Cover with ⅓ inch (1 cm) dirt. Feel free to cover the pot with plastic wrap and poke holes in the plastic so that the seeds can grow in a temperate environment. Coriander has a tendency to blossom fast. After blossoming the leaves never go back, so make sure that you don't wait too long with the harvest. If you want access to coriander all summer long, the best way is to sow in rounds. The variety "Slowbolt" blossoms somewhat slower than the others and is therefore a good choice.

DILL

Anethum graveolens

A real Swedish classic, it is just as beautiful as it is tasty. It is wise to choose a dill variety that has both crown dill and leaf dill, such as the variety with the fun name "common dill." You can then harvest leaves when they are fresh and small and later allow some of the plants to develop with their crowns. Even if you don't use them as a spice, they look beautiful as decorative flowers or just as an ornament in the vegetable garden.

SOW AND HARVEST
Dill can be sowed as soon as the soil is ready in spring and it is sowed directly onto the growth site. So ⅓ inch (1 cm) deep and not to tight together. If the soil is weed-free you can sow in patches. If not, it is better to sow in rows so that you know where you can expect the dill to emerge. All weeds should be removed as soon as they show up. Keep the seedlings moist. One tip is to cover with a fiber cloth until the plants show.

PARSLEY

Petroselinum crispum

Parsley can have both curly leaves and smooth leaves. The latter variety has become very popular in cooking during later years. I like them both. The smooth parsley is more flavorful and the curly is incredibly beautiful as a border growth with its nonchalant way of growing. It does, for instance, enjoy growing with tomatoes. The parsley is a biannual growth that can sometimes survive winter.

SOW AND HARVEST
The parsley is sowed in a pot, plug, or directly in the vegetable garden. If you sow it outside, then start in the middle of May. Sow the seeds on the surface and keep the soil moist. The seeds grow slowly so be patient. I usually let them grow to little plants in a tray and then move them outside as a border plant. If that's the case, you sow four to five seeds in each plug so that you get sturdy, small plants to move outside.

Harvest the leaves continuously. If the parsley lasts over winter you can harvest the leaves from early spring to about midsummer the following year. After this, the plant will blossom and the quality of the leaves will decrease.

SHISO

Perilla frutescens

An Asian spice growth with a sweet and spicy curry flavor with a hint of mint. The plant can have red leaves or green leaves and the leaves can be less or more curly. The leaves are eaten fresh or in soups and stews.

SOW AND HARVEST
Sow in a shallow depth in porous soil in a pot or tray. Shiso grows slowly so be patient. Sow eight weeks before you wish to plant them outside, and you should wait until the risk of frost is completely over. The plants are replanted when they are about an inch (couple of cm) tall, and they are planted with an 8–10 inch (20–25 cm) distance between each plant. You can also cultivate shiso as a pot growth. The leaves can be carefully harvested one at a time or you can cut the top off right above a set of leaves so that the plant develops new leaves.

Tip! *Let the basil grow in slight shadow. If the leaves are exposed to strong sun they can become rubbery and get a slight bitter taste.*

GOOD STALKS

Fennel, celery, asparagus and rhubarb . . . good stems are a motley crew of vegetables that have nothing more in common besides the fact that they are all good stalks that enhance the mood of kitchen. They are somewhat odd, and many of them are most unusual in our kitchens. Still, these are some of the plants that I most look forward to harvesting and preparing, with their unique flavors and clear seasonal character. The asparagus, for instance, and the rhubarb are both biennial growths whose meager sprouts are a clear sign that the beginning of summer has arrived.

I HAVE GOTTEN more familiar with asparagus since I started cultivating in Spain, where it also grows wild on every hill. In Swedish vegetable gardens, however, it needs light and nutrient-rich soil to be comfortable. It peeks out with its pointy sprouts when spring arrives, and every fall it stands proud in bright yellow as small pointy bushes.

The rhubarb is different. I've lost touch with this plant after I moved her. This is because it belongs to a group of growths that does not only endure cold, but also needs cold to grow well. But the hunt for varieties that withstand heat continues, because it is deeply missed in my Spanish garden.

The rhubarb crop back home in Tyresö gave many ideas for tasty dinners. The most common is to pinch a few stalks for a pie and cream at the beginning of summer and then afterwards, we are done with it. But this unique growth can be used in many other delicious ways: spicey chutneys, lamb stews, compote with nutmeg and cloves for the cheese plate, fill for a nice tenderloin, cold summer drinks with vodka and lime, and vanilla-boiled rhubarb juice—just to name a few. The rhubarb plant can get quite old, and even if you don't look after them, they will grow and give a decent crop for multiple years. But if you really want to take care of it, you should add fertilizer and move and rotate plants now and then to keep them fresh and energized.

Two other stalks worth mentioning are celery and fennel. Both of these are annual growths. They also have strong characters and their presence on the plate does not go unnoticed. We know fennel best from dishes with fish and seafood, wine-boiled mussels with fennel, or in the bouillabaisse—the filling fish soup from the south of France. But in my opinion it is great on its own as well. Oven-baked with a little olive oil and salt is a delicacy.

Celery is a rather demanding growth, but if you get it to grow, the bouquets are quite sturdy. Because of its strong flavor, you may only use one or two stalks now and then. This means that a couple pots on the windowsill can provide enough celery for the entire year.

CULTIVATING GOOD STALKS

FENNEL

Foeniculum vulgare

The base, or bulb, of fennel can be eaten raw or cooked. It has a slight anise flavor. It is filling and both sweet and a little shot. The dill-like leaves can be picked continuously and used as a spice in salads or fish dishes.

PREPARING THE GROWTH SITE

Choose a warm and sheltered spot in the garden. Fennel enjoys a moist and humus-rich soil. Use manure and stone meal as a base fertilizer.

SOW

WHEN? Should be pre-cultivated, but can also be sowed directly in warmer climates. Pre-cultivation happens four to six weeks before planned planting, which is when the risk of frost is completely gone and the soil holds a temperature of at least 50°F (10°C). You can sow it directly in midsummer. The fennel is sensitive to cold in combination with a lot of light. It may shoot up and blossom without developing a nice base. It is therefore good to wait a while into a summer before you sow. By then the temperature is more stable and the days are shorter.

HOW? The fennel has a sensitive root system that wants as little disturbance as possible. It is therefore best to sow directly in a root trainer/growing tray that can be planted directly out in the garden without replanting. Fill the trays three-fourths full with soil. Lightly press it into place, drop a couple of seeds in each plug, and cover with soil and water. Keep the seeds moist. Remove the weakest plant in each plug early on. Plant with a 14 inch (35 cm) distance between the rows and an 8–10 inch (20–25 cm) plant distance.

If you sow directly in the garden it is easiest to make a rut, about an inch (2 cm) deep, with about 14 inches (35 cm) between the rows. Water the rut and sow the seeds with 2 inches (5 cm) distance. When the plants appear, you cull them to a distance of 8 inches (20 cm). Be careful not to disturb the roots. If you bother the plant it might blossom too quickly before the base is properly developed.

NURTURE

Feel free to cup a little soil around the base of the plant during growth to make it more stable. Covering the soil is perfect as the root system doesn't like a stir and it needs even moisture. There is usually no need for support fertilization, but if the summer is very dry you have to make sure that the plants receive enough water as they easily dry out.

HARVEST

WHEN? The bases are harvested when they have swelled and are fleshy, usually in late summer, early fall.

HOW? Cut the entire base with a sharp knife from its root. Be careful not to cut too high, so that you get all the stalks nicely gathered. Top the plant so that the green stalks poke up 2–4 inches (5–10 cm) above the base. The fennel can be stored in a cold place for a couple of weeks. If you want to make the plant last you

It is the swelled stem base that has the strongest flavor of the fennel, but you can also harvest and use the leaves as a spice.

can cover it with some leaves or straw to protect it against frost.

PROBLEMS THAT MAY ARISE

Fennel is not difficult to grow. It rarely gets sick as long as it has received a good base fertilization and plenty of water. The main threat to the growth is shifts in temperatures or periods of drought. When the plants are small, it is a good idea to have filter cloth at hand to cover them with on cold nights.

The fennel can be attacked by the same nematodes or fungal diseases as other bouquet growths (such as carrots, dill, parsley, root parsley, celeriac, and celery) so be meticulous about the crop rotation when you sow. Furthermore, the fennel is somewhat of a loner and they say that it grows best on its own, at least it doesn't seem like any other plant really likes growing by its side.

MY FAVORITES

'Finocchio di Parma sel. Prado'
A very white and beautiful Italian fennel that works excellent in the Nordic climate, but should be pre-cultivated. Sweet and mild flavor, which makes it tasty raw as well.

'Zefa Fino'
A fast-growing fennel that is especially ideal because it develops even if you sow a while into summer. Gives a nice, flat, swelled base.

CELERY/CELERY STALKS

Apium graveolens var. *dulce*

Celery is cultivated for it leaves and its stalks, in contrast to it relative, celeriac. The celery grows a bouquet with clearly bent, crispy stalks. Celery is not among the easiest plants to cultivate, first and foremost because it takes so long to develop, but also because it demands a stable climate to be comfortable. On the other hand, it is rarely affected by disease, so if you manage to get it to grow, the chances of a nice crop are great.

SOW

WHEN? The celery should be pre-cultivated to make sure that it has time to develop. Sow about three months before you plan to plant it in early summer. This demands that you can add extra light during the growing.

HOW? Sow in a shallow depth, with just a couple of millimeters of cover and preferably cover with perlite that lets light through. Another option is to not cover the seeds at all but rather bind transparent plastic over the seeds and make airholes in it. Keep the soil moist and around 68°F (20°C). The germination can take a while, but don't give up. When the plants have appeared you can lower the temperature a few degrees, but continue to give them extra light.

Celery needs time to develop pretty stalks.

PREPARING THE GROWTH SITE

Celery wants to be a little spoiled and likes a warm, humus-rich, well-fertilized spot where it has good access to moisture. A mineral-rich soil is important and you prepare the soil best by fertilizing with both manure and Algomin or stone meal.

PLANTING OUTSIDE

Harden the plants meticulously and you can even start preparing the plants by slowly lowering the temperature inside. Move them once or twice and plant them when all the risk of frost is gone and the temperature has reached 55–60°F (13–15°C).

Dips in temperature can make the growth of the celery come to a halt. Plant in rows with a 14–18 inch (35–45 cm) distance, and about 10 inches between the plants.

NURTURE

There are two kinds of celery: the one that bleaches itself and the other that needs a little help. The self-bleaching type is obviously a little easier to cultivate. If you choose a variety that needs help, you have to cover the stalks during the growth season so that the sunrays don't reach them. You do this by twisting carton or burlap around the stalks; alternatively, you can cup dirt up around the plant regularly.

HARVEST

WHEN? Celery is usually ready to harvest in early fall and can stand until the frost hits. If you want to make the crop last longer, you have to cover the plants as protection against the cold. You can pick the leaves continuously, like parsley.

HOW? Either you break off single stalks from the plant, or you can harvest the whole plant by cutting it loose from its root with a sharp knife. If it is kept in a cool place it can keep for a couple of weeks, but it's not made for long storage. If you want to keep it for a long time, it will keep best chopped and frozen.

MY FAVORITE

'Golden self-blanching'
This is, to be honest, the only celery I have ever cultivated, but I had good results. It is self-bleaching and gives light-yellow, good, crisp stalks.

ASPARAGUS

Asparagus officinalis

Asparagus is both nice and fun to cultivate. It is biennial and a relatively modest growth, but it is rather demanding to prepare the growth site and it requires patience to wait a couple of years before you can start harvesting. If you have room, I usually recommend that you plant a whole little hedge once you're at it, so you will have a real crop once you can harvest them. Green and white asparagus are the same plant, but the color depends on whether or not you bleach it.

A young asparagus plant that will grow more and more stalks to harvest as years go by

PREPARING THE GROWTH SITE

Since asparagus are biennial, you need to be considerate when you choose a spot for them. It is a rather beautiful plant that gets a beautiful fall color, so it does not have to be hidden under the garage. It likes to grow in a warm and sheltered spot. The soil should be light, sandy, and humus-rich. Deep-dig and generously fertilize with manure before you plant the asparagus. If you do the work in springtime, you can decrease the fertilizer and replace some of it with compost. Feel free to blend in some sand up to 8 mm deep. Loosening the soil on the deep is very important.

SOW

Asparagus is easiest to buy in springtime as finished plants. You can sow the seeds yourself, but as I mentioned, this will take some time. For the first year they will only germinate and then you can plant them the following spring.

WHEN? Sow inside in February and March or outside in a hotbed in April and May.

HOW? The seeds are sowed about an inch (a couple of centimeters) deep and are blended with a mixture of dirt and sifted soil. If you sow in root trainers, you can sow a couple of seeds in each plug and later remove the weakest sprout. After a couple of months the plants will need to be replanted. Place them in compost-fertilized soil. In late spring you can move the plants out to a cultivation bed where they will grow. Cover with straw and leaves during winter. The following year, you dig them up when the sprout peeks up about an inch (a couple of cm) above the ground and move them to their growth site.

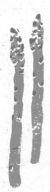

TIP!

There are both male and female asparagus plants. The females grow small flowers that distribute seeds. If you cut them down and remove everything before fall hits and the seeds have ripened, you can avoid wild plants in your crop.

PLANTING OUTSIDE

The plants are planted in springtime as soon as the soil is workable; April-May is usually about right. If you dig up your own small plants that have been germinating you choose the strongest plants with the most developed roots. The weak and underdeveloped are placed on the compost. The asparagus needs at least 12–16 inches (30–40 cm) distance between the plants and about 40 inches (1 meter) between the rows. The row distance may seem excessive in the beginning, but the leaves will spread out over time. Make an 8 inch (20 cm) deep trenches in the ground that you fill with 4 inches (1 decimeter) of porous soil. Place the plants on the small hill with the roots spread out downwards, then cover with about 2 inches (5 cm) of soil. As the plant grows you add more soil until the entire trench is full. Afterwards, you cover around the plants with clippings or seaweed.

NURTURE

When you cultivate with a cover of fresh organic material, you automatically ensure nutrients and moisture for the plants. During the first two years you can let the plants take care of themselves. Remove withered and dead material but don't harvest. If the growth seems weak, you can fertilize with nettle water in June. Two years after planting, you can harvest for the first time. Afterwards, when autumn approaches and the plants have turned yellow, you cut them down to a short stump.

HARVEST

WHEN? After planting you should wait for two years before you start harvesting. The reason for this is that the plants needs a large and well-developed root system to handle the stress of the harvest, as you will want new crops after harvest. The sprouts are cut off when they grow above the surface, but let them get 6–8 inches (15–20 cm) long. Harvest up until midsummer, but not longer as the plant needs to recuperate for the rest of the season.

HOW? If you want to eat the asparagus green, you simply let it grow as it is and cut the spears off with a sharp knife. If you want to harvest white asparagus, you have to bleach them. You bleach them by covering the spears with soil as they grow. When the pile of soil is about 8–10 inches (20–25 cm) deep, you can dig up the bleached asparagus and cut them loose.

PROBLEMS THAT MAY ARISE

Asparagus is nice to cultivate because diseases rarely affect it. As long as it is allowed to grow well-hydrated, it will keep fresh for years in the same spot.

However, asparagus rust can occur. This is a fungi disease that is difficult to get rid of once it has taken hold of the plant. The best thing to do is to prevent the disease by being meticulous about cutting the plant in the fall and burning the flowers, as well as making sure that the cover material is removed and composted in the spring or is folded in with the soil. The soil needs to breathe fresh spring air and later be covered with new light material once it is warm enough.

MY FAVORITES

'Primaverde'
A rather new variety of fresh and sweet asparagus with a light green color. Only male plants.

'Rambo'
A robust and sturdy variety that grows good green spears early in the season. Usually recommended as one of the best varieties for home cultivating.

'Rhapsody'
A medium-sized asparagus that you may grow as both white and green.

RHUBARB

Rheum rhabarbarum

Rhubarb is biennial, grows in large crops, and demands a lot of space. The stalks are harvested young and crisp and vary in color depending on the variety, everything from light green to cherry red. Rhubarb contain oxalic acid, which is not healthy in large amounts, but there are varieties with lower levels of oxalic acid and the thinner the stalks are when you harvest, the less acid they contain.

DIVIDING

It is most common and easiest to buy finished rhubarb plants, or that you get a piece of your neighbor's plant. This is also a way of lessening the waiting time until harvest, because after planting you have to wait at least one year before you can harvest. If you sow, you have to extend the waiting time to two years. When you divide rhubarb, the mother plant is dug up and the root system divided with a sharp and clean knife. Each new plant should have at least one leaf bud, a piece of soil stem, and root system. Let the cut surface dry a little bit before you place the plant in the ground. You can plant them in fall or spring, but they find it easiest to establish in spring.

PREPARING THE GROWTH SITE

Rhubarb is most comfortable in humid and nutrient-rich soil, as it needs much of both. Clay soils are fine as long as they are watered well. If you have a heavy clay soil you should, however, fold in some humus. Humus-rich light clay seems to be the ideal. The rhubarb will spread out over time and each plant needs about 10 square feet (1 square meter) of personal space. It enjoys the sun, but it can grow in walking shade as well. The soil should be clinically cleansed of weeds, as the rhubarb does not want competition. If you are planting in the spring, you should prepare the soil the fall prior.

SOW

Sowing is cheaper than buying ready plants, and if you want to plant a lot you can consider it. The selection of varieties decreases though, as it is hard to find real variety-stable seeds.

WHEN? Pre-cultivate in March and April or sow directly in the ground from April-June.

HOW? Sow the seeds about an inch (2 cm) below the surface and keep humid. If you choose to pre-cultivate you can sow directly in 3 ½ inch (9 cm) pots with a blend of planting soil and sifted soil. When the plants are showing, you can add some compost or nettle water. Plant them out on the growth site or in a hotbed in May and June. You can plant the rhubarb as soon as the soil is ready and you can dig in it. Plant with about 30 inches (75 cm) of distance between the plants.

NURTURE
Rhubarb needs a lot of nutrients and it needs constant access to humidity. Most people that grow rhubarb don't take care of it at all, and it still keeps coming back every year, but with minimal nurturing you can get a better crop and the plant will keep longer. Fertilize every year with manure and support fertilize with stone meal or Algomin during summer. Feel free to cover with clippings around the plants and remove weeds.

HARVEST
WHEN? Harvest the first rhubarb as soon as the stalks have developed in spring. It is at its very best then. You can usually harvest a couple of times during spring and early summer. Later the plant will need rest if it should stand a chance of providing a crop in autumn as well.

HOW? The stalks are harvested by twisting them lightly so that they let go of the base. Always choose the freshest stalks. They contain the least oxalic acid and taste the best. If you use a knife, be careful so that you don't cut the root and damage the plant.

PROBLEMS THAT MAY ARISE
The largest problem is most often biennial weeds that make the plants weaken over time. Make sure that the soil is free of weeds when you plant the rhubarb and later cover cultivate systematically.

Rhubarb can also attract aphids. These are most easily removed by spraying soapy water or a hard stream of water. The largest problem with the aphids is that they can be carriers of a virus. You should therefore fight aphids as best as possible, even if they seem harmless. Lice attacks will often occur during droughts, when the plants are stressed because of a lack of water. Be meticulous with your watering routine and cover your seedlings and you will decrease the risk of unhealthy plants.

MY FAVORITES

'Elmblitz'
A good alternative if you want a variety with less oxalic content. It gives red-green stalks and large harvests. Can be bought as seeds.

'Elmsfeuer'
Flavorful rhubarb with beautiful red stalks. Makes great squash.

'Spangsbjerg'
A favorite with my rhubarb-cultivating colleague. It is red through and through and grows long thin stalks that are easy to use in cooking.

'Viktoria'
A green rhubarb that's fresh and worthy for its rich harvest and good taste. It's a real workhorse, and is often found in old gardens. You can buy this variety as seeds as well.

Rhubarb Cream

2–3 Servings

9 oz/ 2–3 stalks (250 g) rhubarb
1 cup (2 dl) water
¼ cup (0.5 dl) sugar
1½ tbsp potato flour

1. Rinse and peel the rhubarb. Cut in smaller pieces, about an inch (2 cm).

2. Boil water and sugar. Add the rhubarb. Let it boil for 4–5 minutes until the rhubarb starts dividing.

3. Stir the potato flour in with a little cold water. Pour into the pot in a thin ray, while stirring. Let the cream come to a boil, when you see the first bubble it is ready.

Serve with milk.

Fresón
De Puerto Serrano
(Cádiz)

TOMATO

I have a love affair with the tomato. The first time I tried to cultivate my own tomatoes, I was sold. I like every single moment in the process—from reading seed catalogues to harvesting. Choose varieties, sow in small clay pots, educate the small plants, bind them, trim, and later harvest. The tomato plant needs a lot of care, and if you are careless with watering, fertilizing, or trimming, it will show immediately. This plant demands attention, but the reward after a good effort is better than any other.

FEW OTHER VEGETABLES are so distinctly different when you grow them at home compared to when you buy them. When you place a sun-ripened, lukewarm tomato in your mouth, you can't help but feel happy. Tomatoes should always taste that way—sweet, tart, and warm, with thin skin and soft fruit meat. Children are honest. They are usually good at pushing the sliced tomatoes on their plates away, but if they are placed in front of a Sungold plant with small mini tomatoes that taste like sunshine, they will eat them like candy.

My tomatoes have grown in the vegetable garden, in pots, in bags, in hotbeds, in heightened beds, in sunken beds, in Sweden and in Spain. The possibilities are endless, which also makes them a vegetable for everyone. They have been with me through all of my cultivation spots. And I've always learned something new about how they work and how they like things.

The tomato is a diva, and you can't avoid that fact. It likes standing in the warmth of the sun and stretching. It needs regular watering and refills of nutrients. You have to trim some of the varieties so that they can focus all of their energy on making fruit. The tomato is really a climbing growth, and you can tell. If you don't limit it, it will grow out of proportion. This is how it looks in my Spanish vegetable garden, as there is no need to restrain it here; there are enough warm days for it to continue giving fruit even if I don't cut it.

Even if the harvest season is short, you can get a generous amount of tomatoes. This is never an issue because you can use them in an infinite number of ways. You can dry them in the oven, make chili sauce, marmalades, chutneys, and other preserves, and you can even freeze them. However, in my experience, most of the small tomatoes go straight from the plant to the mouth. The short-lived luxury of eating sun-ripe tomatoes from the garden is hard to tire of.

CULTIVATING TOMATOES

SOW

WHEN? You can grow tomatoes (*Solanum lycopersicum*) both outside and in greenhouses. You should sow about eight weeks before planting outside. If you are growing them in a greenhouse, February and March is usually fine, but if they are going directly into the ground you should wait till March and April. If you don't have optimal conditions for growing plants then you might want to wait until April. By then the light is back and you have a greater change of growing strong and fine plants without extra light.

HOW? Tomato seeds are easy to work with and can be sowed in trays, directly in small pots, or in root trainers an inch (a few centimeters) deep. The seeds want a lot of warmth to grow, around 75°F (25°C). Once they've broken the surface they need a lot of light, and as soon as they've developed character leaves you can move them into a cooler environment. This cools them down a little so that they don't loose control and grow long and thin.

EDUCATION

When the plant has developed character leaves you can move it into a pot if you have many in one tray. If you have them in small pots or plugs you can wait until the plant is 2–3 inches (5–7 cm) before you move them into a larger pot. The tomatoes develop roots from the stem, which means that you can set the little plant deeper in the soil than what it was before. It will then develop a steady root system. If the plants are long and thin you can remove the leaves and place the whole stem under the soil in the pot so that only the tip of the plant is visible. This way you increase the chance of a fine and steady plant. Just make sure that the soil stays humid.

PREPARING THE GROWTH SITE

Tomatoes can grow in pots, in sacks, in the garden, in the yard, or in a greenhouse. What you choose depends on your possibilities, but also what kind of tomato you are growing, and if you plan to grow the same kind of tomato multiple years in a row. Tomatoes are unfortunately the kind of vegetable that can attract diseases that they contract from the soil. It is therefore an advantage to change where they are growing each season. If you have a small vegetable garden it can sometimes be a good idea to cultivate the tomatoes in a pot to let the soil rest.

TIP!

Even if you grow your own plants you can buy a couple large plants at your closest trade farm. They give fruit in a timely manner and you lengthen the season.

Do not let green tomatoes go to waste. Make marmalade or chutney with them and spice with, for instance, cinnamon and ginger.

Tomato plants should be stubby and pretty just like this when they are little. These are raised at Rosendal's garden in Stockholm.

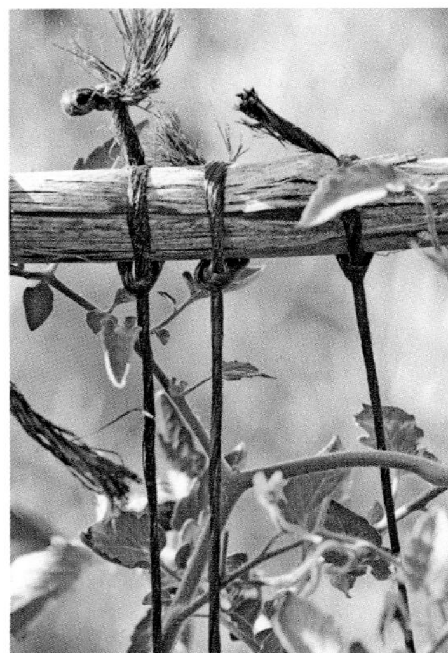

The strings are twisted around the tomato plants, which makes it climb upwards.

Reminder notes are my savior! (It reads: Don't forget to fertilize the tomatoes)

The tomato is a powerful climbing growth and will act like this unless you trim and shorten it.

There are also tomatoes with different ways of growing to choose from: bush tomatoes are low, don't need trimming, and are perfect for pot growing. Similarly, "Hundreds and Thousands" with their hanging branches could be an ornament in a pot or a hanging basket. Other tomatoes grow tall and will demand support and binding.

Tomatoes need a lot of nutrition and water. They want soil that can hold moisture and is mull-rich. Fold in compost and/or well-burned manure in the soil. If you're cultivating in a pot or directly in a sack, choose a soil that is earmarked for large urns that will maintain its structure all through the summer. No matter if you cultivate tomatoes in pots or the garden, make sure that the spot is well drained.

The tomatoes want loads of sun, warmth, and wind shelter. Having them up at a sun-drenched wall is great, and a mound that holds warmth is even better. Remember that each plant needs at least ten liters of soil to grow in. The more soil you give the plant, the better the prospect of meeting the nutrient and water need.

Planting outside

You can move the plants outside when the nightly temperatures are milder. The tomatoes do not tolerate frost and prefer temperatures at around 50°F (10°C) during the night. You can plant them a little deeper than you did in the pots. Give them a growth support right away, such as a bamboo cane, and prepare to bind it as you go. Place them with 20 inches (50 cm) of distance in-between.

NURTURE

As previously mentioned, tomatoes demand a lot of attention and nurturing. Many tomato varieties need to be trimmed. The bag of seeds will most often specify if the plant needs trimming. The trimming means removing all of the new sprouts that shoot out from the fold between the stem and the petiole. This way, the plant won't grow in all directions, but steadily rise upward and can focus its energy on growing fruit. If the plant is getting too tall you can cut the top. Afterwards you can allow new side sprouts to grow further down and create new main stems.

Even if you've given your tomato plants a good base fertilization, you will need to give it some snacks during the season. Support fertilize with Algomin, wood ashes, Chrysene, seaweed, or similar. Tomatoes also love to have the surface covered with straw or clippings. This is beneficial from a nutritional standpoint, to hold moisture, and to protect the outer roots.

Frequent watering is also extremely important. There are growths that can manage if you just

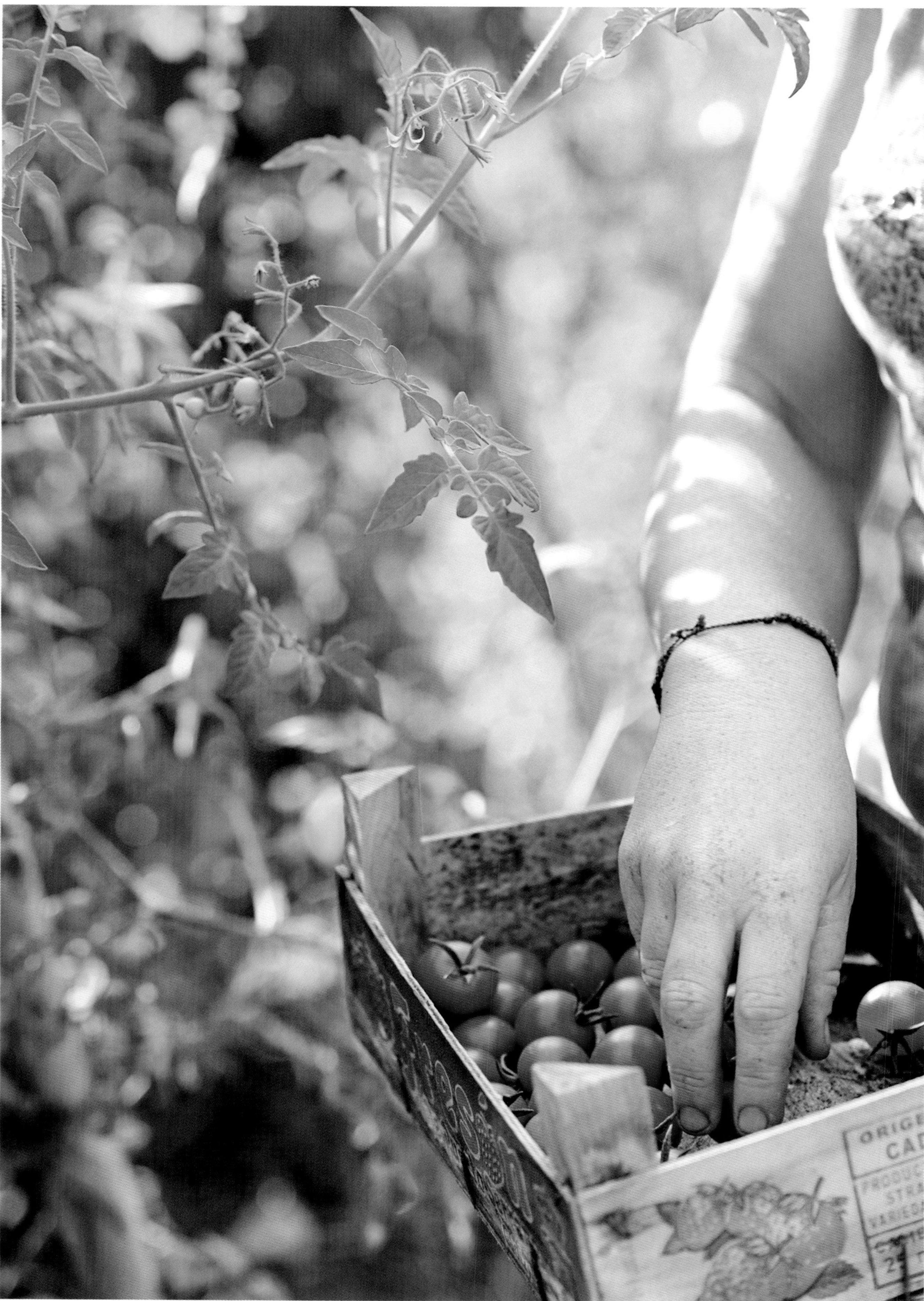

spray a little water now and then when you want to and have time—it is not that kind of plant. Water your tomatoes regularly and make sure that the whole root system has access to water. If you are going away, then install a drop system, or ask a neighbor to help you with the watering. Tomato plants do not like being watered directly on the leaves, so water directly on the soil.

If you take away all of the new shoots projecting from the crease between the stem and leaf stalk, the branches will grow steadily and focus on developing fruit.

HARVEST

WHEN? The tomatoes are at their best when they are completely ripe. They should have developed their color, hardened, and should easily let go of the plant.

HOW? When ripe tomatoes are picked by hand, they let go easily if you bend the stem lightly. If you want to harvest green tomatoes it may be best to use small pruning shears so you don't damage the twigs. At the end of the season when the cold is approaching, you can pick all of the tomatoes and let them ripen inside.

PROBLEMS THAT MAY ARISE

Tomatoes belong to the same category as, among others, potatoes, eggplant, and bell peppers. They can also get the same diseases. That is why you should not grow them in the same spot year after year and preferably not next to each other in the garden either. The most common are mold and other fungi infections, but viruses and nematodes that live in the soil can also ruin things.

Fungi attacks often succeed in humid and cold summers when the leaves don't really have time to dry. The spores are dispersed in the air and it is difficult to avoid them. What you can do is makes sure that the leaves are as dry as possible and that there's air between the plants and branches so that the air can circulate. Infected leaves need to be thrown away immediately and be burned or thrown out—not to be put on the compost.

Another threat to a tomato cultivator is getting bad fruit. Most common is pistil rot, when the tomatoes start rotting in one end. Luckily this is a result of calcium deficiency and not a virus. This can either be due to lack off access to calcium in the soil or uneven watering so that the plant has not been able to absorb the calcium properly. Fertilize with Algomin and be meticulous with watering to avoid, or repair, the problem.

Tip! *Many cultivators say that if the plant has high silicone levels, it will be more resistant to fungi diseases. You can achieve this by, for instance, spraying horsetail tea on the plants. I have treated my small plants with nettle water for many years and horsetail tea to keep them healthy and packed with nurture. To me, this is a way of trying to give them a strong immune system. But there is no guarantee that they won't get sick and when the attack is there, it definitely doesn't help. But I have to admit, that I often have strong and healthy plants . . .*

To decrease the risk of soil-bound diseases, and nematodes, it is most efficient to grow with rotation cultivation.

You should always dig up the whole root system of the plant before winter, and preferably a part of the surrounding soil as well if you cultivate in a greenhouse, and fold in new compost in the cultivation spot. This way you add new fungi and bacteria that can balance out possible pests in the soil.

ORIGEN

MY FAVORITES

1.

2.

3.

'Black Krim'
Makes a beautiful and exciting addition to the tomato selection. Dark fruits from Crimea and as such are good to cultivate in our climate as well. Fresh, sweet and sour fruit meat. A salad favorite. Tall plant that needs to be bound and trimmed.

'Costoluto Fiorentino'
An Italian variety that is reliable even in the North if you grow in a greenhouse or in warm places. Furrowed large fruits with sweet and juicy fruit meat.

1. 'Cuore del Ponente'
One of few steak tomatoes that I like. This ripens completely without cracking. Sweet and juicy meat and extremely beautiful furrowed shape. Grows tall and very strong, is bound and trimmed.

Tip! If you oven-bake the tomatoes slowly or dry them on low heat so that they are half-baked, the fruit will get rid of much of its water and the sweeter flavors will be enhanced. Good as a side, but also in meat sauce or chili sauce.

2. 'Gardener's Delight'
A cherry tomato that never fails, steady and affluent with tasty, intensely red fruits. I use them for everything: salad, drying, salsa, and oven-roasting. Tall plant with fierce growth. Bind and trim.

3. 'San Marzano'
A real Mediterranean tomato that's grown in the slopes of Mount Vesuvius, but you can also grow it in a greenhouse or in warm parts. Elongated fruit with few cores, a lot of meat and thin skin. Supreme in sauces or stews. Tall plant that needs to be bound and trimmed.

4. 'Sungold F1'
Beautiful little olive-shaped cherry tomato. Very fruity and sweet meat, and wonderful in salads. Tall plant that needs to be bound and trimmed.

'Tumbling Tom Red'
'Hundreds and Thousands' tomato with hanging branches. Does not need trimming. Grows loads of small, fine red fruits, sweet and tasty. Perfect for a balcony or veranda.

'Vilma'
A cherry tomato that deserves its place among the favorites because of its flavor and because it's a real balcony-tomato. A short growing, stable, bush that gives many fruits, and does not need to be trimmed.

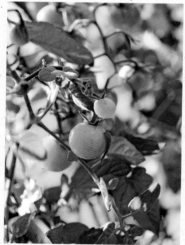

4.

'Zloty Ozarowski'
A good, orange tomato with a lot of flavor and fine fruit meat. Beautiful in salads. Tall plants that are bound and trimmed.

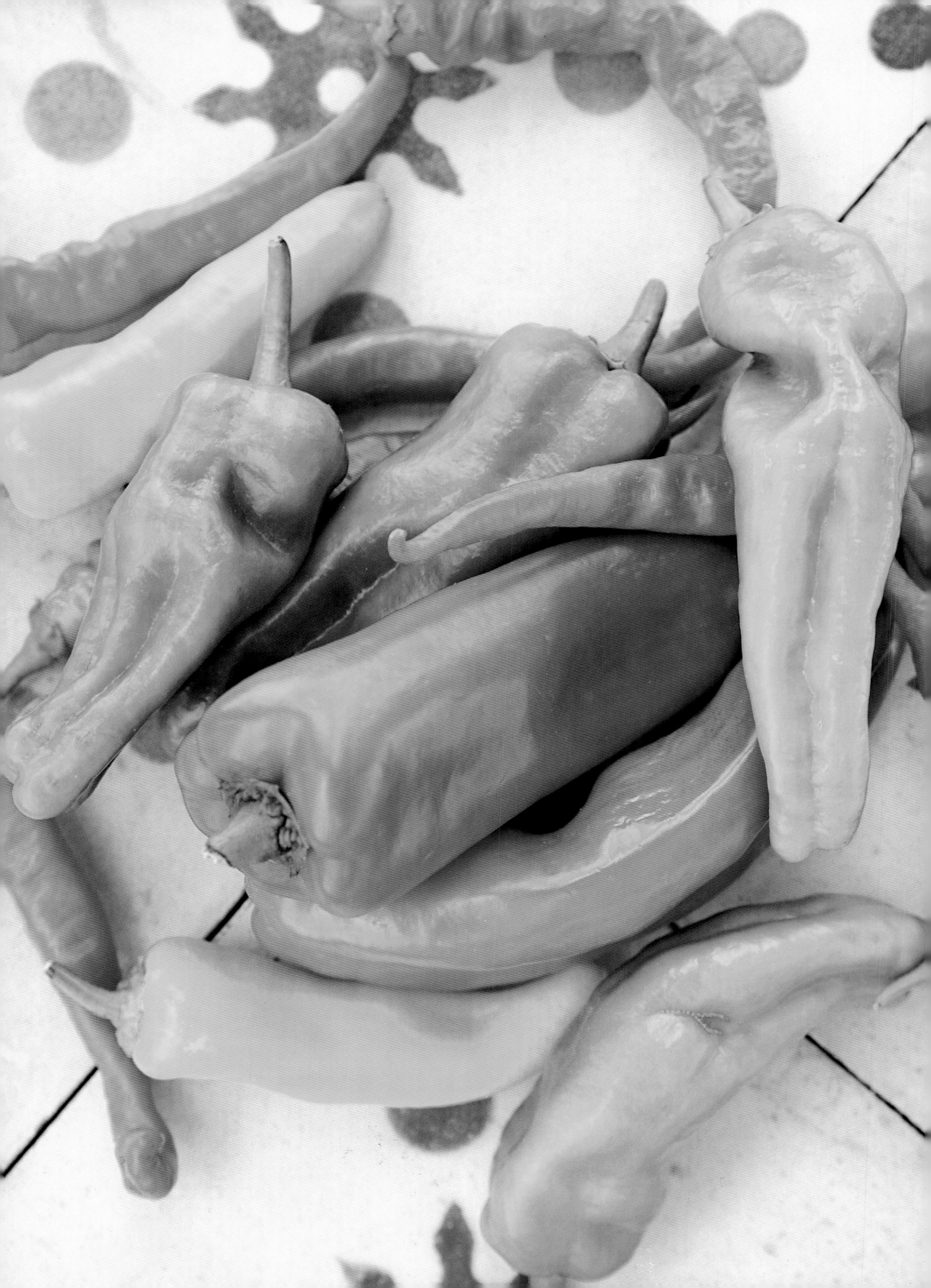

CHILI & BELL PEPPERS

Despite the fact that chili and bell peppers (*Capsicum*) are not among the vegetables that are most natural for us in the North, they do belong to the favorites. In February, when the winter is at its worst, many of us are willing to use multiple days mounting growth lamps and converting our living rooms into sixty degree (16°C) nurseries for tiny chili plants. All just to get a small taste of Mexico or India towards the end of the summer.

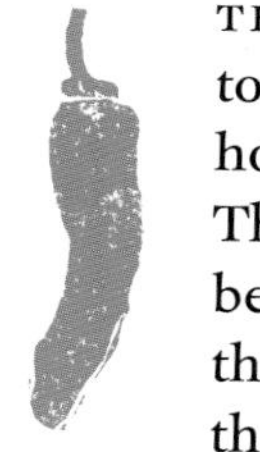

THE BELL PEPPER is most likely to succeed if you have a greenhouse or can cultivate in a hotbed. The climate outside will often become too cold and unstable for the plants to be comfortable and the fruits to have time to ripen and develop their sweetness. But as I said, if you have access to a greenhouse, you can get large, fine plants and a good harvest. I have a small favorite bell pepper, "Mini Bell," that does manage to ripen well in Sweden and grows small, round fruits in various colors. It tastes delicious oven-roasted and is a perfect "first" bell pepper to start out with.

The chili plant is a little tougher than the bell pepper and can grow outside in favorable conditions, but only in warmer climates. If you live further north it will have to decorate the glass veranda, the greenhouse, or the windowsill. It likes sun and warmth and dislikes large changes in climate and hard winds. Just like the bell pepper, the chili is a small bush, and you can cultivate it in a pot. However, certain plants can grow quite tall and may need poles to lean against. The good thing about having them in a pot is that you can move them outside when the sun is out and take them in during the cold nights in the fall to allow the fruits to ripen indoors.

The chili can, with the right circumstances, survive the winter and give a rich second harvest. But it demands attentive nurture, so sometimes it is quite honestly easier to just plant new small plants instead.

Chili is without a doubt, the kitchen vegetable that attracts the most collectors. And that's not very surprising considering all of the varieties there are. You can more or less find a variety with every color and flavor imaginable.

Capsicum (*Capsicum annuum*), Aji (*Capsicum baccatum*), and Yellow Lantern Chili (*Capsicum chinense*) are the largest groups and encompass a whole lot of varieties. For anyone who wishes to dive into the chili world and keep testing new varieties, there are no limits. Furthermore, it is a fruit that can you can do a lot with.

Just on my shelves alone you can find chili paste, chili sauce, chili shreds, preserved chili, smoked chili . . . etc. If you know how to take care of your chili fruits, you can cover your entire terrace with chili plants without ending up with too much. They are decorative and beautiful with their bush-like way of growing, their smooth green leaves, and small star-shaped flowers. If you want to try cultivating chili for the first time, I recommend that you choose a variety that you can dry, and to avoid growing too many of the same kind. They grow a lot of fruit. On the other hand, if you end up with an abundance of chili, there is no greater gift than a little homemade heat.

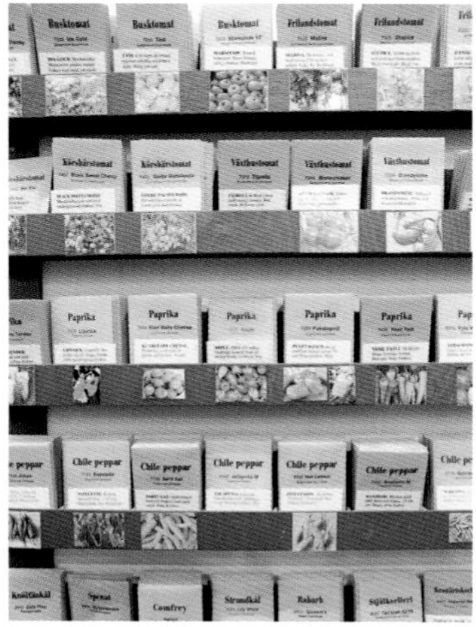

You can find and infinite selection of chili seeds, perfect for plant collectors.

Make sure that you keep the soil in the pots humid and fertilize with liquid fertilizer regularly to get strong plants.

Bell peppers are picky when it comes to heat. Here's the good 'Corno Giallo' that will only grow in greenhouses to be comfortable.

CULTIVATING CHILI & BELL PEPPER

SOW

WHEN? Chili and bell peppers have to be pre-cultivated, and sown indoors, from February-April.

HOW? Broadcast sow in a growing tray or add two seeds in each plug in a root trainer. Place the seeds about an inch (2 cm) deep and keep the soil humid. The temperature should be about 77°F (25°C). After two to three weeks, the small heartleaves will show and you can lower the temperature to 60–70°F (16–20°C). Indoors, most often even in greenhouses, you need extra light to make the plants grow in the right pace.

CULTIVATING

When the character leaves have developed, it is time to move the plants from the tray, so that each plant gets its own plug or little pot. Do not set them in pots that are too large right away, but assume that you will have to replant it once more since it grows to fit the pot it is in. This way a fine and stable root system develops.

The bell pepper plants should finally be placed in a greenhouse or a hotbed. The chili plants can either be planted in a greenhouse, outside in pots, or at a sheltered place in the garden. You can move the plants outside when any risk of frost is gone and the nightly temperature never goes below 50°F (10°C)—not earlier than the middle of June. It is important that you

Most of the bell pepper varieties can be harvested as red or green; it gets sweeter as it reddens.

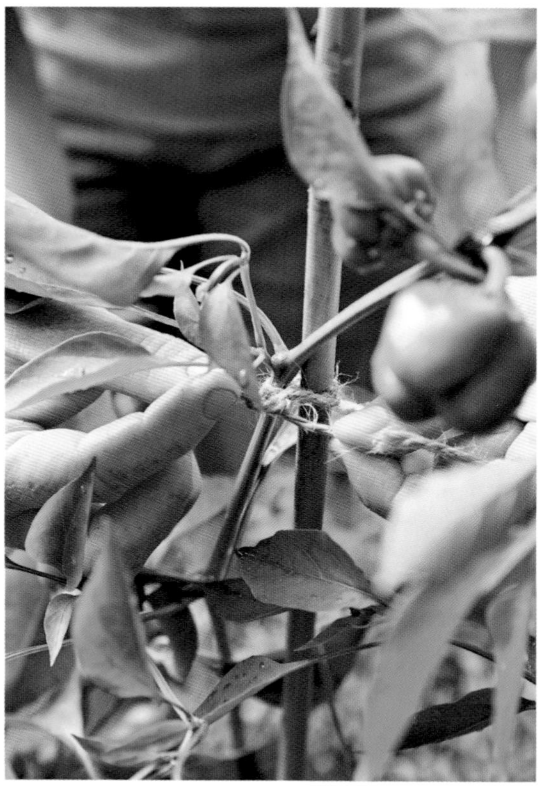

Both bell pepper and chili grow small bushes that may need a support cane, especially when they carry fruit.

Pot cultivating is practical. When fall hits you can move the pot into a warm place. Here bell peppers, eggplant, and thai basil grow together.

gradually train the plants to get used to lower temperatures so that they don't suffer a shock when you set them outside. Keep some fiber cloth on hand in case the temperature suddenly drops.

Both chili and bell pepper wants humus-rich soil that holds moisture. Feel free to do a base fertilization with Algomin and then support with blood meal during the growth season, for instance BioBact, in order to satisfy the plants' high demands for nutrients. If they are growing in a pot they need at least 2 ½ gallons (10 liter) of soil per plant. Buy a fine, nutrient-rich soil, suitable for large pots. The plants do not want to dry out; accordingly, you have to be vigilant with watering, especially if you cultivate in pots where the soil easily dries.

Be prepared to support the plants with a bamboo stick or similar. Even if they have a nice bush-like growth pattern, they do have a tendency to tip over when the fruit sets.

HARVEST

WHEN? The color of the fruit decides when you harvest. All bell peppers go from green to red, orange, yellow, or brown-red. The sweetness develops as the fruit matures, but there are fruits that are good even when they are green and they may therefore be harvested as both green and red. Taste your way or read the recommendations on the seed bag.

The chili has different colors as well, and develops both its fruitiness and strength as it matures. But even here, you can sometimes use the green fruits with good results. If you plan to dry the chili, it should be harvested red and completely ripe. Some varieties with thick fruit meat-walls are not suitable for drying, but should rather be preserved if you wish to keep them over time. Jalapeno is an example of a variety that is suited for preservation.

HOW? Cut or slice the stem of the fruit with a sharp tool.

'Sweet Banana' is a cheeky little bell pepper favorite.

Ajvar relish made with roasted red bell peppers—one of the goodies that you can make out of the bell pepper crop.

PROBLEMS THAT MAY OCCUR

If you cultivate indoors, for instance on a glass veranda, aphids are sometimes a problem. They will most often come when the air is too dry and you can prevent this by showering the plant regularly. Pick the aphids with a peg and squeeze them apart. Shower affected plants with soapy water multiple times. Just like for the tomato pistil, rot may occur. The fruit turns brown and starts to rot along the pistil. This is often a sign of calcium deficiency, which in turn can be a result of uneven watering or unbalanced fertilizing.

Despite the fact that these plants are warmth-loving sun worshippers, they do have a limit. If the air in the greenhouse is too humid and the temperatures pass 86°F (30°C), you have to air out and maybe give the plants some shade to lower the temperature. If not, there is a risk that they won't bear fruits. Overly strong sun that hits the leaves directly is best solved by giving the plants some shade with a net or simply move them to a place with wandering shade.

TIP!

The fruits on one single chili plant can have different strengths. Test the heat of the fruit before you throw it in the stew. The easiest way is to cut off a small part by the stem and carefully test with the tip of your tongue.

Pinch off the first fruits that develop after blossom on the bell pepper plant, as this stimulates the future growth of fruit.

1.

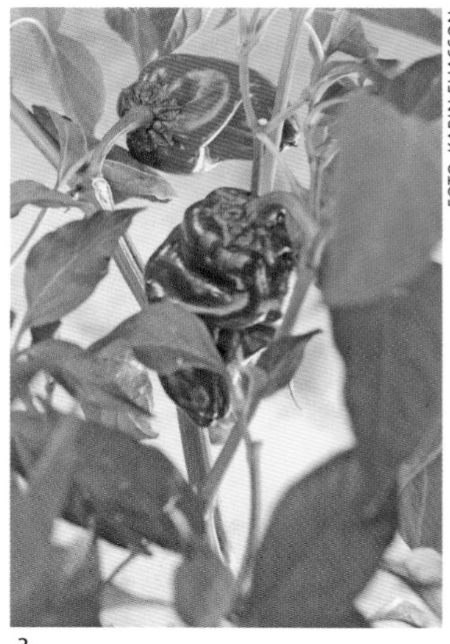

FOTO: KARIN ELIASSON

2.

3.

MY FAVORITES

BELL PEPPER

'Ariane'
A reliable and good variety that gives fresh, fine plants. A good place to start.

'Corbaci'
Also called Sweet Pepper, which is a good name because it looks like chili but has no strength, and it is actually sweet. It provides a lot of fruit and is easy to use. You can cut it and use it in salads or use it whole in stews.

'Liebesapfel'
A nice pumpkin-shaped bell pepper with thick, juicy meat. I like to oven-bake this with green bell peppers as a fill.

1. 'Mini Bell'
Grows many chubby fruits in green, yellow, red and brown-red. The variety has a rather large core, but the bell peppers can be eaten whole if oven-roasted or be used in stews without rinsing them. The development time of the 'Mini Bell' is shorter than most of the other bell peppers.

'Sweet Banana'
A sweet cusped bell pepper. A salad favorite that can be eaten yellow or red. It is easy to grow and gives a nice crop.

CHILI

2. 'Ancho Poblano'
A wonderful chili fruit that you may dry or smoke. It provides a round taste in meat stews.

'Big Jim'
I like this chili because it is mild and very functional. It has a sweet, fruity flavor that lifts salsas, salads, and stews to new heights.

'Inca Berry'
A beautiful little bush that I like looking at, with small oval fruits as pendants. A tasty and not too strong Aji pepper that works with almost anything.

'Jalapeño'
A classic that grows a lot of fruit and is nice to reserve or use in various dishes.

'Kali Mirch'
A hot chili with little acid that works well in woks, noodle salads, and chicken dishes. Fascinating color change when they ripen and go from green to black-purple to red. The plant is worth growing for its beauty alone.

'Monkey Face'
A silly name on a wonderful yellow wrinkly chili fruit, that is not too hot to eat oven-baked with some cream cheese and herbs. But it is also great in salsa and grill sauce.

3. 'Pimiento de Padron'
A Spanish chili favorite that you can stuff with grated cheese or oven-bake as is with a little salt—a Spanish tapa with some hold.

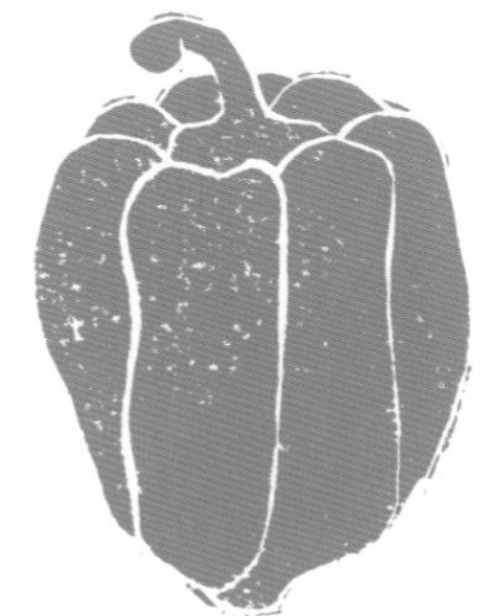

The picture to the right: Most often you can pinch the fruit off of the plant, but a small pair of cutting scissors can be a great help. The better the cut, the less damage on the plant.

BELLOTA
3625

EGGPLANT

This is a real "Thousand and One Night" growth. Exotic, a little difficult to charm in a Swedish climate, but regal. It might just be one of the most beautiful vegetables there is. I like growing them in beautiful pots so that they look like small solitary trees. They need warmth, which can't be overlooked, but as long as you keep it in mind, you can usually find a spot for the plant.

IN COLDER CLIMATES you'll need to find a place on the windowed veranda or in a greenhouse. In warmer climates you can actually successfully grow it outside, but always in a sheltered corner, against a sunny and warm wall. They will like any place where they are showered in warmth and protected against cold and hard winds.

If you satisfy the plant, you will soon be rewarded with fruit. And even if the classic "Black Beauty" both lives up to its name and is a filling and tasty eggplant, there are so many fun and easy varieties to choose from that it would be a shame to limit yourself to just one. Both "Turkish Egg" and "Golden Egg" are small fruits that mature more easily in our unreliable Nordic climate.

Eggplant (*Solanum melongena*) may not belong to the most common vegetables in the kitchen. But if you look a bit further it is one of the world's most appreciated kitchen growths. If you are running out of ideas as to how to prepare it, then a good tip would be to look through a cookbook from the Middle East. You will definitely find something satisfying when it comes to recipes. Baba ghanoush might be the most famous variety of all the sauces you can prepare with the soft grilled eggplant meat, a dip with Middle Eastern flavors such as lemon, garlic, olive oil, and parsley—and if I get to choose—a pinch of smoked bell pepper. But there are so many other ways to prepare it as well: preserves, stews, casseroles, rolls . . . You won't be bored with your crop.

CULTIVATING EGGPLANT

SOW

WHEN? Eggplants need to be sown indoors and be pre-cultivated to have time to develop and give fruit over summer. Sow around March.

HOW? Sow in a root trainer or in small pots, a couple of seeds in each. Extra light can be beneficial, especially if you don't have a glass veranda or greenhouse. During germination, the temperatures should be at 75–85°F (25–35°C). You can make this happen by creating your own little greenhouse out of plastic wrap or bubble wrap and place it, for instance, in a window with an oven underneath. Then let the plants grow in light surroundings with temperatures of about 70°F (20°C). Replant the plants one or two times before you move them outside and make them accustomed to lower temperatures. To achieve a steadier and more branched plant, you can top it off at about 10–12 inches (25–30 cm) height.

CULTIVATING

Eggplants are, like mentioned, warmth-demanding plants. They want to grow sheltered and warm. This is obviously easiest in a greenhouse, but if you have a glass veranda or an outside area with a sheltered sunny corner, that will work almost as well. The plants can only be set out when there is absolutely no danger of frost.

The soil should be humus-rich, so that it can hold humidity, and well fertilized. If you keep the plants in pots you have to give the plants at least 2 ½ gallons (10 liter) of soil to grow in and be prepared to support it when it starts to grow fruits, as it can get heavy and wobbly. Remember that the soil in large pots has to satisfy many requirements. It should maintain its structure and its airiness over a long period of time. Choose a soil that's well put together and suitable for pot cultivating—that will benefit you in the end. If you plant the plants in a greenhouse bed, give them 20 inches (50 cm) of distance between each other.

The eggplants are constantly shooting new sprouts along the leaf folds. Just like with tomatoes, you can pinch these off so that the plant can focus on growing fruits.

Add calcium-rich fertilizer during the season such as calcium-enriched Algomin or wood ashes.

HARVEST

WHEN? The plants will usually start growing fruit at the end of summer in July-August, but it depends on the weather conditions.

HOW? Harvest the fruits with small pruning shears or a knife. Certain fruits are best prepared before they are completely ripe, such as the "Turkish Egg," while others should develop their complete color and shape, like the "Long Purple" and "Black Beauty." Regular harvest stimulates the fruit growth.

PROBLEMS THAT MAY ARISE

The eggplant is related to, among others, the potato, tomato, chili, and bell pepper, and consequently it is vulnerable to the same diseases. Keep track of the order of the plants and don't set them in the same soil as some of these growths was planted in the year before.

The most common problem is that the plants are attacked by fungi diseases. This is hard to treat but you can work to prevent it by avoiding a humid climate in the greenhouse. Make sure that the air circulates and fertilize with mineral-rich fertilizer rather than nitrogen-rich. If leaves are still attacked, then remove them. Burn them and toss them right away. Very damaged plants should ideally be removed from the garden.

Aphids and white flies can also attack the plants. Pick them off by hand and use soapy water to shower the plants continuously for a couple of weeks until the pests give up.

TIP!

Even if you cultivate in a pot, it is smart to have flowers nearby to improve pollination. Here, my majestic 'Black Beauty' is accompanied by a blossoming basil plant.

MY FAVORITES

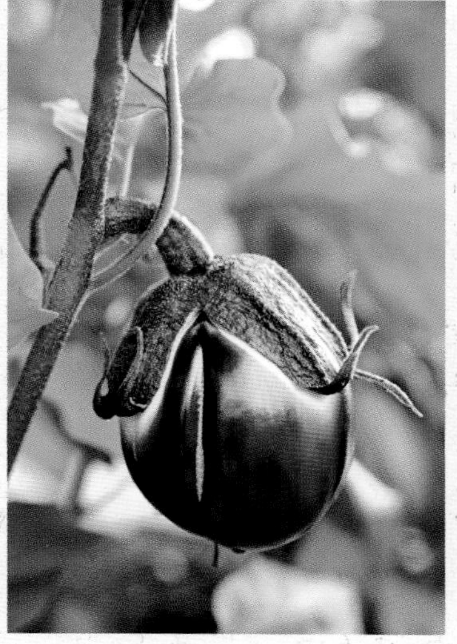
1.

2.

3.

1. 'Black Beauty'
Despite its "commonness" this is a favorite as it gives stable crops of meaty, chubby fruits perfect for oven baking.

'Casper'
A pretty new variety in the Swedish selection. A fine compact plant that gives a good crop of snow-white, elongated fruits with a great flavor.

'Golden Egg'
Perfect to grow in a pot. Offers a load of small egg-shaped fruits that matures from white to yellow.

2. 'Prosperosa'
A classic Italian eggplant with round, very beautiful, dark purple fruits. Excellent for slicing in casseroles or marinated in honey- and soy and grilled.

'Turkish Egg'
A small, round fruit that you may harvest as green or orange. It has a lot of fruit meat with many small seeds. I use this for sauces and stews or sliced in preserves.

The picture on the left: 'Black Beauty.'

'Vista F1'
A modern variety that offers a lot of fruit and has a short development time, which makes it suitable for colder climates.

3. 'Udumalapet'
I like the name of these fruits that have yellow and purple stripes. Tastes a bit nutty and its shapes makes it very functional in many dishes.

Eggplant Sauce

2 eggplants
1 tbsp olive oil
2 scallions, roughly chopped
1 garlic clove, peeled
½ cup (1 dl) leaf parsley
1 tbsp lemon thyme, chopped
¼ cup (0.5 dl) olive oil
1 tsp salt
1 pinch black pepper, freshly ground
1 pinch smoked powdered bell pepper

1. Set the oven to 440°F (225°C). Cut the eggplants in half and turn them in olive oil in an ovenproof dish. Bake in the middle of the oven for about 30 minutes.

2. Scoop the meat out of the eggplants with a spoon. Mix the meat with scallion, garlic, parsley, lemon thyme, and olive oil in a blender or with a handheld blender. Flavor with salt, pepper, and powdered bell pepper.

3. Let cool before serving.

REAL
Cadiz C.F.
BETIS
dani

THE CULTIVATORS OF VILLAMARTIN

Outside of our neighboring city of Villamartin, there is an area with cultivation plots for the retired. This is a very fun place to visit. They cultivate pumpkins, tomatoes, eggplants, bell peppers, radishes, lettuce, and so much more. Here, the biggest vegetable wins. They feel bad for me that I cultivate so many mini tomatoes and usually try to give me some plants of steak tomatoes, so that I will survive the summer. This is a man's world. There is not a single woman in sight, and when you peek into the tool shed, you can easily see that it is used just as much as a male hangout as it is storage for shovels and forks. They decorate the walls with soccer flags and Madonna pictures, there's a razor on the shelf, and the transistor radio is set up on top of the beer stack.

Just this day when I came to visit, they were eagerly discussing yesterday's hail storm and its damage on the crop. The farmer's vulnerability to moody weather is the same no matter where you go in this world.

SQUASH & PUMPKIN

You might remember the pumpkin from Cinderella that through an abracadabra is transformed into a carriage. Or the plant in the movie *Little Shop of Horrors* that lies there hissing "feeeeed meeee." Both of these images enhance the most noticeable properties of these plants: intensive hunger and a potential to grow quickly.

SQUASH AND PUMPKIN are simple, easy, and fun to grow. A great beginner's vegetable. Although I have to admit that it took a while before I tried to grow squash. I thought that the squash I found in the store had a drab taste and was hard to vary in the kitchen, but I had trouble finding the motivation to grow many of these vegetables myself. Maybe it was the curiosity for all of the unknown vegetables in this family that made me decide to finally grow my own squash and pumpkin.

And when they first moved into my vegetable garden, they did so with panache. I made the same lovely mistake as so many others: I was seduced by the abundance. The seed catalogues are like a bag of candy—you can choose small and large, smooth, wavy, bumpy, flat, round, oval, yellow, green, white, orange, vulgarly lumpy in shifting gloomy colors, and beautifully smooth porcelain white fruits. I wanted to try everything at once, planted too much, and had plants with meter long tentacles that crept into strawberry gardens, lettuce crops, bean growths and consequently spat out so much fruit that it was impossible to take care of all of it. But this over abundance creates a childish joy for farming and my desire for squash remained.

Today, I still have my favorites return each year, and they offer flavors from the fresh cucumber-like, through nuts and almonds to the sweet caramel-like. Since certain varieties climb while others are more bush-like, you can, with a little planning, make room for a lot on very little space. You can use walls and pots to organize your squash and pumpkin land.

In taking care of the fruit, the trick is to harvest the summer squash early, like good early vegetables for grilling, marinating, or woking. Winter squash and pumpkin are allowed to grow in limited amounts into fall and then harvested and stored. I use the small "leftover fruits" that I pick off of the plants as summer squash. They still taste fresh and mild. The fruits that are allowed to mature for the entire summer develop a high sugar content and obtain a much broader flavor, which makes them perfect for oven-baking, casseroles, or soups.

CULTIVATING SQUASH & PUMPKIN

A BOTANICAL JUNGLE

Squash and pumpkin are part of a large plant family. There is a myriad of varieties to choose from. The family relationship between various squash and pumpkin is a messy story. The group is divided into the species *Cucurbita pepo* and *Cucurbita maxima,* where Cucurbita pepo includes most of the summer squash, pumpkin, and the Acorn squash., which is a special kind of squash. *Cucurbita maxima,* on the other hand, includes mostly winter squash. Summer squash got its name because it can produce fruit for the entirety of the summer if you continue to harvest while the fruit is still young. The least known variety of summer squash is the zucchini, which is Italian. The winter squash, on the other hand, benefits from its ability to mature over multiple months and develop hard skin and high sweetness, so it can be stored during winter. Pumpkin, which belongs to the summer squash family, has traits similar to the winter squash and should be treated similarly. But, as usual, there are exceptions in each group and it is therefore always important to read the directions on the seed bag to familiarize yourself with how you should proceed to get a nice harvest.

SOW

WHEN? I always recommend pre-cultivating plants, but you can also sow directly in the garden. If you sow directly you have to wait until the soil is warm enough for the seeds to germinate and not rot away, this means at least 60°F (15°C). The winter squash and pumpkin need a long, frost-free season in order to mature properly; it is therefore a good idea to pre-cultivate these in particular. A good rule for sowing is about one month before you plan to plant them. If the plants will be planted in a greenhouse or hotbed, you can start earlier.

Squash and pumpkin are very sensitive to frost and can therefore not be planted until frost nights are definitely over. When you should sow therefore depends on when you figure you can plant them outside.

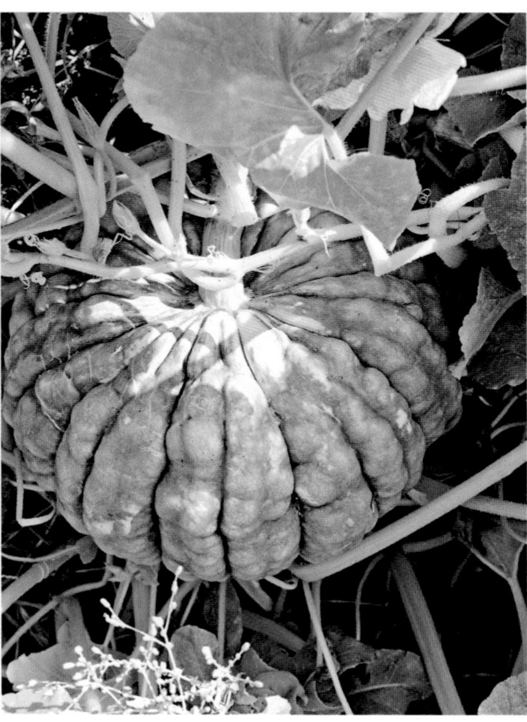

The large pumpkin 'Marina di Chioggia'

Simple and tasty. Shaved summer squash with parmesan, olive oil, and roasted almonds.

HOW? The seeds are large and easy to work with and should be sown directly in big pots, about 3 ½ to 11 inches (9–11 cm) in diameter, in regular planting soil, an inch (2–3 cm) deep. Set the seeds down standing and push them down into the soil, this way they grow easily.

CULTIVATING

Squash and pumpkin want a loose and humus-rich soil. Base fertilize with manure; this way you give the plants a good nutrient base while you also increase the soil's airiness and ability to hold moisture.

Don't be skimpy about space for the plants. It will give less fruit and the plant will more easily attract diseases if they don't have enough air around them. The planting distance varies between 3 to 9 feet (1 and 3 meters), depending on the variety. Check the seed bag. Be careful with the roots of the plants when you replant them outside, as they are sensitive and don't like to be disturbed. Set them out when the risk of frost is over.

Since the roots are sensitive to disturbance, it is a good idea to cover cultivate the crop. Cover around with straw or clippings to avoid weeds so that you won't need to do weeding.

Squash and pumpkin need a lot of nourishment and water, but first and foremost they need potassium for a nice harvest. The basic need can be satisfied through a base fertilization with manure. To satisfy further needs you can, for instance, support fertilize with Algomin, Chrysan or wood ashes during the growth season. You should avoid nitrogen-rich fertilizers, such as blood meal or poultry manure. They promote leaf growth and the risk is that you may end up with large leaves and less fruit.

When the plants are starting to grow fruit you should bed underneath the fruits with straw or fiber cloth to decrease the risk of damages by ground contact.

If the plant looks healthy and fine, you might not need to trim it at all; if possible, it is best if it can grow free. If the leaves start looking ugly or diseased you cut them off by hand. Leaves that have been attacked by fungi often turn yellow with brown spots or they get a grey layer of mildew. The infected leaves are tossed or burned and not added to the compost.

HARVEST

Always use a clean and sharp knife when you harvest. Cut the fruit as close to the stem as possible so that you don't leave "stubs" where bugs can enter and live.

To eat as an early harvest, the squash is harvested when its still small, about 4-8 inches (1—20 cm) and it is usually a good rule of thumb for them to still have their nice premature characteristics intact.

For storing the squash once it is harvested, the fruit meat should be hard and a slight knocking on the fruit should give a hollow sound. The shaft should be woody by the fruit and the skin should be hard. You can test by carefully pushing a fingernail against the skin. It should not leave a mark, and if so, you should leave it for a while longer. The leaves will often be withered by the time you're harvesting, but the fruit may need to lie with the withered plant for a while longer to mature. But watch out for frost—it ruins the fruit. Winter squash usually needs to mature indoors for a couple of weeks after the harvest to develop a cork-like skin. During these weeks, they should preferably be in an airy and warm place. Squash and pumpkin can usually be stored on a shelf in the kitchen. Place them in an airy spot and look after them to

Tip! Feel free to harvest the summer squash while the flower is still there. This is how the zucchini is sold by vegetable vendors on the streets of Paris. It is a sign that the fruit is fresh, but it is also pretty to prepare the squash with the flower still there.

Tip! A French farmer once told me that the best method for storage was to first clean the fruit with a sponge and lukewarm water, then dry the skin carefully and later polish it with a kitchen towel so that it's shiny. This way the fruit's own wax will close all of the open pores in the skin and the fruit will preserve itself.

Male and female flowers look different. The male flower connects directly to the stem of the plant while the female flower develops fruit by the flower bracket.

make sure that none of the fruits have gone bad, and if so, remove it.

Pumpkin seeds are great in bread and salads, to sprinkle on top of stews and rice dishes, or to roast with a little salt and eat as a snack. The hull-less pumpkins have the best seeds, such as Kakai. The pumpkin takes a long time to mature and even needs to sit indoors after harvesting to be completely developed. Afterwards, just poke the seeds out, rinse them, and dry them at room temperature on a paper towel.

Fried squash flowers are an uncommon delicacy in Sweden, but well known in Mediterranean countries. All pumpkin and squash have male and female flowers. The male flowers have long stems and a clear stamen with pollen in the middle of the flower. The female flower has a small beginning fruit that swells out by the mount and has a small round pistil in the center. A good variety for flower harvest is 'Costata Romanesco.' You can use both male and female flowers, but if you take the female flower, you won't get the fruit, so it is therefore preferable to take the male flower. The flowers need to be prepared completely fresh.

PROBLEMS THAT MAY ARISE

Technically, pumpkin and squash are easy to cultivate, but sometimes we still run into problems. The most common is fungal attacks on the leaves. To avoid this you can take some preventative measures (see page 193).

If the fruits shrivel up and fall off before they have time to mature, you are having trouble with the pollination of the plants. This usually happens in greenhouses where there can be a lack of pollinating insects. It is always good to keep flowers near the vegetables to attract pollinators. Also, make sure that the temperature in the greenhouse is not too high, as insect won't want to fly in. During the warmest months in Spain I struggle with insect pollination of the plants and therefore pollinate by hand to be safe. This is easy and rather cozy to do in the morning. When you pollinate, you take the pollen from the male flower with a brush and place it on the pistil of the plant. Or you peel the crown leaves off of the male flower and use the actual stamen to place pollen on the pistil.

1.

FOTO: KARIN ELIASSON

2.

MY FAVORITES

1. 'Yellow Crookneck'
Summer squash, bush variety that is harvested small, fresh nutty flavor, tasty cold marinated.

'Ronde de Nice'
Summer squash, climbing, harvested when it is about 4 inches (10 cm). Perfect to stuff and oven-bake or grill slices.

'Bennings Green Tint'
Summer squash, bush variety with undeniable beautiful shape. Good to harvest somewhat larger. Scoop the meat out. Marinate with salt, olive oil, and herbs. Blend with roasted almonds and arugula. Roughly grate some Parmesan on top. Use the shell as a bowl.

2. 'White Acorn'
Acorn-squash, climbing, unbelievably beautiful fruit, a summer squash that should mature properly and be harvested with hard skin, tasty to stuff and oven-bake in its own peel.

3. 'Chinese Miniature'
Acorn-squash, climbing mini fruit that should be harvested with hard skin, oven-bake whole or eat with a spoonful of butter and salt.

'Buttercup'
Winter squash, climbing, not as beautiful but very tasty, flavor reminiscent of sweet potatoes, good as a soup, casserole, or oven-roasted.

4. 'Connecticut Field'
The climbing, classic Cinderella-pumpkin. It's delicious and beautiful to watch. It was cultivated by the settlers in the American west.

'Fig leaf Gourd'
Cultivated for its beautiful fig-like leaves. It grows quickly, it's climbing, and it offers beautiful fruits that unfortunately are hard to use in the kitchen. Fantastic for framing the vegetable garden.

FOTO: KARIN ELIASSON

3.

4.

CUCUMBER

Cucumbers are fun. They can climb or crawl, be long, short, or round. They are one of our most common sandwich toppings—fresh or pickled. Cucumbers are also one of our most common kitchen vegetables. But I have to admit that it is one of the growths that I've had the most problems with over the years. Yes, it is strange, because they are really happy and glad to grow. But we all have one vegetable that we have struggled with more than others. Withering disease, leaf mildew, and other fungi diseases have attacked my cucumbers over the years and I have had to up my cultivating technique and meticulousness to ultimately win them over.

WITH THESE EXPERIENCES on my mind, I planted an extra crop of cucumbers during my first season in Spain. I thought that I might go through the same disaster again in this new climate. I also received a few extra plants from my kind neighbors. That summer I harvested 45 lbs (20 kg) of cucumbers every day. I was going crazy. My brain was racing to find recipes and other uses for the vegetable. Our nice carpenter was gifted a load every day until one day when he kindly but determinedly said, "No, thank you. No more, my mother grows cucumber as well." My husband desperately tried to sun-dry cucumbers with little success; bitter slices were the result. Either way, a lot of good recipes for soups, sauces, salads, and stews were born that summer. The favorites were cucumber soup with yogurt, ice, and mint, and an Asian variety of pressed cucumber where you use rice vinegar, and some chili and dill, instead of parsley and vinegar.

From this experience we can conclude that yes, cucumbers *(Cucumis sativus)* do have a tendency to become sick, but when they are healthy they give more generously than most plants. Cucumbers come in many varieties. Gherkins are best suited for preserves and can usually be cultivated outside. Among the gherkins we find the famous Västerås cucumber, which is a trustworthy old servant. Common cucumbers are eaten fresh, but they need more heat than gherkins and are most successful in a greenhouse. The Lemon Cucumber is kind of an oddball and a fun complement to the regular varieties. It got its name because of its round shape and yellow-white skin. If you want to plant many plants, variation is always ideal. Gherkins can be harvested very small and crispy to be pickled whole as cornichons, which is a good solution if the plants start growing senseless amounts of fruits.

CULTIVATING CUCUMBERS

SOW

WHEN? I recommend pre-cultivating cucumber plants and that you sow them three to four weeks before you plan to move them outside. The move outdoors can not happen until there is no risk of frost and the plant has at least three leaves. Do not forget to harden the plant so that the leaves don't turn yellow and fall off.

HOW? Sow ⅓ inch (1–2 cm) deep. The seeds are pretty sizable and easy to handle. Set the seeds down standing in the soil so that they grow more easily. Keep the soil humid. Place two seeds in each pot. You can sow them directly in pots of 3 ½–4 inches (9–11 cm).

PREPARING THE GROWTH SITE

Cucumbers are generally heat-dependent just like their relatives, squash and pumpkin. Gherkins have a greater chance of developing well in open land than regular cucumbers. Most cucumbers will need a green-house to be comfortable. All of the cucumbers want a loose and humus-rich soil that can hold moisture and warmth. Prepare the soil through folding in compost and burned manure.

Be careful with the root system when you replant the cucumbers. Do not touch the roots more than necessary and be especially careful with the neck of the root. Do not plant deeper than how it was planted in the pot.

The plants can either grow free on the ground or be bound up. Generally, the gherkin will grow crawling on the ground while the regular cucumber prefers to climb. There will be varieties of this so check the description on the package. If the vines are to crawl on the ground, they need at least 3 feet (1 meter) of space between the rows and about 12 inches between the plants to develop well. If you bind them you can plant them with 20 inches between. Do not feel tempted to set them closer together to have room for more. Cucumbers need a lot of air to avoid attacks from fungi.

NURTURE

If you want branched plants that grow on the ground you can cut the top off of the plants when they've grown four to five leaves; this gives a richer harvest. If you bind them up the opposite advice usually applies: you will want to decrease the side sprouts to make the plant more manageable. Cut the side sprouts back if you don't want them. This way the setting of fruit will be concentrated around the main stem that grows more powerfully. If you think that the main stem is too long, you can cut the top after a while and let a few side sprouts at the bottom grow out instead.

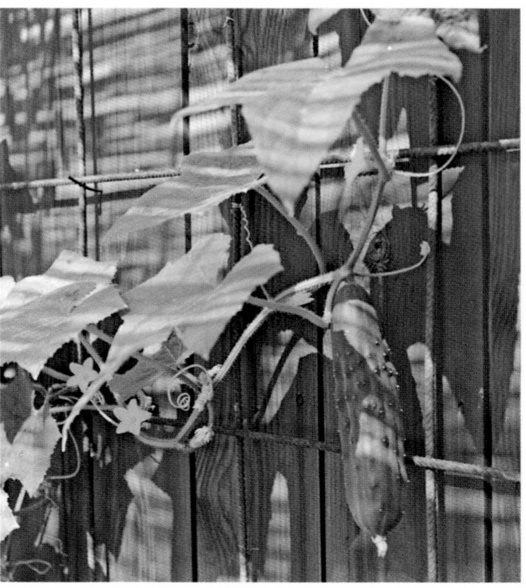

On small plots, it's a good idea to let the cucumbers climb to save space.

The plants want a continuous influx of water and are very fond of drop watering. Feel free to cover the soil to avoid damaging the roots with raking, but also to maintain the humidity in the soil. If you cover the soil around plants that crawl on the ground, it will also keep the cucumbers clean from soil and it decreases the risk of attacks by fungi and insects.

Fertilize with potassium-rich fertilizer, such as wood ashes, and be careful with nitrogen fertilizers. Too much nitrogen will promote fungi diseases and gives abnormal leaf growth and poor flavor of the cucumber.

HARVEST

WHEN? The fruits should be firm and the gherkins between 2–6 inches (5–15 cm) in size, the common cucumber longer, about 6–12 inches (15–30 cm) depending on the variety. Harvest continuously to get as large a crop as possible. It is very important that you harvest the first cucumbers as soon as they are ripe and don't let them hang on the plant for too long. This will halt the entire plant and it will give fewer fruits. **HOW?** Cut or slice the cucumbers off with garden shears, scissors, or a knife.

PROBLEMS THAT MAY ARISE

The most common problems you run into are fungi diseases, leaf mildew, and virus. The easiest way to avoid virus is to be meticulous about the crop rotation, and never plant the same plant in the same place closer than every fourth year. Pick off aphids and other attackers that can carry bacteria. One virus that often attacks cucumber is cucumber mosaic, which makes the leaves mosaic-patterned. To prevent this you can choose resistant varieties, such as "Market More" and "Lemon."

Fungi diseases are avoided by, among other things, keeping fresh air around the plants, removing sick and withered leaves, avoiding watering on the leaves, and maintaining an even and good climate in the greenhouse. Certain fungi diseases, like withering disease, often occur because the plant is suffering under poor cultivating conditions. When the plant was young it might have been planted too wet, too cold, it lacked nutrients, or something similar.

To avoid disease as much as possible you should be vigilant about cleaning harvesting knives and other tools regularly.

Greenhouse spinning mites are very troublesome. Always clean the greenhouse between seasons and don't let the plants dry out. To prevent the problem you should shade the greenhouse if it gets too warm, for instance, through whitewashing the windows or hanging a fabric on the inside of the glass. If the plants are still attacked, you can try regularly showering the leaves with soapy water and possibly fight the mite biologically through planting their enemy Phytoseiulus, which you can buy online.

MY FAVORITES

COMMON CUCUMBERS

1. 'Market More'
Stable, fresh, and generous cucumber that can handle a northern climate. Perfect for cultivating outside.

'Suyo Long'
My absolute favorite cucumber, with long, dark fruits that are bowed and lumpy. It has a good fruity flavor and is best for binding up. Sometimes sold under the name 'Soo Yow'.

1.

2.

FOTO: KARIN ELIASSON

GHERKINS

'Double Yield'
An old fine gherkin that has rarely disappointed me. Fine small, crispy fruits for preserves. Can be cultivated outside and gives a large harvest during the entire season. Grow on the ground.

'Vert de Massy'
A real all-around cucumber that can used for cornichon-preserves, regular preserves, or be eaten fresh. It can both climb and crawl on the ground. Great variety!

OTHER CUCUMBERS

'Jungle Cucumber'
Also called 'Gurania makoyana.' Pretty, small, striped cucumbers that should be harvested small and firm. Good to cut in half and throw in the noodle wok.

2. 'Lemon'
The Lemon cucumber is different, but very useful and tasty fresh. It has small, round, lightly yellow-green fruits and a white, fresh, and sweet fruit cucumber meat. Can be grown on the ground or climbing, in greenhouses or outside. Also called 'Crystal Apple.'

Tip!

Cucumbers have a surface root system—water often and a little instead of rarely and a lot.

CORN

Corn brings us to warmer shores and Mexican hats. But it is very possible to grow corn in colder climates as well. It is even pretty easy, as long as you keep in mind that corn needs a little extra warmth and shelter from the wind to feel at home. In southern and middle Sweden they cultivate a lot of sweet corn *(Zea mays* var. *saccharata),* which is the most common corn to cultivate in the garden, but it's also a food source for animals. Self-picking is also common. Even though I've started to grow my own corn to secure a few well-filled plastic bags in the freezer, I can still find charm in the large corn fields. I gladly take a stroll among the tall plants now and then to experience the sensation of being lost. As a child, I would keep an eye on my mother's legs on the row next to mine, so that the fear that I would never get out would decrease. The fields are intriguing.

CORN IS DEFINITELY one of the growths I often place in the children's garden corner. Most children like corn, no matter if they're large corn cobs or cute mini kernels. Furthermore, the seeds are large and even small children's hands manage to stick them in the right place. Since the corn preferably grows in large groups, you can play with the shapes when you set them out and make wavy roads between the groups. The corn (*Zea mays everta*) used for popcorn is especially exciting. Imagine growing your own popcorn! It is a somewhat different corn cob than the ones we are used to eating, a smaller and tightknit cob with tiny kernels. It needs a little more time to mature, so if you don't live in a more temperate climate you should grow them in a greenhouse or start pre-cultivating early.

Since corn is one of the world's most cultivated seeds, there is obviously a whole sea of varieties. Cultivating in the North does, however, set certain requirements that the corn cannot be too sensitive to cold and that the fruit grow early and ripen fast. It is therefore best to keep to the varieties that are already tested in your climate.

CULTIVATING CORN

Corn plants create lushness in the garden.

PREPARING THE GROWTH SITE

Corn is, as previously mentioned, dependent on warmth and needs a little extra attention to reap a nice harvest in colder climates. Make sure that it grows in a sheltered, sunny spot. The best way to secure warmth around the root system is to make sure that the soil is well-drained, light, and humus-rich. If the spring is particularly cold you can warm the soil with a plastic cover before sowing or planting. Fertilize the soil with manure and compost. The corn wants a lot of nutrients and water, and if you can cover cultivate with organic material, that's ideal. Corn likes to be cross-fertilized. To sow the best corn possible, you should therefore keep to one variety at a time. Choose your variety with care and keep to one variety every year.

SOW

WHEN? I always recommend pre-cultivating corn to win time. In southern parts of Sweden, and warmer climates, you can sow directly in the ground, but the soil temperature must be at least 60°F (15°C) and when the plant has appeared, any risk of frost must be gone. If you pre-cultivate, start four to five weeks before you plan to plant them outside, and wait until there is no chance of frost.

HOW? The corn quickly develops a large root system and should therefore be sown in deep root trainers. If you want to save space you can first broadcast sow the seeds in trays and then replant them when they are about 2 inches (5 cm) tall. Fill the trays with a blend of planting soil and sifted soil. Push the seeds 1–2 inches (2–4 cm) deep and makes sure that the soil is lightly packed. Water the soil properly. Let the seeds germinate and the plants appear when the temperature is about 77°F (25°C). Later you can lower the temperature somewhat when they start growing properly.

When you sow directly in the ground, the easiest way is to make a 2 inch (5 cm) deep trench in the soil and water it. Add the seeds, cover with soil, and water everything again. The corn will pollinate better and get more fruit if it grows in groups instead of rows. Make large circles or squares and sow the corn with 8–10 inches (20–25 cm) distance between each plant in every direction.

Tip! Corn and beans are friends, not only in the Latin American kitchen but also in the vegetable garden. If you leave a little extra space between the corn plants, you can let a few bush beans work as good soil cover.

PLANTING OUTSIDE AND NURTURE

The plants are not moved outside until the risk of frost is completely over. The hardening process is very important. Have fiber cloth at hand in case there are surprising cold nights.

Keep weeds away from the corn. It doesn't like competition and cover cultivating is preferred from this perspective as well.

Support fertilize with stone meal or Algomin when it blossoms. When the corn is about to

A corn variety that is made into flour and cultivated because the cobs are so beautiful. It's often called 'Painted Mountain'.

pollinate, you can help them out by gently shaking the plants a little so that the seed flour rains down on them.

Be extra vigilant with watering once the fruits have appeared. Remove side sprouts that shoot out from the base of the plant. They just steal energy, and they rarely turn into nice fruits. Let only two or three corn cobs develop on each plant unless you are cultivating a mini-corn variety. In those cases you can expect 10–15 cobs per plant. Upwards cup some dirt against the stem when the plant is about 20 inches (50 cm) tall so that it gets extra support around the base. Repeat as you go if needed.

HARVEST

WHEN? Regular corn is ready for harvest at the end of summer. The threads at the top of the cob should be withered and if you carefully peel back the leaves, a light pointed push against the corn kernel should release a white corn juice. If the juice is transparent, the corn is not ready. Mini corn is harvested before the kernels develop. Open the peel and carefully peek to get a sense of how mature the corn is. Regular harvest encourages greater crops. Popping-corn should be left until the kernels are dry. After which, they should be harvested and dried even more spread out in a warm room indoors.

HOW? Harvest, prepare, eat. The cobs are easy to break off of the plant by hand. You should not let many minutes pass after you harvest them till they're boiling in the pot. Corn that is left for a long while after harvest loses flavor and elasticity as the sugar transforms into starch quickly. It is also great to grill corn. If you grill them fresh you don't have to remove the peel, just polish them and remove the threads. If you grill them peeled, maybe even slightly blanched, you may brush them with some chipotle glaze for a spicy and smoky taste. Corn is best stored in the freezer.

MY FAVORITES

'Early Extra Sweet'
One of the oldest and best corn varieties. It doesn't grow very tall, which can sometimes be preferable.

'Golden Bantam'
Gives really tall plants with slim, very tasty cobs.

'Minor F1'
A mini corn that is harvested small and underdeveloped. Good for boiling or in a wok.

'Minipop F1'
A popcorn-variety that can also be harvested as mini corn. It is always a good option if your vegetable garden is not particularly large. The plant only grows about 3 feet (1 meter) tall, which makes it easy to place and easy to use.

'Sweet Nugget'
Sweet, flavorful cobs with large corn kernels. It gives a stable amount of cobs on each plant and is suited for the Nordic climate.

'Tom Thumb'
Fine small corn cobs for popcorn. Don't be scared of the tiny size of the kernels. They still make great popcorn.

BEANS & PEAS

The Bean-man—he was quite a mystery; one of those people that showed up out of nowhere with an interest in beans and created a space where he could cultivate his interest. I was an apprentice at Rosendal's Garden in Stockholm at that time and that is where I met him. "This is the Bean-man," one of the garden masters said. "If there's anything he doesn't know about beans, it is not worth knowing." And that was really true. He gave a lecture about beans for us at Rosendal. When he was standing there in the row of his flag-high plants, it was with a loving touch that he showed us red-striped borlotti beans from Italian seeds. He told us about the darkest purple bean he had ever seen, almost black, and about an almost 12 inch (30 cm) long wax bean of the variety "Neckar Gold."

THIS ENTHUSIASM WAS contagious. That late summer, when every day between 7 a.m. and 9 p.m. was spent on harvesting for stores and kitchens, I preferred to disappear in the rows of bush beans. Despite the fact that I got both wet and cold from the caress of the plants along my legs, I liked this corner of the garden. To carefully move the leaf aside with my left hand and pick long rows of purple beans with my right hand. They kept giving that summer, the beans.

I still like beans and peas and I can't decide if I like the plants the best or the actual harvest. These plants invite you to be imaginative. And the result is purple-colored bean towers, circles of sugar snaps with sunflowers in the middle, heavy mesh walls of tall growing peas that separate the cosmos from the dill and verbena. I love climbing plants! They add another dimension to the garden and they save room on the ground. It is perfect for those who lack space.

The challenge is not finding varieties, but deciding among them. You can begin by deciding if you want peas or beans for fresh-consumption—like broad beans and wax beans, sugar peas, marrowfats, blauwschokkers, and haricot verts—or if you'd like to dry your harvest or store it. In that case you should choose a borlotti bean and a garden pea. After this you can also decide if you want a tall-growing plant or a shorter variety, depending on the cultivation conditions. And then you can choose the color and shape among the ones that emerge.

One cultivation favorite is also the broad bean with its compact, sturdy, and willing plants. Add a little extra when you draw up the space for broad beans. Plant a real hedge so that you get a good harvest. You will want a lot of broad beans when you are actually making food. They are great in stews and summer salads of all varieties, but I also like to eat them as snacks. Small light-green beans, quickly heated and later turned in a little olive oil, lemon juice, salt, and chopped mint. Bean-snack royale!

Panting sugar peas outside. Always be careful with the root system.

The climbing support for tall peas and beans should already be in place when you move the plants outside.

You can bind broad beans with a string to give it support.

CULTIVATING BEANS & PEAS

Garden beans is a category that includes all of the varieties I will now dive into: haricot verts, snap beans, and borlotti beans.

HARICOT VERTS

Phaseolus vulgaris

The name "haricot verts" really only means "green beans." These beans are indeed green, as well as round, and of somewhat varying lengths. You eat the whole bean, both the seeds and the sheath, and it is preferably harvested while small. The haricot verts come as tall-growing, large beans, and as short-growing, bush beans.

SOW

WHEN? These beans are sensitive to early planting. If the soil is too cold or too wet, the seeds will not germinate, but rather rot. If you want to get started with your broad bean crop early on, your best option is to pre-cultivate. March to May is usually suitable. If you sow directly onto the growth site the soil should hold a temperature of at least 53–60°F (12–16°C).

HOW? Beans have large seeds that are easy to work with. Set them in 2–3 inch (5–7 cm) pots, in root trainers, or in toilet paper rolls so that they have a lot of room to start with. Fill every pot to the rim with soil and then carefully pack it into place. Then push the seeds down at least an inch (3 cm) deep and water well. If you sow directly in the ground outside the easiest way is to make a 2 inch (5 cm) deep trench in the soil. Water the trench and set the beans out with 6 inches (15 cm) between each plant. Then cover with soil and water again. Leave 12–18 inches (30–45 cm) between each row. Sow four to six stalk beans around each support.

Climbing towers are the easiest and smartest supports for stalk beans.

PREPARING THE GROWTH SITE

Beans like well-drained soil with high humus-content. Since they don't have high demands when it comes to fertilizers you can fold in, for instance, compost and decomposed bark humus if you want to add humus to the soil. Beans do not only find it difficult to grow in low temperatures, the are also sensitive to cold at all times, and can have trouble with windy places. Therefore, you should choose a warm place in the garden and, if possible, a sheltered spot. Feel free to heat the soil by covering it with plastic before you sow to secure a good soil temperature. High growing beans, such as stalk beans, need a climbing support that is about 6 feet tall (2 m). This can be a trellis, thin rope that's tied to some construction, or wooden poles that are set in a triangle and tilt against each other on top. This is the most stable way of offering support to the beans.

Tip! *Beans have a tendency to stand a bit unsteady and break easily. Cup a little soil against the stem regularly during the growth season. This is a nice support for the plant.*

PLANTING OUTSIDE

Plant the beans outside when the risk of frost is over. Bush beans can be set with 6–8 inches (15–20 cm) between each plant and 12–14 inches (30–45 cm) between the rows. For stalk beans it is usually suitable with four to six beans around each pole, alternatively 12 inches (30 cm) between the plants along a trellis. These growths will later grow up by twisting around the support against the sun. If the plants end up being too heavy, you can fasten them to the climbing support with extra string.

NURTURE

Just like all legumes, beans have a way of fixating their own nitrogen. Nitrogen-fixating bacteria in the soil enter symbiosis with the growth's roots where an exchange of nitrogen and carbohydrates occur. This then means that you don't have to fertilize these growths with any significant amount of nitrogen, and on the contrary, over fertilizing with nitrogen can lead to problems like fungi attacks. The only time you might need to add nitrogen is in the beginning before the roots have formed, and in that case, use poultry manure. Other than that I recommend support fertilizing with wood ash or Algomin. You can fertilize in one or two rounds during the growth period.

HARVEST

WHEN? You eat the beans whole, both seeds and pod. They are best if you eat them completely fresh right after harvest, but you can also blanch and freeze them. All of the varieties of haricot verts benefit from an early harvest. Harvest them when they're crisp and thin. Regular harvest will stimulate new growth of fruit.

HOW? The bean stems can get a little rubbery, so it is best to use a small pair of scissors or garden shears when you harvest.

WAX BEAN

Phaseolus vulgaris

The wax bean is very similar to haricot verts, but they are yellow-white instead of green. Sow, cultivate, harvest, and eat like haricot verts.

PURPLE BEAN

Phaseolus vulgaris

The purple bean is another variety of haricot verts. It has a dark purple color and its leaves have dark stems and veins that look beautiful against the white flowers. The bean's red color turns to green when you heat it.

Sow, cultivate, harvest and prepare purple beans just like haricot verts.

THE SNAP BEAN

Phaseolus vulgaris

The snap bean has a flat pod and can be yellow, green, or purple. If it is yellow, it's called snap wax bean. Sow, cultivate, harvest and eat the snap bean like haricot verts.

SPLIT BEANS

Phaseolus vulgaris

Borlotti beans should be opened. You don't eat the pod in itself, but the seeds inside. You can choose if you want to harvest while the seeds are still young and relatively soft or wait until they are mature and dry.

Sow and cultivate the borlotti bean like haricot verts, but if you want to harvest the borlotti bean for storage you should wait until the pods have dried up. Then you cut the entire plant and hang it in a warm, airy, and dry place until all the pods are completely dry. Later, you open the pods and take out the beans. Spread the beans out and let them dry a little longer before you place them in cans in the cupboard to be used as cooking beans. In colder climates it can be difficult for the borlotti bean to have time to dry completely unless they grow in a greenhouse.

FLAGEOLET BEAN

Phaseolus vulgaris

The flageolet bean is a bit special as it can be used at any stage of development. This, combined with its good flavor, makes many say that if you can only cultivate one bean, it should be this one.

Sow and cultivate like haricot verts. You can harvest it as a small haricot vert and eat it directly or you can open it and eat it as small fresh beans in sauces, salads, and stews, or harvest them completely ripe and dry for storage. You can choose whatever suits you.

RUNNER BEAN

Phaseolus coccineus

This bean is tall growing, and noticeably so. It can be used to dress whole pergolas in summer clothes. With its unusually beautiful, colorful flowers, many cultivate it more as a decorative plant than as a food plant and it is sometimes also called flower bean. However, the beans are edible, and very good, so don't miss your chance to harvest. You harvest and prepare these like haricot verts. Sometimes their meat can get a

Picture to the right: The beautiful purple stalk bean 'Blauhilde'.

Borlotto lingua
Capella 2010

little woody, but not when they're young and tender. Sow and cultivate like haricot verts.

BROAD BEAN

Vicia faba

The broad beans grow as small bushes and usually grow about 3 feet (1 m) tall. They are nice to grow in a colder climate since they are a little more robust than other bean plants. They tolerate both cold and wind better. Eat the beans fresh or dried.

SOW

WHEN? Can both pre-cultivate and sow directly in the growth site. You can sow them while the soil is still cold, around 39–40°F (4–5°C) is not problem. You can pre-cultivate about a month before you plan on planting them, which you can also do early since the plants can handle frostbite.

HOW? Sow the broad bean like other beans. But do leave a little extra space between the rows, 16–20 inches (40–50 cm), or sow in double rows, or in other words, two rows with six inches (15 cm) in between. Then leave 20 inches (50 cm) before the next pair. This way you obtain more lush and steady plants and you can make practical harvest paths between the double rows.

PREPARING THE GROWTH SITE

The broad bean can grow in most soils, but it cannot dry out. Therefore you should prepare the soil by adding humus as a blend of compost, manure, and bark humus. The broad bean would like to be kick-started with nitrogen-fertilizer so that it can later manage just fine with the help of the nitrogen-fixating bacteria around the root threads. Because of this reason, farm manure is a good base fertilizer, but you can also use poultry manure or bone meal.

Tip! Let the broad beans grow up through twigs sunken in the ground to give them extra support.

Picture top left: Runner bean in blossom.
Picture top right: Asparagus beans.
Picture bottom left: Borlotti beans from my own harvest.
Picture bottom right: Stalk snap waxbean 'Goldfield.'

Freshly harvested young broad beans are delicious!

PLANTING OUTSIDE

Plant in the beginning of summer when the frost risk is no longer too big. They can deal with one or two frost nights, but make sure that you harden them; pre-cultivated plants are always more sensitive then the ones that were sowed directly. Plant the broad beans according to the distances listed for sowing.

NURTURE

Support-fertilize with a little wood ash or Algomin during the pre-season and place sticks for support as the plant has a tendency to fold. Feel free to cut the top of the plants when blossoming and setting fruit is over. It is the young fresh leaves in the top that attracts black leaf lice.

HARVEST

WHEN? The beans can be harvested regularly over the summer and, in principle, eaten in all stages of development.

HOW? You can eat really small young pods whole, boiled, or woked. After more time you can harvest plump pods, open them, and eat the little beans inside. If you want to harvest for storage you should wait until the pod is starting to shrink a little. Then you take out the mature seeds and spread them out to dry in a warm and airy place. You can also blanch and freeze broad beans. If the beans are really ripe, the outer shell may fall off during boiling. Feel free to remove it. It is the inside that counts. The outer shell can have a slight bitter taste in mature beans.

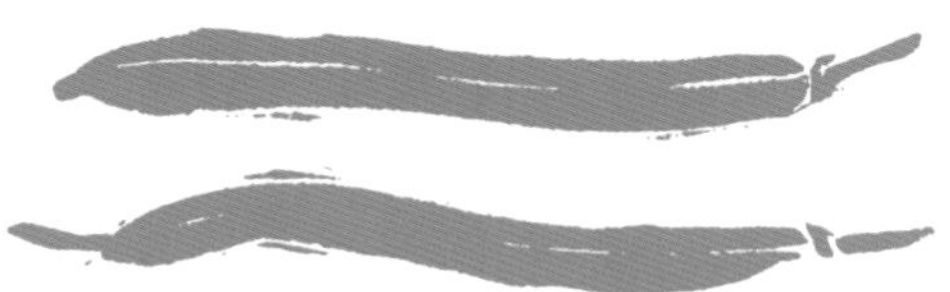

SUGAR PEA AND OTHER PEAS

Pisum sativum

SOW

WHEN? You can sow sugar peas and other varieties early, as soon as it is possible to work with the soil. You can also pre-cultivate them, and in that case you sow three to four weeks before planned planting.

HOW? You sow peas just like you sow garden beans (see haricot verts on page 122). But you can sow them a little closer together, 2–4 inches (5–10 cm) is a good distance for sowing directly in the growth site, depending on the variety. You can also sow pea growths in double rows, like the broad bean.

PREPARING THE GROWTH SITE AND PLANTING OUTSIDE

The peas are not as sensitive to cold as beans, but other than that, they want the same growth conditions. See haricot verts. Pre-cultivated plants can be set out early, often in May. If there is still a risk of frost, you should remember to harden the plants carefully and cover them with fiber cloth under really cold nights.

Tip! To prevent birds from pulling up small plants you can lay out birch twigs around the plants. This usually confuses the birds.

NURTURE

Fertilize the pea plants as beans. Feel free to use a cover material so that the humidity around the plants is secured, so they cannot dry out. In my experience most pea plants need some kind of support, short or tall. They can easily fall over if they don't have, for instance, a little bamboo stick to lean up against. Medium tall and tall plants needs stable nets they can climb against, where they can get a good grip. Climbing pea plants can get pretty ugly around the bottom after a while, so it might be a good idea to plant something in front that will cover the withered bottom of the plant in the long run, such as marigolds.

HARVEST

WHEN? The sugar pea, that's eaten with the pod, is best harvested as small and crispy when you still can't see the contours of the peas inside the pod. Harvest regularly during summer.

HOW? Peas are often easy to pick by hand, but if it is hard to release it, you should rather use garden shears than pulling too hard. Peas can be stored blanched and frozen.

SUGAR SNAP

The sugar snaps are small, lumpy pods that you can eat whole with the peas inside. For this you wait until the pea is round, full, and well-developed inside the pods. They came to be through a cross between the sugar pea and marrowfats, which you can recognize when you see them. They are crispy, sweet, and super tasty.

You sow, cultivate, and harvest the sugar snap as sugar peas, but with the difference that they would like a soil temperature of 50°F (10°C) before they're sowed outside. And as I said, let it mature more than the sugar pea before harvesting.

Picture to the right: Sugar pea in bloom.

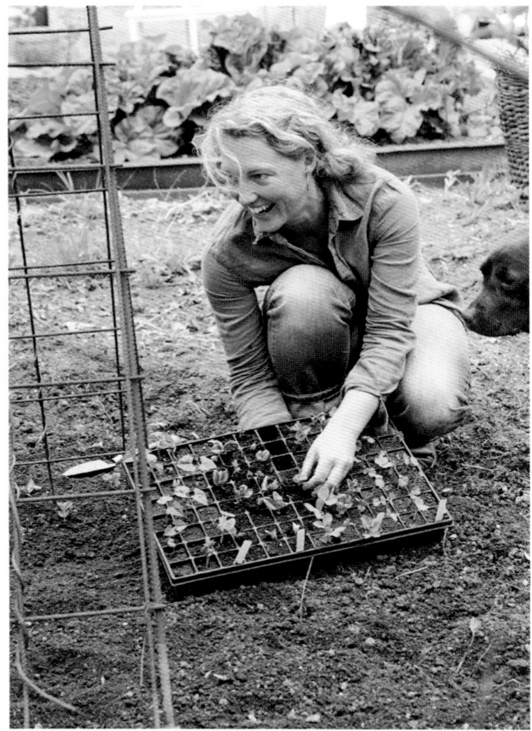

Sugar peas can handle cold pretty well and can be planted early. But protect them from night frost.

MARROWFATS

This is what we usually call green beans. You harvest the pods when the peas are still green and, in actuality, not ripe. You don't eat the pod in itself but the peas inside. Marrowfats have a sweet flavor and a soft, and somewhat smooth texture. They can be opened, blanched, and frozen for storing.

Sow and cultivate as sugar peas. Harvest continuously, but not until the peas are developed in the pod.

SPLIT PEA

The split pea is another type of pea where you eat only the pea and not the pod. Harvest and eat just like the marrowfats. These peas are different from the marrowfats in that they have a more mealy texture, but on the other hand, they can hang on the plant for a long time after they've matured without being ruined, and they are more robust than the marrowfats.

Sow and cultivate the split peas as sugar peas, but it wants warmer soil before you sow it directly in the soil. Let the temperature reach 50°F (10°C) before you sow.

GARDEN PEAS

These peas, that you can soak and boil to make a classic pea soup, are not as common in home gardening anymore, but they are still a part of commercial cultivation. If you want to sow them you can still find seeds from some seed distributors. One of the few varieties you can find in the store and that you can grow as garden peas is "Blauwschokkers." Sow and cultivate the garden peas like sugar peas. Let them mature completely before you harvest them, then split them and let them dry indoors.

PROBLEMS THAT MAY ARISE

Both beans and peas are sensitive to fungal attacks, most often in the form of rust or leaf mildew. Rust emerges as brown-yellow spots on the leaves while the leaf mildew looks like a dull layer over the leaves. The best thing to do to prevent the problem is to avoid planting too tight, watch over the plants, and burn infected leaves. Be careful not to fertilize too much with nitrogen-rich fertilizers, as an excess of nitrogen invites fungal attacks.

Bacterial brown spot used to be a common problem. It later disappeared as a result of vigilant control of seeds. Unfortunately it now looks like it is making a comeback. The disease looks like round, indented, dark spots on the pods. It is often spread through seeds. The best way of protecting yourself from this is to buy controlled and fresh seeds.

Black flies are small insects that suck nutrients from the leaves and pods of the growths. The pods will usually get a grey, shiny, transparent look. If you discover the attack early on, you can usually save the plants by spraying soapy water.

The broad beans can attract black leaf lice. You can easily get rid of these by spraying them off with hard water jets or soapy water. When the blossoming and fruit set is over, you can cut the tops off, and the attacks will then decrease significantly. Other bean plants can suffer from lice attacks as well and you should treat it the same way. Even access to moisture is important to avoid lice attacks on the beans.

MY FAVORITES

1.

FOTO: KARIN ELIASSON

2.

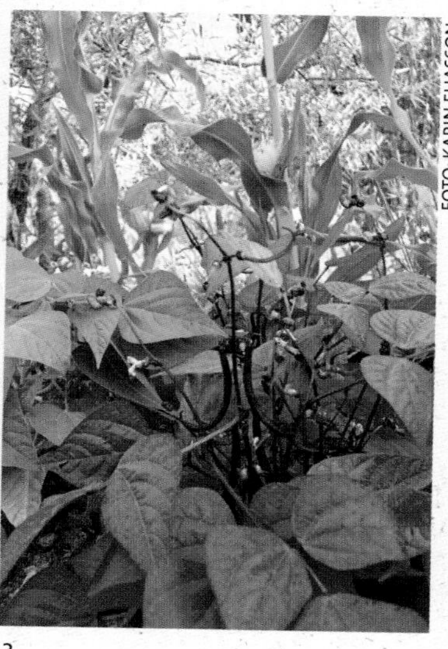
FOTO: KARIN ELIASSON

3.

1. 'Borlotto Lamon'
Split bean/stalk. The borlotti bean from Italy. You can use it in any way imaginable. Grows willingly, gives good crops, and tastes good. One of the few beans that I dry and store. Should be pre-cultivated.

2. 'Chevrier Vert'
Flageolet bean/bush. A French tasty bean that you can eat at every stage of development. Grows easy and willingly.

'Dragon Langerie'
Wax bean/bush. A new discovery that I fell for. Actually one of the best beans I've ever tasted.

'Marga'
Haricot Vert/stalk. A vigorous annual bean in my vegetable garden. Long, thin, green, juicy, threadless beans that you can harvest for a long time.

3. Royalty
Purple bean/bush. Very pretty leaves, flowers, and beans. It has a dark purple color when it is raw, but turns green when you heat it. A beloved border growth.

'Kelvedon Stringless'
Runner bean/bush. It has an incredibly beautiful red-orange flower and is like an exclamation point among the bean growths. It gets going early with a strong growth. It is also great as a decorative plant in a pergola. It has delicious pods and you pick them relatively small and young.

'Imperial Green Longpod'
A fresh and reliable broad bean that gives pods packed with many peas, which I like. It can become quite tall and needs a little support to carry its pods towards the end.

'Blauwschokker'
Blue pea/split pea and garden pea. This is a fun variety that you can either use as a split pea or dry and eat like a garden pea. It is very beautiful with its blue-purple pods, it grows tall, and is easy to grow. One of the few kinds in the store that you can grow as a garden pea.

'Carouby de Maussane'
Marrowfat/medium tall. Gives small, evenly round peas that are easy to harvest. A stable pea plant that climbs better than most.

'Sugar Snap'
Haricot verts/medium tall. Common in cultivating as deserved. It is reliable, tasty, sweet, and crispy.

Save leftover seeds for next year. They will usually keep well, but the ability to germinate can decrease somewhat.

Tip! *Stalks and leaves on the artichoke can be quite bitter. When you've harvested and cleaned the fruits you should clean your hands and later hold all of the rinsed fruits under running water, and possibly add some lemon, before you cook them. If not they'll be bitter.*

EDIBLE THISTLES

Artichokes command respect when you plant them in your vegetable garden. It is like there is something noble about them, as if they know that there is no other plant that can compare to their beauty. They can grow 6 ½ feet (2 meters) tall, spread over 5 square feet (½ sq.m) per plant, and shoot flower vines like crown jewels over the frilly, green leaves. They are often allowed to dwell in the middle of the vegetable garden in a large, heightened, well-drained circle with large verbena. If a plant could be proud, I would say that the artichoke is just that.

THE PLANT IS really biennial, but in colder climates you will may have to make due with one crop a year. It's important to choose seeds of varieties that blossom the first year. Some seed brands are full of artichoke varieties, so test your way through. But if you want to be certain that you will be able to harvest the first year, then look for that information on the packet. In colder climates it is safest to cultivate the artichoke in a greenhouse.

Its relative, the cardoon, is not as sensitive. It doesn't need to blossom as its stalks are what we want to eat. The cardoon grows with even more powerful leaves than the artichoke, but if you grow to eat it, there is no need to wait too long before you bleach the stalks and harvest. The bleaching is without a doubt an extra workload in the cultivation. Many growths should be protected against the sun before you harvest to give them enhanced flavors. Some of us like that extra challenge to achieve the exact taste we want, and if so, the cardoon is a fun plant to try. You can, of course, leave a couple of plants because they are so beautiful. They can form a hedge that shelter sensitive plants from the wind, be a silver background to plants in purple, blue, and shock pink. The leaves on the cardoon can be used for so much more than eating.

Both the artichoke and the cardoon are forgiving to grow, despite the fact that they really belong in warmer climates. But they are thistles after all, and thistles have good growing power. The only thing you can't avoid is the pre-cultivation. They can't be sowed directly if they are to receive enough time to mature well. If you don't have the time to pre-cultivate yourself, then buy plants to win time, so that you don't miss the peak of the crop.

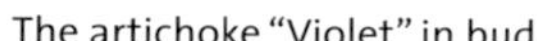
The artichoke "Violet" in bud.

A groovy cardoon plant that's been left unbleached.

CULTIVATING EDIBLE THISTLES

ARTICHOKE

Cynara scolymus

You eat the flowers of the artichoke while they are still buds. If you want, you can harvest them really small and tender, but they should always have some fruit meat, so make sure that they are firm and full in their bottom before you harvest and prepare.

SOW

WHEN? Pre-cultivation is a must since the artichoke has a long development time. Sow eight weeks before planting them outside, which should be when the risk of frost is over.

HOW? It is easiest to sow in a tray. Sow a couple of seeds in each plug and remove the weakest plant if both germinate. Fill the trays about three-fourths full with a blend of planting soil and sifted soil. Lightly push the soil in place, place the seeds on the soil, and cover with about an inch (a couple of centimeters) so that the trays are full. Water thoroughly. Let the seeds sit in a temperature of about 65°F (18°C). Lower the temperature a little when the plants start to show. When the root system reaches the walls of the plug, replant in larger pots. Fertilize the small plants with compost during replanting. Water from underneath.

PREPARING THE GROWTH SITE

The growth site should be sunny. These thistles need a lot of space, so make sure that they have room to spread out. You can plant them as a hedge to give shelter to more sensitive late summer and fall growths. The soil should be

Tender artichokes that have been prepared with olive oil, butter, and lemon.

'Violetta de Chioggia'

fertilized, humus-rich, and moisture retaining. Base fertilize with manure and stone meal. This is usually enough nutrients for one season.

PLANTING OUTSIDE AND NURTURE

Harden the plants thoroughly. Certain varieties can survive some frost, but I recommend that you always plant them when the risk of frost is over. The plants can't stand in cold soil so if it's late spring you can speed up the warming process by covering the soil with plastic. Plant the plants with 23–32 inch (60–80 cm) distance in between the plant in every direction.

Make sure that you keep the soil humid. These growths do not want to dry out. Artichokes usually grow fast once they get going and they need access to nutrients. If the soil is very light you can add a little fertilizer when they are getting ready to blossom, for instance bone meal or Algomin. Cover the ground to help keep the soil humid. If the lower leaves wither and grow ugly then cut them off as you go.

HARVEST

WHEN? The artichokes are harvested as they ripen, from the end of July until the frost arrives. It depends on the variety. You should harvest them before they fully blossom.

HOW? Cut the flower bud with a piece of the stem. Place them in a cool place if you are not preparing them right away. Artichokes keep for a couple of days in the refrigerator, but they're always best fresh.

Tip! To help the water run off of winter covered plants, and prevent that they rot, you can place a few tiles or similar around the stems on top of the cover material.

The most common way of preparing artichokes is to boil them whole. You can then break off the leaves and dip the white fleshy end in butter or vinaigrette, enjoying the inner, meaty part of each leaf. (It's easiest to use your teeth to pull out the delicious, purply insides.) Once you've devoured all the leaves, with a knife or spoon you can scrape out and discard the inedible fuzzy part (called the "choke") covering the artichoke heart. The remaining bottom of the artichoke is the heart. Cut into pieces and dip into sauce to eat.

WINTERING

In warmer climates you can cultivate the artichoke as biennial. Most often they will need to be covered over winter to survive the cold. The plant needs to be well-drained. Only the stem is left over winter and it will shoot new buds in spring. When the harvest is over in fall, cut the plant to 8–12 inches (20–30 cm) above ground. Scoop soil up around the base of the plant and cover with a light and warm blend of leaves, compost, and straw. The cover should happen right before the cold arrives. If it's a wet winter, you have to lift the cover now and then and make sure that the root system gets air, so they don't rot. In spring, when the sun starts warming, remove the cover material completely. If not, it will isolate the cold and prevent the sun from heating the soil.

PROBLEMS THAT MAY ARISE

This growth is relatively unproblematic. The most difficult challenge you'll meet is usually aphids. You can usually spray this off with water.

Wintering the plants can sometimes result in mold attacks and root damage, which makes the whole plant rot. This happens when the roots are too wet and don't have access to enough air. Make sure that the roots get air during cultivation. Do not use a material that is too heavy or dense when you cover.

MY FAVORITES

'Green Globe'
One of the most common artichokes, especially in Sweden. It gives a secure harvest of medium sized, round artichokes. Definitely worth cultivating and tasty.

'Gros Vert de Laon'
A French artichoke that is extremely tasty with an unusually large, developed heart. It should be cultivated as biennial and is also suitable for warmer climates. The first year doesn't give much of a harvest, and you should harvest the flowers that grow while they are still very small to allow the plant to establish itself.

'Violetto'
Gives pretty, small artichokes with violet features. Gets a slightly more open bud than the green globe. Harvest as soon as the outer leaves give an impression of starting to fold outwards.

'Violetta de Chioggia'
Another south European, an Italian artichoke. This grows large, filling artichokes beginning the second year, but already the first year it gives small, Bordeaux-colored buds that are harvested while still tiny and taste amazing. A beauty in the garden.

CARDOON

Cynara cardunculus

You eat the leaf stalks on the cardoon. They need to be bleached before you harvest them so that they develop the soft and fresh taste we're looking for. The cardoon is sowed and cultivated the same way as the artichoke.

HARVEST

WHEN? The whole plant is harvested at the same time, since that is easiest when you are bleaching. Let the stalks develop so that they are meaty and fine, but harvest before the frost and they will become woody and rough. A height of 20–27 inches (50–70 cm) should be just right.

HOW? About one month before you harvest you should start bleaching the stalks so that they have time to get good and tender. The bleaching is done by protecting them from sunlight. You can do this by binding the plant together and folding a little burlap around the plant. Scoop up a bit of soil around the "package" by the base so that it stays steady and stable. You can also use cardboard or, if you have, rhubarb pots for bleaching.

Later you cut the whole plant off and the outer rougher stalks are removed before you boil and eat it. There are only a few equivalent varieties on the market.

Picture to the right: Picturesque sampling of 'Green Globe' and summer flowers.

ONION PLANTS

I wonder if there was ever a vegetable that has revolutionized the flavors of cooking like the onion has. It was one of the vegetables that the pioneer farmers on the beaches of the Euphrates and Tigris brought in from the wild to grow and refine more than five thousand years ago. Ever since then, the onion has had a central role in cooking all over the world in all its shapes and forms. In Sweden we have spiced our herring preserves with onion for hundreds of years, made onion sauce for pork, and cut chives on top of the sour cream. Today, the onion is a given part of the modern kitchen.

ONION GROWTHS (*Allium*) is a straggly family and the ones we know as our most common food onions vary with multiple colors and shapes. Ranging from the regular onions (yellow onion, red onion, pickled onion, and silver onion) with their swelled bodies to the elongated leeks, the cloven garlic, and the straw-shaped chives. I would like to give an extra mention of those loyal growths and Chinese relatives, that are a little more seasonal, but still biennial growths—the ones that you finely chop and sprinkle on top of various dishes to give a fresh flavor and scent. They can be added to soups, in cold sauces, woks, and placed as beautiful straws in Chinese spring rolls. Not to mention the fact that they grow so beautifully in tufts, preferably in a pot on the stairs, and they grow beautiful violet flowers.

Despite my love for this fresh leaf onion, I have to admit that it is the "regular" onion, the yellow and red onion, I use on a daily basis. Since I moved to Spain I use it even more. Here, the onion has become a base for almost everything. Melted in olive oil and spiced with all kinds of spices until it turns creamy and can be a terrific base for stews, sauces, and meat dishes.

On of the reasons why the onion is a base vegetable is that it is so easy to store. Good and plump yellow onions, red onions, silver onions, shallots, and garlic can actually be stored year-long as long as we are careful when we harvest and dry it. Dry, dry, dry all that you can, otherwise mold will attack. But if you manage the critical drying you can have fine onions throughout the winter. We can't forget about the leek either, that bravely withstands winter and can offer fresh fruit into the winter months, which allows us to taste soup with fresh leeks even in December.

In my tribute speech to the onion, I am now going to add that it is easy to cultivate.

The most important thing to remember is that the soil should not be too heavy. Onions, no matter what kind, want to grow without the soil clumping and sticking to their roots or against the onion itself. A mull-rich, porous soil is preferable, so use a bit more time on the preparation of the soil. With the exception of the leek, the onion is very fuzzy when it comes to nutrients. Furthermore, there are varieties that, with their shallow root system, can grow many places where other vegetables cannot. In other words, the onion deserves a place in the vegetable garden and on the plate.

Tip! The slightly strong taste and scent of the onion that we look for in our cooking is a result of the fact that it contains sulfur onion oil. In certain onion varieties it can be sharp enough that it is hard to eat the onion raw. But if you squeeze the sliced onion with balsamic vinegar or lemon, salt, and sugar and marinate it for a while before serving, the worst sting of the powerful onion oil will disappear and you end up with a mild, fine onion to eat in your daily salad. Or in your wok. Or with grilled chicken.

CULTIVATING ONION

YELLOW ONION, RED ONION, SILVER ONION, PICKLED ONION, AND SHALLOT

Allium cepa
Allium cepa var. *aggregatum*

The cepa onions have a swelled, more or less round body and they grow in singles. The shallot *(Allium cepa* var. *aggregatum)* belongs to a special branch of the cepa family. It distinguishes itself by growing a bit differently and growing multiple onions on each plant, almost like wedges. All of the cepa onions are not just as suitable for storing. Read the information for each variety to know how to use them the best way.

SOW

You can sow onions with seeds or plant small ready onions. In most places in Sweden it is beneficial to plant onions since you would have to sow very early for the onion to have time to develop. But seeds are cheaper, and there are certain varieties that you can only get as seeds. Furthermore, many cultivators say that onion that's cultivated from seeds is tougher and more mold-resistant than those that are cultivated from onion. So if you live in the southern parts of Sweden and have time for pre-cultivation, than it might be a good idea to try.

WHEN? If you are planting with an onion, set it out in May, when you can work with the soil. Sow indoors in February to April.

HOW? The onion is placed in the soil with the base facing downwards and only the tip visible above ground. You can also cover the onions completely with ⅙ inch (0.5 cm) if you are bothered by birds that jerks the onions from the ground. Set the onions with 4–10 inches (10–20 cm) distance between and 12–16 inches (30–40) between the rows. The shallot wants a more narrow distance between the rows, 8–10 inches (20–30 cm) and pickled onions can be planted with an inche (2 cm) distance between the plants and 2 inches (5 cm) between the rows. Gently push the onions down so they stay in place.

Broadcast sow the seeds sparsely, and about ⅓ inch (1 cm) deep in a tray with sowing soil. Make sure that the temperature is 68–77°F (20–25°C) during germination. When the seeds start growing you can lower the temperature to 60°F (16°C). Replant the plants when they are 2 inches (five cm) tall. You can still keep them in a tray, but with planting soil. Set them in rows with an inch (2 centimeters) of space between. When the plants have matured a little you can move them into a root trainer

Decorative vegetable garden where perennials are sowed with onions, beans, and red beets.

so that they get their own plug to grow in. This way you'll have a steady little plant to work with when you are moving them outside.

PREPARING THE GROWTH SITE

Onions are, as previously mentioned, an uncomplicated kitchen growth, but they prefer light and humus-rich soil. If you have muddy soil you best enhance this by adding compost and manure. But to avoid a powerful fertilization, which the onion doesn't like, you should do the base fertilization the fall before you'll set the onion. Choose a sunny and warm part of the vegetable garden. In spring you can blend some Algomin or stone meal and compost and fold it in with the soil as a lighter fertilizer. The root systems are shallow, which means that the plants can grow in places where the soil-depth is poor. Regular onions need about 6 inches (15 cm), while pickled onion can manage with 4 inches (10 cm).

The leaves create a nice contrast against the beautiful leaf-shapes in the vegetable garden, here planted between cabbage and beans.

PLANTING THE ONIONS OUTSIDE

Small onion plants can be planted outside with 4 inches (10 cm) distance and 12–16 inches (30–40 cm) between the rows. The distance can vary a little bit with the size of the varieties.

NURTURE

Onions generally don't need much watering. You only need to water if there are long periods of drought. But onions are very sensitive to weeds, so you should remove weeds regularly. Onions don't like dry or hard surfaces either, which can occur in muddy soils. This is easily prevented though cover cultivation with clippings or straw. This way the surface where the shallow root systems are developing will stay humid. If it is too wet it will increase the risk that the onion rot or is affected by mold. You can also gently loosen the soil, but watch out for the roots.

HARVEST

WHEN? If you want to use fresh onion, you can harvest it as soon as it has swelled and obtained some volume. If you want to store it you have to wait until the withering stage, when the tops start turning yellow. When this happens, and a large part of the crop have yellow tops, you can help the rest of the onions by knocking on the tops and later waiting a couple of days before you take them up to dry.

HOW? You can remove a leaf here and there from the onion without damaging the plant and use it in salads as chives. When you harvest the entire onion it is very important that it gets to dry. Spread the onion out in a place that's protected from nightly humidity and rain, in a place where air can circulate freely, such as in a greenhouse or under a roof on the balcony. If you have a room with dry and warm air, that's even better, for instance, a boiler room. The tops should be completely dry before you polish the onion. Free

TIP! *All of the onion growths benefit from cutting the tops back to 2 inches (5–6 cm) a couple of times during growth to strengthen the root system. This gives strong, stable, and fine plants.*

from dirt, skin, and cut off long root threads and dry tops. If the tops are not completely dry the onion will go bad very soon. If you want to make preserves of pickled onion, it should hang in a dark place during drying to keep its pretty white color.

PROBLEMS THAT MAY ARISE

The most common problems when cultivating onions are the onion fly and onion mildew.

The onion fly lays eggs on the onion leaves or in the soil surrounding the plant. The larvae then enter the onion and ruin it. Over time the whole plant will wither and die. The larvae of the onion fly can also pupate and survive winter in the soil. If you don't change the onion's growth place, the attacks may gradually worsen.

The best protection against the onion fly is to cultivate under a fiber cloth at the beginning of the season and possibly place the fiber cloth over the plants again at the end of summer. The onion fly lays its eggs in May and also in July-August. This is when the danger of an attack is greatest. Rinse the crop properly after harvest so that there are no scraps left in the soil over winter; these will often make nests for the fly larvae over the winter months.

Covering the soil around the budding onion with grass clippings is a good way to keep the soil moist.

Onion leaf mildew is caused by tight cultivation, humidity, and cold. The attacks create yellow leaf tops and later yellow-brown spots on the entire top. To decrease the risk of attacks it is important to let air circulate between the plants in the crop, to keep weeds away, and not water too much, especially not the tops. Attacked onions are harvested right away and consumed before the onion goes bad. The tops are burned or tossed.

MY FAVORITES

'Banana Shallot'
An oblong shallot that is easy to cultivate and tastes great both raw and cooked. Great for storing.

'de Barletta'
A pickling onion that grows quickly and happily. Grows small, even, onions that are suitable for preserves, but you can also eat them fresh or marinate them and grill them on skewers.

'Long Red Florence'
An Italian, long and narrow red onion with a dark violet skin. It is incredibly tasty raw in salads or in yogurt sauces. It is easy to cultivate, but it can be difficult to store for the entire winter, so don't leave it for too long.

'Pompeii'
A mild and sweet silver onion that you harvest at about 2 inches (5 cm). It is easy to cultivate and grows relatively quickly. It can be stored for months.

'Red Baron'
A round red onion that is easy to cultivate, good, and stable. It can be stored and is red all the way through.

'North Holland Blood Red'
A red onion that is best fresh as a salad onion or as mature red onion. It doesn't keep very well.

'Sturon'
A yellow onion that never disappoints in growing, storing, or flavor. Large yellow round onions with brown-yellow skin that keeps for a long time.

LEEK AND SCALLION

Allium porrum, Allium fistulosum och Allium cepa

Leeks and scallions are similar, both in cultivation demands and look. But the scallion is smaller and is harvested as a baby. Leek is an umbrella term for onions that are cultivated first and foremost for their tops. The varieties either belong to *Allium fistulosum* or *Allium cepa. Allium fistulosum* and also exist as a wintering variety that is called Welsh Onion. It grows in tufts and is harvested as chives. The non-resistant varieties are cultivated as annual scallions and we harvest the entire onion, like the chive.

SOW

WHEN? Chives and scallions should be sowed as seeds. You can choose to grow small plants and replant them outside or sow directly on the growth site. If you want to pre-cultivate it is fitting to do so in March-April under the same temperature circumstances as regular onions. If you sow directly, then wait until the middle of May or when the soil feels good to work with. It is common to sow scallions in rounds from May to July and harvest them small.

HOW? If you pre-cultivate the plant, you can sow directly in the soil in a hotbed or in a tray, the same way you did for the cepa onion. Sow them an inch (2 cm) deep and with about an inch (2 cm) distance between each plant. When they poke up about 2 inches (5 cm), it is time to replant them. If it is still too early to move them outside, plant them back in the tray but more spread out, with 2 inches (5 cm) distance between the plants for leeks and about an inch (2 cm) for the shallot should be fine. Just like with the regular onions, you can cut the top one time during growth to obtain better plants.

If you sow shallots directly, you can sow at the same depth, but with an inch (2 cm) between the plants and 8–10 inches (20–25 cm) between the rows. You do not have to cull these. The leek needs 5–8 inches (5–20 cm) between the plants when it grows, but it can be set more closely and then culled. The row distance should be 12–20 inches (30–50 cm).

PREPARING THE GROWTH SITE

The leek and shallot are different from other onions in that they need more nutrients. Base fertilize with cow or horse manure that you blend well with the soil and support fertilize over the summer with bone meal or poultry manure. You should cup both of the onions a couple of times during the growth period to achieve the pale tender lower part of the onion. (See nurture, below). It is therefore most convenient to sow in light soil. A heavier, muddy soil will clump up and stick to the onion. You can make heavy soil lighter with rough sand, compost, and bark humus.

PLANTING OUTSIDE

You can move the plants outside when the danger of frost is over. It is rarely beneficial to rush the planting outside. The risk is that the plant develops poorly or starts seeding too soon. The plants should be planted deep, about 2 inches (5 cm) into the ground.

NURTURE

Since leeks and shallots need a lot of nutrients, it is a good idea to cover cultivate. Cover right away or when the plant is about 4 inches (10 cm) tall. Don't pack the cover material around the top, but leave a small circle around the plant for air circulation. Feel free to add more cover material once the plant has grown to twice its size. These onions need to be cupped, which means that you scoop soil up around the plant so that the neck of the onion is partly protected against sunlight. This way it's bleached and will become tender and good. Cupping also stimulates the growth of the onion. You usually need to do this twice during the growth season, but it can vary depending on whether or not it rains and if the soil sinks down. You simply have to keep an eye on them. If you cover cultivate, it is best to remove the cover material around the plant and cup up clean soil. This is to avoid a tight and humid environment around the onion so that it might get mildew. If it is difficult to scoop up some of the soil then you can add new soil around the neck of the plant instead. Use soil with lots of sand for the ultimate airiness. Support fertilize during the summer with bone meal or poultry manure. If you cover cultivate with clippings or growth waste, you should be careful with additional fertilization so that the onion doesn't overdose. Watering is usually unnecessary, but, as usual, this depends on the soil and rain. Do not let the soil dry out completely.

HARVEST

WHEN? The shallot is usually harvested when it is 8–10 inches (20–25 cm) tall and between one-third and one inch thick, but there's nothing in the way of harvesting it earlier. The leek is harvested in late fall. Most of the varieties can stand into winter, just as long as the soil around the onion doesn't freeze so that you can't pull it up. If you want to try to leave it out you should cover the soil with straw or leaves. To avoid rot in the wet winter soil, it is still a good idea to move them inside and keep them in a controlled environment; set them in a box of sand in a cool cellar, for instance. If you have a greenhouse you can replant them in the greenhouse beds. There is no risk of them being damaged by water in there.

HOW? The harvest is easy; you twist the onion a little and then slowly pull them upwards so that it lets go. If it is really stuck you can loosen the surrounding soil with a garden fork first and then try to release the onion from the soil. You can freeze leeks fresh or, even better, blanched.

Both scallions and leeks can be cupped so that the stalk is bleached and so it obtains a milder flavor.

PROBLEMS THAT MAY ARISE

Both the leek and the shallot are relatively problem-free. What can be bothersome is the onion fly (see p. 187) and leek moth. To avoid attacks from leek moths you can cover the crop with fiber cloth and pick the larvae if you see them. The attack will show on the top at first, which will be shattered. If you discover the attack early on, merely cut the upper part of the plant and burn it. If you don't discover it in time the insects will find their way into the stem and the onion will rot.

Leek.

MY FAVORITES

'Ishikura Long'
An incredibly tasty and mild shallot. You can cultivate this in rounds during the summer and eat small.

'Prenora'
A leek favorite for its stability and good taste, as well as its ability to handle cold. It grows fast and straight up, and it gets a rather long neck, which I think is beautiful.

'Red Beard'
Another beauty in the vegetable garden. A shallot with a red striped onion neck, best when it's still small. It is easy to cultivate, but not very good with cold.

'St. Victor'
This leek is just as beautiful as it is good. It develops violet stripes in late fall and is incredibly pretty with violet cabbage varieties. Furthermore, it is easy to cultivate and forgiving.

GARLIC

Allium sativum

Garlic may just be one of our most loved and commonly used onion growths. Not only is garlic healthy, but it has an oil that prevents bacteria growth. Garlic is, in other words, both food and medicine that is good to keep in your garden. It is easy to cultivate and should be planted in the fall.

PREPARING THE GROWTH SITE

In contrast to most everything else in the vegetable garden, garlic is planted in late fall. The reason is that it needs a long time to establish and start growing. Choose a part of the garden where the spring sun warms early. Fold in compost and loosen the soil properly. In Spring you can add stone meal or Algomin.

PLANTING

WHEN? Garlic should be planted with a planting onion in your climate. September-November is a good time to plant garlic.

HOW? You use the cloves from garlic the same way you do when planting onions. You can usually just use regular garlic that you bought in the store, as long as it is not heat-treated. But I do recommend using a controlled onion to make sure that its fresh. The cloves are best planted in small hills of soil. The largest threat against garlic that's planted in fall is humidity. The risk for it to rot in the winter wet is looming. By placing the cloves in a hill of soil, you guarantee drainage around the garlic.

Shape low hills, about 2 inches (5 cm) tall, and 12–16 inches (30–40 cm) apart. Set the onion 2 inches (5 cm) deep in the hills with 6 inches (15 cm) distance between the plants. Cover the soil with leaves and straw.

PRE-CULTIVATING AND PLANTING THE GARLIC OUTSIDE

If you are late to set your garlic and the soil is difficult to work with, you can always pre-cultivate the garlic by placing them in toilet paper rolls in a cultivating tray. Fill with soil, place one clove in each roll and water. Cover with straw and keep away from frost, for instance on a closed veranda, or a greenhouse, until spring, when you can plant them outside.

Garlic needs to get going early. You therefore need to be quick to get it planted in spring if you want to give it a good start. Warm the soil where you are planting the garlic with the help of transparent plastic. As soon as the soil settles down and you can work with it, cut holes in the plastic and plant the paper roll, or the lump of soil, with the clove. Leave the plastic for a while so that the garlic has a nice and warm environment. In early summer you can remove the plastic and cover with organic material instead.

NURTURE

Garlic is not difficult. You only need to water it after a long drought, but for the purposes of keeping the surface loose and fine, I greatly recommend a cover. It grows smoothly all through the season if you give it a little Algomin or stone meal in spring. Just be careful when you weed and rake around the onion as it has a shallow root system.

HARVEST

WHEN? We mostly harvest garlic in August, when the top has started yellowing and the onion is swelled and well-developed.

HOW? You pull up garlic just like any other onion and leave it out to dry in the sun so that the white-pink peel dries out completely. Store the garlic in a dark and dry place. If you want, you can make braids out of the garlic and hang it on the wall. In that case, save the top so that it is long enough for braiding.

PROBLEMS THAT MAY ARISE

Garlic can sometimes be attacked by the onion fly (see p. 187), but is generally spared more often than the regular onion.

MY FAVORITES

'Isle of Wight'
A variety made for the somewhat grayer and more humid climate in the north. It is safe to cultivate and has a nice development even with cooler summers.

'Rosso di Sulmona'
A beautiful Italian garlic with violet cloves that give the garlic a nice pink gleam. Tasty, beautiful, and good for storing.

Budding chives

CHIVES AND CHINESE CHIVES

Allium schoenoprasum och Allium tuberosum

Both of these are among my onion favorites, much because of their taste and usefulness, but also because they are a biennial act in the garden. You sow them, harvest them, and use them the exact same way, but there is a slight difference in flavor. The Chinese chive is somewhat sharper and is more reminiscent of the garlic. I like this the best when chopped and sprinkled on top of warm dishes, while the chive is great for colder dishes.

SOW

WHEN? The plants are biennial and you therefore don't need to plant them every year, but to secure a fresh crop it could be a good idea to sow anew every four years. You can sow directly on the growth site in May-June or pre-cultivate beginning a couple of months earlier.

HOW? The seeds are set in tussocks or in rows, with about ⅓ inch (1 cm) soil covering the seeds. Keep the seedlings moist and cover with a fiber cloth. If you pre-cultivate, you can sow the seeds directly in a 3½ inch (9 cm) sized pot and later plant the entire lump of soil in the garden.

PREPARING THE GROWTH SITE

Both of these onion varieties prefer a humus-rich, light soil to grow in. Since they are going to stay for multiple years, you should prepare the soil a little extra and make sure that it is well-drained. Deep fork the soil and fold in manure and compost. Fertilize with some Algomin to stimulate the plant. Both regular chive and the Chinese chive will grow fine in a pot as well, and

A wheel of onion and flowers is pretty as a centerpiece in the vegetable garden.

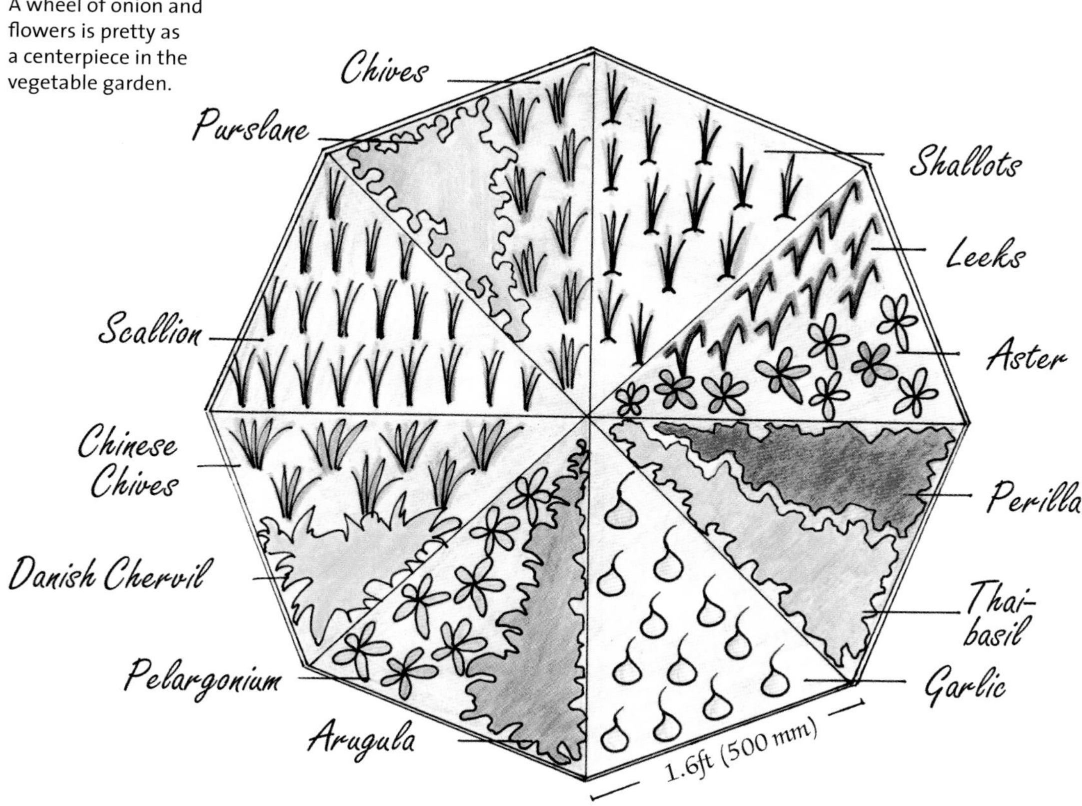

they both grow beautiful flowers, that should be cut before they start seeding so that the onion doesn't spread uncontrollably.

PLANTING OUTSIDE
Pre-cultivated plants are set out when the risk of frost is completely over and they are planted either in a group or in a row. I think it is nice to use tussocks of chives with summer flowers in the garden or as a border in some of the beds.

NURTURE
These plants are not affected by disease or pests and don't need any notable nurture, but they should not be subjected to long-lasting drought. Fertilize with Algomin once a year. If you let them go into complete blossom, the leaves turn rough and are not as fun to eat. You can cut the plant down completely a few times to stimulate new leaves. Generally the plants survive the winter the best in the reservation or the garden, even if you've had them in a pot during summer. Cover the Chinese chive with straw or leaves to give it the best possible conditions for wintering.

If there are a lot of hard winters where you live, it is best to keep the onion in the pot and winter it in a room sheltered from frost.

HARVEST
Cut the leaves continuously by cutting them 2 inches (5 cm) above ground. You can cut the leaves and freeze them, although it will lose some of its original taste. If you harvest all the time, it won't blossom.

Tip! *The chive tussocks can grow quite large and tired over the years. If you separate them, they will get new energy and grow more leaves. You can always give the excess half away to a friend or a neighbor.*

Cut the flowers off the chive and place them in a vase on the kitchen. This way you prevent them from spreading seeds and you still get to enjoy the beautiful plants.

POTATOES

My grandmother Beata would always compete with her neighbors and relatives to grow the finest Dahlias. But it wasn't only about growing the biggest or lushest plants, but just as much about who got their Dahlias to blossom earliest in the season. My grandmother would win often, maybe because she took it so seriously. Nobody really spoke about the competition; it was just understood. During family events, you could hear my grandmother in the kitchen saying, "Oh, so yours haven't blossomed yet? Oh, well that's only natural. It is still early, but mine are blossoming just fine, but it can differ sometimes... it definitely can."

I OFTEN THINK about this competition when the potato season starts. You see notes in the newspaper announcing, "The new potatoes are already here!" with a smiling farmer on the accompanying picture who almost risked his entire crop by planting the potatoes two weeks before everyone else—but then he also got to be FIRST. And we all want to be the first with fresh potatoes. Maybe not as much for the prestige, but because we want to make the season as long as possible and get potatoes during that time when potatoes, salt, and butter can be an entire meal.

Potatoes, with the botanical name *Solanum tuberosum,* come in so many flavors. Nowadays, there's a whole sea of fun varieties to try. Most of them are sold in small portions so that you can try many different ones. Firm, mealy, round, lumpy, oblong, sweet, chestnut-flavored, light, fresh . . . etc.

Many of the varieties that I used to buy abroad can now be found on the Swedish market. There's a potato for every taste, and each year there are new and exciting varieties. My random favorites are all small, firm, sweet varieties that goes well in balmy summer salads—with herring and lemon-marinated red onion, with parsley and Serrano ham, with chopped chervil and smoked salmon. They are early potatoes that should be harvested in summer and preferably enjoyed right away. But there are certainly real goodies among the slower varieties, the ones that need to grow in the soil into fall and develop a skin that allows them to be stored over winter.

The potatoes have always been close to my heart. I think they taste great, the plant is beautiful, and I like the variety of tubers. Besides, the potato is a forgiving kitchen growth that anyone can grow in a bucket on the balcony, in a sack, in a hotbed, or straight in the garden. It is most comfortable in warm, light, soils, but if you have muddy soil, don't be discouraged. With manure, compost, and a sunny spot, you can create a pretty potato patch almost anywhere.

The plants grow quickly and give a deep green lushness to the garden, and soon white or purple star-shaped flowers will pop up among the green. Wait until the flowers have blossomed and then you can start looking for small tubers. If you are going to eat them as fresh potatoes, you don't have to wait for the peel to grow and give the potato a protective shield. Carefully grope under the soil around a plant and see how the potato looks. You can harvest it as soon as they are an okay size, despite the fact that the peel may still be thin as silk. Harvest, boil, eat, and be happy.

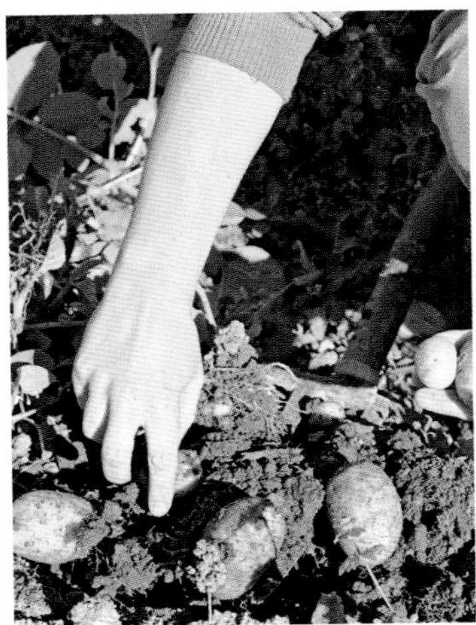

Potatoes—one of our most loved...

...and cultivated vegetables.

Potato basket in modern packaging

CULTIVATING POTATOES

PRE-GROWING

WHEN? It is not necessary to pre-grow the potatoes, but it is beneficial to do so, as the plant will get started earlier and you can harvest sooner. You pre-grow by placing the potatoes in light three to four weeks before planting is usually fine.

HOW? Place them in a little peat humus or in an egg carton in a window. After a couple of weeks, you'll see the green sprouts peeking out here and there on the potato. Let the sprouts become ⅓–1 inch long (1–2 cm). The potato should preferably be planted when the soil temperature is above 46°F (8°C). The soil temperature is important in order for the tubers to start growing right away and not stagnate in cold soil, which increases the risk for attacks and weak growth. The beginning of May is usually a good time for moderate to warmer climates.

PREPARE THE GROWING SITE

Choose a sunny, airy, and well-drained spot for your potato crop. The potato is most comfortable in light soil that can hold moisture. And sandy humus-rich soil is perfect. Prepare the soil by loosening it well, about 8–10 inches (20–25 cm) deep. If you have a very muddy soil you should blend in some bark humus or compost to make it easier to work with and well-drained. Base fertilize with burned manure and add a little extra fertilizer with a high sulfur and potassium content, such as wood ashes. Be careful with nitrogen-rich fertilizers—they make a watery potato and too much above ground blossoming in comparison to the tubers. Make sure that there hasn't been another growth from the potato family at that spot during the last three years, like tomatoes or eggplants.

PLANT THE POTATOES

Plant the potatoes in rows, about 4 inches (10 cm) deep. There should be about 12–16 inches (30–40 cm) between the tubers and 20–28 inches (50–70 cm) between the rows. A good row distance is important so that you can cup the soil in a good way later on. Early potatoes can be planted somewhat tighter together, while fall and winter potatoes need a greater distance, as they are going to stay longer and the tubers grow larger.

The plant is sensitive to frost. It is therefore a good idea to keep fiber cloth on hand just when the top peaks out, in case the frost returns.

CUPPING

When the plants are 6 inches (15 cm) tall, you cup upwards for the first time. Scoop up dirt around the plant, while avoiding the actual leaves. You do this to prevent the potato from daylight. If it does, it develops the poisonous substance called Solanine and turns green and inedible. The cupping also helps keep the humidity around the fruits. Cup at least once during the growth.

WATERING

Potatoes need good access to water to develop a large amount of tubers. If you cultivate in very sandy soil, you have to watch the ground carefully so that it doesn't dry out. The less you water the top, the better. If you, for some reason, have to water the tops, do it in the morning. This way they can dry during the day; at night the humidity will stay longer. It is most important that the plant does not dry when it is blossoming. Be attentive with the watering when you see that the plants are growing buds and blossoming is near.

HARVEST

WHEN? Normally, it takes two to three months before early potatoes are ready for harvest. It depends, among other things, on whether or not you pre-grew it. You usually start harvesting the fresh potatoes during blossom. Carefully grope around the plant and look to see how they look before you turn the entire root system upside down. Even if you want a small potato, it should have developed a little color and size to have a good flavor.

HOW? You can choose to harvest the entire crop at once or you can gradually pick the tubers. If you harvest the entire plant, it is easiest to use a garden fork that you push down along the edge of the crop. Turn up the whole root system with the fork and then pick the potatoes from the root threads. If you would rather pick gradually, you have to be careful and just scratch away the soil around the plant and remove ready tubers. Afterwards, you move the soil back over the roots and tubers so that they can grow in peace and quiet.

Fall and winter potatoes are harvested from September to October. Cut off the top a couple of weeks before you are planning to harvest. This helps the potatoes develop a thicker peel and increases their storing abilities.

PROBLEMS THAT MAY ARISE

The most common problems are mildew and other fungal diseases, with rot on the tubers as a result. If your tops get brown spots that spread, you should immediately cut them off and burn them or toss them in the trash to prevent the disease

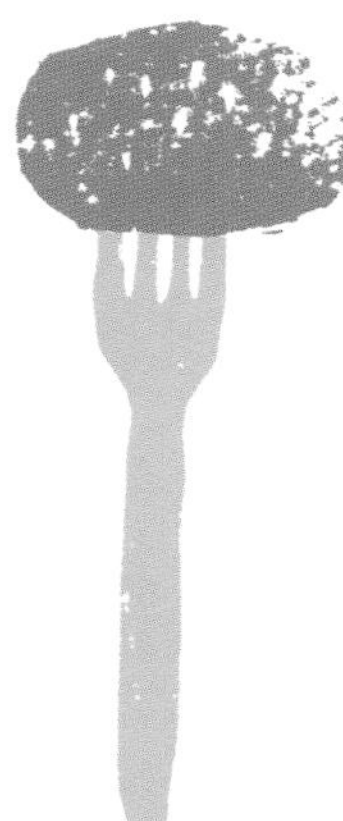

TIP!

You can cultivate the potatoes in a bucket. Make sure that the bucket has holes in the bottom so that it is well-drained. If not, water can gather in the bottom. Empty four inches (10 cm) soil in the bucket. Add the potatoes and cover with two inches (5 cm) soil. When the top has come to about four inches (10 cm) above ground you fill more soil in so that it reaches the leaves. Continue adding soil as the top grows, so that the root system and tubers gradually develop from the stems. Harvest when the plant has blossomed.

from spreading to the tubers or to other growths. Do not let the potatoes you are storing come in contact with infected tops or infected growth parts on the surface.

To decrease the risk of this kind of disease it is important that the potato is in the sun so that the top isn't humid. Do not water the top, only the soil, and avoid planting too tight so that you prevent air from circulating around the plants.

Scurf is another problem that might occur. This is usually a result of poor watering, but it can also be because of the pH values. Potatoes are not comfortable in lime-rich soils; they ideally want a pH value of about 6–7. Do not use lime-rich fertilizer on the potato crop.

Potato cysts are a nuisance that can occur in soils where a lot of potatoes have been cultivated. Nematodes hinder the plant's nutrition uptake. The plants become scrawny, the harvest is poor, and the potatoes are of bad quality. The solution is to stop growing potatoes in that spot. To prevent this problem, it is best to be vigilant about rotating.

In addition to these two, you can be visited by wireworms and snails that make holes in the potato and ruin it. The larvae live off of roots from grass and other natural growths and naturally inhibit the growth. The problem will most often be the most severe the first year if you have established a new vegetable garden. As you start removing weeds and continually work the soil, these problems will lessen. The best way to prevent this is by not growing the potato close to tall grass or other lush vegetation and remove weeds continuously.

MY FAVORITES

Buy fresh and cultivation-controlled potatoes.

'Amandine'
An early variety with oblong, medium-sized tubers, firm and fine with a filling buttery taste.

'Asterix'
A fall and winter potato that I first encountered in France. It is a real goodie that grows many tubers with even shapes, It has firm meat and nutty flavor.

'Cherie'
A small, early, red favorite. The meat is firm and it has a soft flavor of chestnut or acorn.

'Golden Wonder'
A fall and winter potato. A casserole favorite with very flavorful white-yellow meat, great to store. A winter savior.

'Juliette'
Is early and has small round tubers. Soft and very tasty.

'Leoni'
An early potato and a rather new and reliable friend with tasty small, yellow tubers. It is said that it tolerates drought better than the other varieties, which could be an advantage if you need to travel for a period of time.

'Marine'
An early, pretty new variety that is worth trying for all of you that deal with cold nights for a long time. It tolerates frost better than others and it has light yellow meat. It is versatile, firm, tasty and has a little sweetness to its flavor.

'Ratte Potato'
A fantastic fall potato with a buttery, round flavor. I like it boiled and can eat it without anything else. It is also good oven-baked. A little darling.

Dansk
Asparges
Leoni
Cherie
Juliette
Marine
Asterix
Amandine

ROOT VEGETABLES

My debut as a carrot cultivator was in my villa garden in Harplinge, Sweden, where I grew up. It was, to be honest, my mother that planted and nurtured, and I harvested. I harvested the carrots all too small; they were small yellow-orange shives that I rubbed against the grass until all the dirt was gone and later chewed through. Or refined. My sister's and my specialty was carrot rolls: tiny, tiny carrots wrapped in a lettuce leaf with wild strawberries, and was later sold by our gate for 50 cents to happy neighbors.

I STILL LOVE pulling up carrots and red beets when they are still tiny and eat them as an early-season snack. You can even leave the timid top and eat them oven-roasted with a little butter and salt.

Root fruits are special. It is a very broad group. To start with, we have the hardy classics: carrot, red beet, and radish. Today there are so many varieties that it is bothersome how difficult it is to choose seeds. Pointy white radishes, round and multi-colored carrots, striped red beets—it is a cavalcade of fantasy and playfulness, a given participant in the children's vegetable garden. Guaranteed success.

Then we have the more advanced, slow root vegetables: swede, celeriac, parsnips, salsify and more. They are really not more difficult to grow, but they take longer to develop. But once they're done they taste amazing.

In many ways the slow root vegetables are perfect for the cultivators that aren't home for the entire summer. There's no danger of losing the crop; it will be waiting for you when you return. And you don't need to pour fertilizer on them all summer long. In spring you prepare a nice growth site, and then they will take care of themselves into fall. In contrast, you will have to cull them once, loosen the soil if there's a lot of rain, and water if there's a drought. If you leave, this is best solved through cover cultivation and drop watering.

Root vegetables are a large part of the fall Swedish harvest. Going out and harvesting these aromatic, hard, lumpy vegetables, and with cold fingers, feeling how the cultivating season is coming to an end—this is fall. Even the colors have an autumn-stroke, the orange with the moss green, beige, and wine red. And, despite my love for early harvests, there is a sense of abundance to harvest as you fill up boxes for storage.

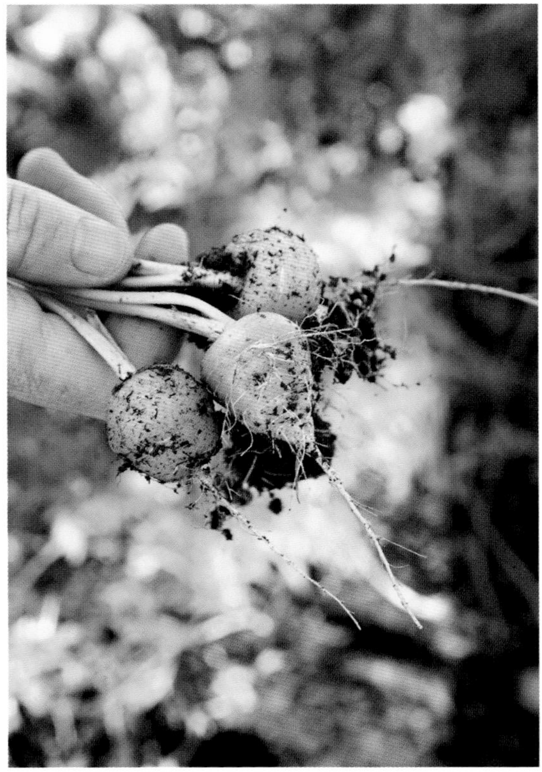

Marble carrots can even grow in the balcony box.

CULTIVATING ROOT VEGETABLES

SWEDE

Brassica napus

The swede is a cabbage growth, but since we use the root, it belongs with the root vegetables. Round and tasty and chockfull of Vitamin C, it is worthy of its nickname "The Orange of the North."

SOW AND NURTURE

It is easiest to sow swedes directly in free land when the soil is possible to work with in spring. It grows at temperatures as low as 46–50°F (8–10°C) in soil temperature. Place the seeds about one inch (a few cm) below ground and cover with fertilized and humus-rich soil. Leave 6–8 inches (15–20 cm) between the plants and 16 inches (40 cm) between the rows. It is important to not be skimpy on space as the swede needs good access to light. If you don't, the top will lose control and grow at the roots expense. Make sure that the soil holds even moisture and that there are no weeds along the tuber—it disturbs the growth of the plant.

HARVEST

Swede is to most, a given autumn food, but don't miss the chance to eat small early growths earlier in the season. You can harvest them from when they are about one inch (a couple of centimeters) in diameter. Divide them and oven-roast them with a little honey, salt, and rosemary.

If you prefer to wait to harvest, that presents no problem at all. The swede tolerates frost, but needs to thaw before it is pulled up like all other root vegetables. Later you can keep it in spacious bags or in a bed of sand in a cool place.

PROBLEMS THAT MAY ARISE

The kale fly can be a nuance for the swedes. If you want to lower the risk of attack, delay the planting to the middle of summer when the flies are less aggressive. Or try cultivating under fiber cloth.

MY FAVORITES

'Krasnoselskaja'
A Russian variety with yellow-green drawings and nice yellow meat. I like it for its even, good flavor quality.

'Magres'
A beautiful variety from England. It grows yellow fruits with a wine-red neck, spherical with a small tip. Sweet and tasty without a hint of bitterness.

CARROT

Daucus carota ssp. sativus

The carrot is a biennial plant, but we always harvest it after one year, when the root is tasty and packed with nutrients. You can find carrots in multiple varieties and they can look very different. There's the early summer carrots that are harvested and consumed right away and are not suitable for storing, and then there's the fall carrots that are sturdy and can be stored over winter. Among the summer carrots we can find anything from spherical or short and blunt, to pencil-thin elegant varieties. Why not try a little of each?

Tip! If you need to cull in the carrot row, you can use nail scissors and cut the tops off of them instead of pulling up the excess roots. If they're standing close to each other and you decide to pull a few of them up, you can rub against the ones that are left, and since carrots have very sensitive roots, be careful!

SOW AND NURTURE

The carrot wants a light, sandy, humus-rich soil. If you have sturdier soil, you can benefit from choosing a carrot variety that is short and stubby. The thin, long varieties will have trouble developing in a heavy soil.

Sow directly in a kitchen garden or hotbed in spring and early summer; germinate at a soil temperature as low as 45°F (7°C). Sow about an inch (a few centimeters) deep, and not too tight. If you're sowing early carrots, you can sow a little tighter, 1–2 inches (2–4 cm) between the plants, but the fall carrots need more room to grow, 2–4 inches (4–6 cm) between the plants, and 10 inches (25 cm) between the rows should be just right. It is common to sow carrots too tight and then have to cull afterwards. You save a lot of time and seeds by giving them enough space to begin with. Water the row before you sow, cover with soil, and carefully water the surface with a watering can. Keep the soil humid and loose so the plant can break though the soil easily.

Since the carrot seeds grow slowly, the weeds will often manage to grow before the carrot top peeks out, which can be worrisome. You can wait a couple of weeks extra to sow the carrots and allow the weeds to grow one round so you can easily remove them. Harrow the soil with a cultivator and then sow the carrots. This way you decrease the risk of weeds.

To prevent the carrots from getting green necks, regularly cup soil upwards along their neck.

HARVEST

Harvest the early carrots as soon as they have developed a real color. They are at their best when they've just matured. If you leave them for too long they can crack and lose their freshness. The fall varieties benefit from standing for a longer time. They have their best growth period in fall when the air has turned cool and humid. The tops should be nice and green when you harvest. If they are starting to look sad, it is better to pull the carrots up and store them. If the tops look fine when the cold arrives, you can let them sit a while longer, cover the crop with grass or straw, and continue harvesting even when the cold is really biting. If it is difficult pull the carrots up you can lightly yank with a fork in the ground before you pull them up, so that the root doesn't fall off. If you want to store them, then do so in a cool room covered by sand.

PROBLEMS THAT MAY ARISE

The largest threat against the carrot crop is the carrot fly and the carrot flea. The most effective way of avoiding attacks is to cultivate under a fiber cloth or in a windy spot. This disturbs the attackers. Cover cultivation with grass clippings also reduces the risk of a carrot flea attack. It is the scent of the carrot that attracts the pests. Therefore, planting with strongly scented growths such as tagetes, marigold, and onion may confuse them. You can also powder the tops with lime, crushed Algomin, or wood ash to avoid attacks.

MY FAVORITES

'Autumn King'
I've fallen in love with this fall carrot. Even quality, beautiful shape, and orange color. Crisp, juicy, and keeps well. Not too picky when it comes to soil either.

'Early Nantes'
An early but resistant carrot. It can remain in the soil without cracking and retains its flavor and nice color. Cylindrical, orange, juicy, and good.

'Parabell'
An orange delicacy carrot that should be consumed completely fresh. It is spherical and is therefore possible to cultivate in heavier soils as well, even in a pot. Pretty, tasty, and easy to cultivate.

'Purple Haze'
Unbelievably beautiful and tasty. Slim, tender, purple carrots that every chef longs for.

PARSNIP

Pastinaca sativa

This white cousin of the carrot is a real gem. The parsnip is, however, a little more difficult to cultivate. It sets higher demands for the soil than the carrot and it takes longer to develop. But just like other root vegetables, it is very suitable for our Nordic climate and is well worth a try.

SOW AND NURTURE

To succeed with a crop of parsnips, you have to have a soil that can hold humidity and nutrients without being too tight or hard. If you have a light, sandy soil, you have to be prepared to fertilize and water over the summer to get well-developed roots. The largest growth happens late in the season and it is very important that they have nutrients then, so don't forget to add grass clippings and maybe a little wood ash towards the end of summer.

Tip! To win cultivation space, you can plant a couple of radishes in between the parsnip plants. The radishes germinate and develop faster and can be harvested just when the parsnip needs more room.

Root Vegetable potpourri of celeriac, various beets, and carrots

You should sow as early as possible, in free land, when the soil is at least 40°F (5°C). In moderate it could be a good idea to pre-cultivate so that you win a little time. Be careful with the roots when you replant the small plants. Similar to the carrot, the parsnip doesn't like when we toy with its feet. Leave 4–6 inches (10–15 cm) between the plants, and 12 inches (30 cm) between the rows.

HARVEST

Assume that the parsnips will need four months to develop from seed to harvest. The parsnip benefits from a bit of frostbite, as the taste is enhanced and it becomes sweeter. Therefore, you should harvest as late as possible in fall. If you want to store them, do so in a cellar climate and protected by sand.

PROBLEMS THAT MAY ARISE

The largest problem is usually trying to get the roots to develop evenly without cracking. This has to do with the quality of the soil and access to humidity; dry soil gives woody and cracked roots; too hard soil gives short, branchlike roots. Cover cultivate with grass clippings. The parsnip can also be attacked by the carrot fly.

MY FAVORITES

'Gladiator'
I tried this one as seeds from London and it has given me large, fine crops and many tasty soups. The shape can be somewhat uneven, but the taste and crispiness is perfect.

'White Gem'
Is not one of the most cultivated parsnips in Sweden for nothing, it maintains an even and high quality. A safe and good variety.

PARSLEY ROOT

Petroselinum crispum var. *tuberosum*

The parsley root is reminiscent of the parsnip both in looks and how it's cultivated. The taste isn't that different from the parsnip either, but it has a clear hint of parsley that makes the root fresh and a little spicy. You can use the leaves as a spice as well. It tastes like a blend of parsley, chervil, and celery and it really lifts the vegetable soup. Sow, nurture, and harvest just like the parsnip.

Celeriac

Radishes always benefit from an early harvest.

HORSERADISH

Armoracia rusticana

I first got to know the horseradish when I took over a crop at an abandoned clay patch in Sormland, Sweden. The only sign of culture growths after the years was the horseradish. However, it had really enjoyed itself and was spread all over. The horseradish is also a biennial growth that spreads through side roots. If you've managed to make it comfortable, it is hard to get rid of it. Therefore choose your growing site carefully. It likes humid and nutrient-rich soil.

PLANTING

If you want to eat horseradish you can buy a small fresh root and set it in spring. You can use a small piece from the grocery store, but it is always best if you can get a hold of someone that sells them specifically for planting. Slant one end with a knife, unless it is already done, and place it on the ground with the slant facing downwards. The top should be at least two inches (5 cm) under the surface. Make sure that the soil is humid and loose all over.

HARVEST

When the root has settled, the plant grows quickly, but I advice you to wait a year before you harvest your first horseradish. You can harvest all through the growth season, but the spring harvest tends to have more of a sting. Pick new root pieces and leave the old that are often woody and tasteless. If you want to store the horseradish over winter, then harvest in fall and keep the roots as carrots. Or harvest in spring and freeze fresh pieces.

Tip! If you want to limit the horseradish plant then plant it in a buried barrel or a large pot so that the roots can't spread.

CELERIAC

Apium graveolens var. *rapaceum*

The celeriac is robust, beautiful, and tasty. It is a forgiving plant because it doesn't attract many diseases, but rather keeps healthy and good quite easily. It is different from its relative celery in that instead of good stalks and leaves it develops a sturdy tuber that's packed with flavor and vitamins. The trick is getting it to grow at all. It is quite the prima donna, and all of you that are drawn to growths that need a little extra attention will love celeriac.

SOW AND NURTURE

As mentioned, celeriac might not be the plant I recommend for beginners. It demands a little extra attention and patience. To begin with it develops slowly, which demands pre-cultivation. You should sow ten to twelve weeks before you are planning to plant them, which means that you should begin as early as March. The seeds need light and warmth to germinate, sow shallow, and cover with perlite. Keep the soil lightly humid and around 70°F (20°C). The germination can take up to three weeks, so you need to be patient. When the plants have come out, you can lower the temperature a little, but you have to make sure that there's still light. Replant once or twice and do not plant it outside until the danger of frost is completely gone. The plant should be planted at ground level—not deeper.

The celeriac wants to believe that it is by the sea. It is comfortable in sandy soil with even humidity and good access to nutrients, and according to many cultivators, it loves algae fertilizers and seaweed. If you have access to seaweed, feel free to cover with that instead of grass. Prepare the cultivation site by properly loosening the soil and make sure that you base fertilize with manure and compost.

HARVEST

Harvest in fall right before the frost. If you want beautiful, even roots, you can devote the very end of the season to cleaning the roots free from rootlets on the upper half of the tuber, and then allowing it to remain and grow some more. You can store celeriac, like most root vegetables, best in a cellar or cool cupboard, in a spacious sack, or sand bed.

MY FAVORITE

'Mars'

Gives a firm and white meat with intensive flavor. Grows beautifully with a large and gathered leaf bouquet on a rather tall-grown head.

RADISH

Raphanus sativus

Radishes are perfect for you if you want a small crop at the beginning or the end of the season. You can sow them early and they develop quickly; you will be able to harvest within five weeks after sowing. Radishes can be round, oblong, pointy, blunt, pink, yellow, purple, or white. It looks

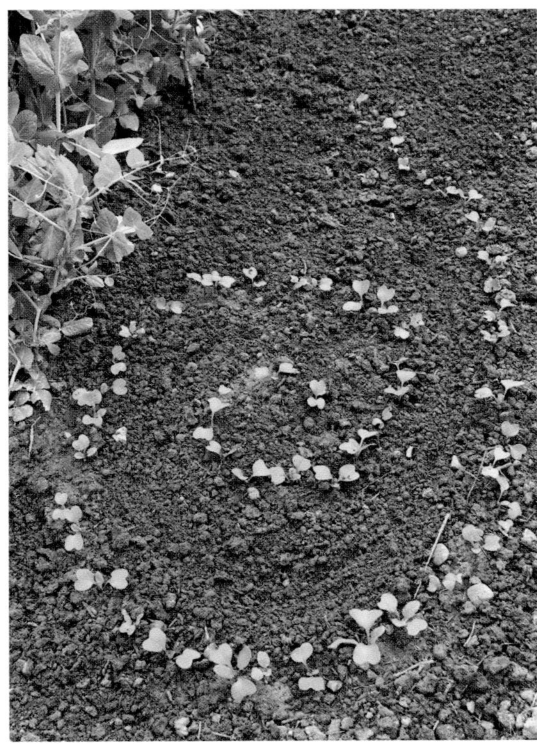

Radishes grow fast and can be used to mark the patterned planting of other vegetables.

pretty to use various kinds in cooking. They are all best when they are small and crispy.

SOW AND NURTURE

Radishes want a light, sandy, and humus-rich soil. Sow directly in a hotbed, vegetable garden, or balcony case from May-September. Sow ⅓ inch - 1 inch deep (1–2 cm) in rows, with about an inch (2 cm) between the plants, and 6 inches (15 cm) between the rows. Radishes turn out the best in pre-summer or late fall. In high summer they can often overmature and become woody.

Make sure that the soil does not dry out. Feel free to cover cultivate once the plants peek out. Radishes want even watering and weather conditions so that they don't halt their development, which can give them a woody flavor.

HARVEST

Harvest them small and crispy and don't let them sit too long once they've matured. If you want to save them for a couple of days, the idea is to keep them in a bowl of cold water in the refrigerator.

PROBLEMS THAT MAY ARISE
Soil fleas and cabbage flies can be troublesome. To avoid them you can sprinkle Algomin or lime on the leaves regularly.

MY FAVORITES

'Cherry Bell'
A round, crispy radish with the perfect pepper strength in its flavor. My absolute favorite.

'French Breakfast'
An oblong variety with a white tip, nice texture of the meat and a fresh and good taste. It is best when it is small.

'Plum Purple'
A purple-pink pretty radish that doesn't get spongy fruitmeat. Good, crispy, and very worth growing.

BLACK RADISH

Raphanus sativa var. *niger*

DAIKON

Raphanus sativus var. *longipinnatus*

You could say that the black radish is a longer, rougher, and stronger version of the radish. It takes a lot longer to develop, but in exchange, it can be stored over winter, which the radish cannot. The Daikon is an Asian variety of the black radish, which grows very quickly and is forgiving to cultivate.

SOW AND NURTURE
The trick to getting fine, well-developed roots is to avoid sowing too early. Wait until midsummer, (end of June/beginning of July) to avoid the plants blossoming. Plant the seeds a small inch (a few centimeters) deep and water. Leave 6–8 inches (15–20 cm) between the plants and 12–16 inches (35–40 cm) between the rows.

Generally, the black radish and daikon needs deep-dug loose soil, and you should cover cultivate with grass clippings to keep the soil humid.

HARVEST
In fifty to sixty days, you'll get a fully developed root. If you want to store the radish, remember that it is better the later you harvest and plan your planting accordingly. If you let the black radish grow overly mature, it will lightly crack and become spongy. Harvest when it is still firm, energized, and fine.

MY FAVORITES

'China Rose'
Pink-white oblong black radish that benefits from being harvested when it is about 8 inches (20 cm) long. It looks like a small pink icicle and it is crisp, peppery, and fresh.

'Red Meat'
A more beautiful vegetable is hard to find! This daikon variety has a white skin with light green areas towards the top and a completely shock pink fruit meat. Invites many possibilities in the kitchen, for instance sliced raw with spicy avocado dip, woked, or freshly grated in fajitas.

RED BEET

Beta vulgaris var. *conditiva*

The red beet is just as loved as it is practical. It can be harvested early to be eaten or to be stored and can be eaten raw or prepared, fresh or preserved. Despite its name, there are red beets in many

different colors and varying shapes. And as a bonus, you can also use the small leaves on top as a lettuce.

SOW AND NURTURE

Red beets prefer a light but humus-rich soil that can hold moisture and nutrients. This means that the best way to prepare the growth site is to fold in compost blended with, for instance, wood ash to satisfy the red beet's potassium need. Do not sow too early. If it is too cold you risk that the plant blossoms instead of developing a nice beet. It is better to wait a while into the pre-summer weeks. Plant the seeds a small inch (2 cm) deep. Leave about 2 inches (5 cm) between the plants and 12 inches (30 cm) between the rows. Multiple plants will grow from one seed, so they can't be planted too tight together. Red beets belong to those who can develop even though they stand tight together, the opposite of, for instance, carrots that will start too twist around each other. If you want a very even size on you beets, you should cull so that each plant gets its own space.

Potassium is important for healthy beets, but do not add too much nitrogen. The red beet likes Algomin or seaweed. The beet has a pretty shallow root system that makes it dependent on watering during dry periods. If you cover cultivate it will help maintain the right humidity.

HARVEST

Harvest the red beet when it has found its shape but is still small. Late red beets should be harvested when the beet is completely developed, but before the frost hits. If you want to store beets, you cut the tops about 2 inches (5 cm) above the beet, remove the smallest roots and store the beets in sand or similar soil climate.

PROBLEMS THAT MAY ARISE

Dry spells make the red beets colorless and weak. Many root vegetables suffer badly if there's a borax deficiency, such as the red beet and swede. It manifests as rot damage—soft, brown spots inside the root vegetable. The best way to avoid mineral deficiency is generally to fertilize the soil with manure and furthermore use various types of support manure to get as much variety as possible. You should also alternate the plants on the growth site so there's a smaller risk of deficiency diseases.

MY FAVORITES

'Boltardy'
Fine, round beet with thin skin and good sweet meat. It is easy to cultivate and has a stable quality.

'Burpee's Golden'
This variety is an old yellow beet variety that gives uneven beets. It can be a bit difficult to get it to grow, but it is worth the effort. Personally, I don't like the modern versions of Burpee's as much as this one, even if they do look prettier.

'Chioggia'
Actually not a favorite when it comes to flavor, but it decorates the salad and the plate. Candy cane-striped, easy to cultivate and very beautiful.

SALSIFY

The salsify usually becomes a favorite with those who taste it and then start cultivating it. They are tasty, tender, sweet, and easy to cultivate. You can eat them as asparagus, lightly boiled with a little salt, or you can use them in casseroles.

SOW AND NURTURE

To grow salsify you need well-fertilized, deep-dug, and humus-rich soil. You sow the seeds in spring or fall and plant them a small inch deep (a couple of centimeters). Leave 8–10 inches (20–25 cm) between the rows and cull the plants to a distance of about 2 inches (5 cm).

Make sure that you keep the bed clean of weeds that will otherwise compete against the roots. Support fertilize with stone meal, wood ash, or Algomin at some point during the season. You have to water and loosen the soil in dry weather.

HARVEST

The salsify is biennial, which means that it develops leaves and roots during the first year. You can harvest as soon as the first fall, but if you don't a flower will develop from the leaf rosette during the second year and the root will grow even more. You can still harvest, and the blossoming doesn't damage the vegetable. Be careful and use a garden fork when you pull the roots up so that they don't break, as they are sensitive.

JERUSALEM ARTICHOKE

Helianthus tuberosus

The Jerusalem artichoke is a tuber that grows underground. It has a sweet and round flavor, a cross between an artichoke and salsify. It has red, white, or yellow skin, but the meat is always white. It is related to the sunflower, which is clear both in its appearance and its height. The plants usually grow to become more than 6 feet (2 m) tall. They are beautiful and are nice even as just a decorative plant in the garden. The one thing you should keep in mind is that it has a tendency to spread. The tubers winter well in the soil and shoot new plants the next year if they're not harvested. They can be used as wind protection, but preferably facing north so that they don't create shade and leave the other plants in the shadows.

PREPARING THE GROWTH SITE

The Jerusalem artichoke is not very picky when it comes to soil, but the ideal is a humus-rich and pretty light soil. Prepare the growth site in fall so that you can set the tubers in early spring. Fold manure and compost in with the soil. Since the plants may spread, it is a good idea to cultivate in a hotbed. It should be about 16 inches deep (40 cm). Fill the bed in fall with a blend of soil, manure, bark humus, and sand.

PLANTING AND NURTURE

Jerusalem artichokes are planted as tubers, just like potatoes, either in fall or in spring as soon as the soil settles, usually April-May. Then you can either buy new pieces to sow or you can use some of the harvested from the year before, that is to say, pull up all of the old ones and choose a lucky few that you will plant as new. You set them 5–6 inches deep (12–15 cm) in a group or in a row, and 12–20 inches between the tubers should be right.

Feel free to cover cultivate with grass or straw, and be extra meticulous with watering if you cultivate in a hotbed. The plants have stable stems, but if there's really tough wind they may need support.

HARVEST

WHEN? Close to fall, often in September, the plants will blossom and after that you can start harvesting the tubers. Later, you can harvest in March-April, as long as the ground doesn't freeze. There are varieties without flowers and in those cases, you have until the end of September, as a rule of thumb, for the beginning of harvest.

HOW? Harvest the tubers exactly like potatoes: lift the root system with a garden fork and pick the tubers. If you have an opportunity to cover the ground with leaves and straw and keep it snow free, you can leave the plants in the ground and harvest all winter. An alternative is harvesting as late as possible in fall and keep them in sand, cold but without frost, during winter. However, they may have a tendency to wrinkle somewhat. The artichokes can be prepared in every way imaginable. They are reminiscent of potatoes but fall apart more during cooking. They are great to make soups, to fry, or blend in the potato mash with a reindeer filet.

PROBLEMS THAT MAY OCCUR

The Jerusalem artichoke grows strongly and problem free. However, voles like them. If you get a problem with voles, it is best to cultivate in a hot bed and place a ground cloth in the bottom. Feel free to blend some crushed stones in the soil as well. The vole will think it is uncomfortable to move.

Picture on the right: Visiting the cultivating patches close to the Skarpnäcks area south of Stockholm to spring-harvest Jerusalem artichokes.

Tip! If you think it is tiresome to peel the artichokes then wash them and cut them in half. Oven-bake the halves for a little while and eat them with a spoon and a good spice butter on the side.

MY FAVORITES

There are not that many varieties to choose from. The most common is **'Bianca,'** which is stable and secure. It gives lumpy artichokes with a good, sweet flavor and blossom in fall.

'Regular Red' Found in many home gardens, but I've had trouble finding planting tubers. I am sure you can ask for it in a gardening forum. There are usually a few kind souls that are willing to share.

'Helianthus strumosus' is another species that shares the same cultivation needs and flavor as the regular artichoke. It gives even, straight tubers that reminds me of sweet potatoes, which makes it easier to handle in the kitchen. It doesn't blossom. You can sometimes find sowing tubers with southern European seed companies.

KALE/CABBAGE GROWTHS

Kale soup, kale rolls, kale pudding, stewed kale, lamb in kale . . . kale is deeply rooted in our kitchens and the cultivation tradition. Today, many would maybe say that they know kale through side-dishes and soups and not so much pudding. No matter, food traditions change. And so does cultivation trends. Surely the white kale head was one of the most common parts of vegetable gardens before, but now they are replaced by other kale growths like broccoli, vegetable turnip, and Tucan kale. It is a good thing when the palette we use to paint vegetables change now and then.

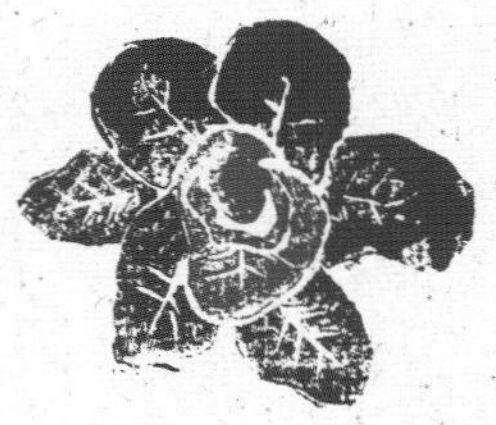

KALE GROWTHS LOVE, cool, and often somewhat humid weather, and many varieties love the long days of daylight that summer offers. Actually, it is only the Chinese family members, like choy sum and Chinese broccoli that are aggravated by the never-ending daylight. They are more comfortable closer to fall. Furthermore, kale is a beach growth that tolerates salt splashes and that feels at home when it is fertilized with seaweed from our coasts. It is simply ideal for cultivating in Sweden, and costal areas. What might make many resistant to growing kale are all of the diseases they can contract (see p. 187). But this shouldn't scare you. Yes, you have to take care. It is not the kind of crop that you can just leave to fight its own battles, but as long as you are prepared, there are many ways you can prevent the problems. As a reward, you get something to harvest all the way into the dark winter months.

The green kale has a tendency to attract less disease than other kale varieties. With its bright green, blue-green, or Bordeaux-red leaves, it is just as popular as a decorative plant as it is as a vegetable. In the summer, these colorful leaves create a fine contrast to the yellow rudbeckias and Mexican sunflowers. This is often used as a decoration on plates where the curly plumes give a look of freshness. In my opinion, it is not best stewed or boiled like Dutch kale, but rather when it has some chewing resistance left still. Like the Hollander I am, I still have to defend the green kale's rightful place on the plates. Frosted, shredded for salads, creamed with squeezed orange, and blanched with roasted hazelnuts and crumbled blue cheese—a wintery, delicate, appetizer.

In addition to classics like green kale, cabbage and savoy cabbage, I definitely think the Asian kale growths are worth a try. Especially if you like simple cooking like wok, steaming, and marinating. These kale varieties are smaller, grow quicker, and are harvested smaller than most of the others. They are slightly peppery, chockfull of vitamins, and have a nice, crunchy texture.

Choose between fine seeds

Time to replant the green cabbage

White cabbage flower

CULTIVATING KALE GROWTHS

WHITE KALE

Brassica oleracea var. *capitata*

The white kale grows as large, leafy heads close to the ground and are commonly called summer, fall, or winter kale. In reality, they are all the same kind of kale, but the different varieties take different amounts of time to mature and the names help us understand when we can expect to harvest.

PREPARING THE GROWTH SITE

Kale is one of the growths that preferably grow in muddy fields. It is important that the site is well drained, though. Water-sick soil is a catastrophe for kale. Fertilize the soil with a blend of manure and Algomin. When you grow kale it is vital to make sure that the soil has a high pH value of at least 7.0–7.5. Sour or slightly acidic soils can promote some of the serious infections the kale can contract, such as clubroot. Cultivate the plants in a windy spot so the wind can help make it an unwelcoming environment for the damaging insects.

SOW

WHEN? You can choose if you want to pre-cultivate or sow directly on the growth site. It is most common to pre-cultivate so that the plants get started before they are planted outside where they will meet pests and other dangers. If you pre-cultivate, then sow four to six weeks before planting outside, and that you may do when the risk of frost is no longer great. Kale plants can, however, tolerate a frost bite. Sow directly when the soil has reached a temperature of 46–50°F (8–10°C) and is easy to work with.

HOW? When you pre-cultivate, it is easiest to sow in a root trainer. Use sowing soil blended with planting soil or compost and sow ⅓ inch (1 cm) deep. Let the seeds germinate in 68–78°F (20–25°C). Lower the heat to about 40°F (5°C) when the plants are showing. You sow in the same depth outside, with 12–20 inches (30–50 cm) distance between the plants depending on the variety and 20 inches (50 cm) between the rows. Keep the seedlings slightly humid.

PLANTING OUTSIDE

Always harden the plants before you move them outside. If you've done this however, they can tolerate frostbite, even if it is best with a relatively steady, frost-free pre-summer temperature when you plant them outside. Place the little plants a little deeper than how you planted them in their plugs and pack the soil around. Cover the ground immediately with grass clippings or similar to retain humidity. Plant with 12–20 inches (30–50 cm) distance between the plants depending on how large the head of the variety is and leave 20 inches (50 cm) between the rows.

NURTURE

Kale should never be in need of nutrients or water. To secure access to nutrients, you can fertilize the plants with a fertilizer that doesn't contain much nitrogen a couple of times during the growth season. Kale likes, for instance, stone meal and Algomin, and it loves seaweed. Fertilizer with a lot of nitrogen, such as poultry manure, can give very leafy, loose heads that go bad quickly.

HARVEST

WHEN? The summer and fall white kale should be harvested when they have matured. If you let it stay too long, the leaves will start cracking. The winter kale that is harvested in late fall can be left for a while after they've ripened and still maintain their fine tight heads. It can be left even when the temperature go below 32°F (0°C), but always let it thaw before you harvest.

HOW? Harvest the kale heads gently. They may look strong and robust, but they are quite sensitive to touch and over-handling. Use a sharp and strong knife and cut the stem off so that you get a nice head with a few extra leaves as protection. Summer kale, which often gives a somewhat looser and greener head, is not suitable for storage; eat it right away. It is a wonderful, soft kale that you can eat as lettuce and that doesn't give the same crisp texture as the fall and winter varieties. You can store the whole winter kale heads if you keep them in a cool place, only 35-40°F (2-4°C) and airy. If you want to save kale over a long period of time the best way is to make sour kale. I am not very good at this myself, but every time I am invited somewhere and the kale is sour, I remember why I should get familiar with this preparation method.

MY FAVORITES

'Danish Ballhead'
This winter kale is great if you want to store kale. It gives smooth, round heads that can sit in the soil and wait for harvest far into the fall.

'Golden Acre'
Golden Acre is a tricky summer kale as it can't be left in the ground for too long, but if it is harvested in time it is the best kale you can get.

'Minicole F1'
This summer and fall kale gives small heads that you can hold in one hand. It has a great quality and is very good. It is great if you don't have much space to cultivate. You can plant it tighter than regular white kale.

RED CABBAGE

Brassica oleracea var. *capitata ruba*

Red cabbage grows just like the white cabbage, but has a wine-red color. It has a slightly longer beginning stage than the white kale and therefore it usually doesn't mature until fall, but by then it has developed traits for storing that are just as good as the white kale.

For advice regarding sowing, cultivating, and harvesting, you can follow the advice for white kale.

MY FAVORITE

'Cabeza'
A good red-violet cabbage that yeilds a stable harvest. Harvested pretty late and can be stored over winter.

Savoy cabbage

The purple green kale 'redbor'

Red cabbage

SAVOY CABBAGE

Brassica oleracea var. *sabauda*

The savoy cabbage is one of my favorites in the cabbage family. I often use it in Asian cooking to make steamed dumplings. Similar to white kale, its head grows but it has curly, dented, green outer leaves and a butter-yellow inside. The cabbage taste is milder that the other head cabbage vegetables. It might be coincidental, but in my experience, the savoy cabbage is not infected by disease as much as the others.

For advice about sowing, cultivating, and harvesting, follow the advice for white kale. The savoy cabbage can tolerate a lot of cold and you can leave it outside into late fall, but harvest thawed. The savoy cabbage keeps best if it can stand outside until you are going to use it, and it can also be stored in a cellar for a few months.

MY FAVORITES

'Best of all'
An English savoy cabbage that lives up to its name. It is easy to grow and yields medium-sized heads, but above all it has a nice mild taste and can be used to treat dandruff.

'Vorbote'
A French savoy kale grows dark green leaves and yellow, curly insides. It is easy to cultivate and grows quickly, tasty, and beautiful.

WHITE CABBAGE

Brassica oleracea var. *capitata conica*

The white cabbage is pointy. Along the cabbage leaves, a white-green head develops. It can be compared to summer kale, and has a clear decorative value. Many prefer this cabbage instead of the regular kale.

For advice about sowing, cultivating, and harvesting this plant, follow the advice for white kale. The white cabbage cannot be stored for a long time.

MY FAVORITE

'Winningstadt'
A rather large white cabbage that gives powerful green cones without disrupting the taste sensation.

CAULIFLOWER

Brassica oleracea var. *botrytis*

The cauliflower gives lumpy, tight heads that are made out of many small flower bouquets that are easy to break apart and prepare. The most common is the white cauliflower, but you can also find them in green and purple nuances that can have a nice effect in the garden.

For advice regarding sowing and cultivating, follow the advice for white kale. Be even more diligent with watering and fertilizing with Algomin, as the cauliflower is a bit more difficult than many other cabbage varieties and can stop developing or just not develop a head at all if something is off. It is the "princess" of the cabbage growths. But they are beautiful, good, and actually not that hard to cultivate, and the heads definitely deserve a place in the cabbage land.

Harvesting cauliflower happens when the heads are nicely swelled and tight, before they start dividing or changing color. To prevent the white cauliflower heads from yellowing at the end of maturing, you can protect them against the sun by covering them with a few large kale leaves. Cauliflower is not easy to store fresh, but you can make sour cauliflower or freeze it in bouquets. Either way, it is absolutely best to eat it fresh. A favorite is frying small bouquets in a little butter, food oil, hot curry, rough brown mustard seeds, and grated coconut and serve with a lime wedge and a scoop of Greek Yogurt.

Cauliflower in Indian clothes with curry, cumin, and grated coconut.

MY FAVORITES

'Igloo'
A rather small and nice cauliflower that give tight, white heads.

'Purple Cape'
A purple-red variety of cauliflower that is fun if you want a change. It has the same good taste as the white varieties and you can harvest it late, sometimes even in January in warmer climates.

'Snowball'
Has quite large heads. The variety provides a safe harvest, but the plants can develop at varying speeds, which is not necessarily a bad thing when you cultivate for private use.

BROCCOLI

Brassica oleracea var. *italic*

Broccoli is also one of my returning friends in the vegetable garden. I see no limit to its use. It is healthy and the taste is superb; enjoy both the crown of the green bouquets and along the sides. The bouquets grow in slightly different sizes and shapes, and are harvested at different times depending on the variety. Feel free to try unknown varieties that may not give the largest or most even bouquets, but do yield a large crop of small bouquets. They often have a different crispness and sweetness to them. Broccoli is easy to cultivate and good practice for first-timers of cultivating cabbage.

For advice about sowing and cultivating, you should follow the advice for white kale, while keeping in mind that broccoli can be planted in rounds over the summer to lengthen the harvest.

You harvest when the bouquets are well developed, but the buds still haven't opened. Be attentive, because broccoli can move fast, and will blossom suddenly. Varieties that give generous side shoots can be stimulated to form more and better bouquets from the sides if you cut the crown before it is completely done. You can harvest regularly as long as the plant keeps growing bouquets. The broccoli tolerates frost and can give harvest long into fall. The best way of storing is to blanch the bouquets quickly and then freeze them.

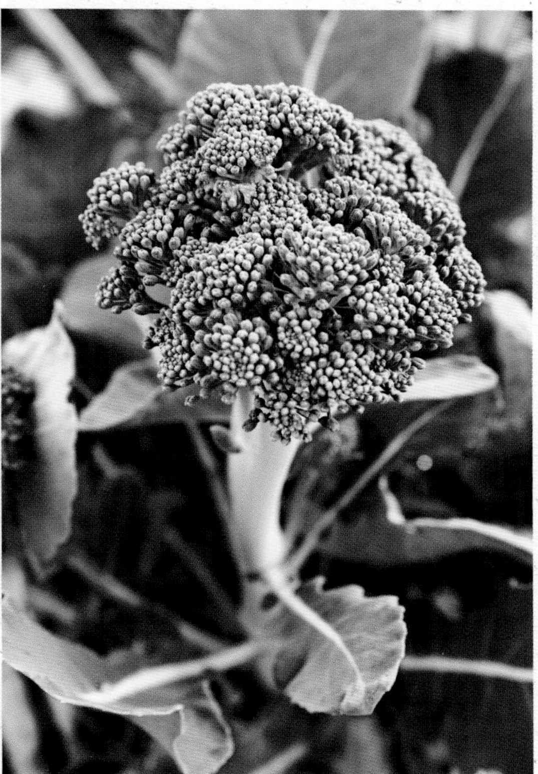

Broccoli

MY FAVORITES

'Calabrese' (Green Sprouting)
A super tasty broccoli that you can harvest for a long time. Not only beautiful and has a crown, but also lots of side sprouts, and it is definitely a cultivation favorite.

'Red Arrow Purple Sprouting'
An English broccoli variety that also give lots of side sprouts in the shape of small crisp purple broccoli bouquets. It is best in late fall.

'Thompson'
Gives tight fine crowns that are followed by the development of many side bouquets that you can continuously harvest. It is pretty new but has received a warm welcome.

BROCCOLO

Brassica oleracea var. *(botrytis x italica)*

Broccolo is a beautiful vegetable that is very common in Italy. I find it strange that it's not a more popular crop because it is tasty, easy to cultivate, and practical. It gives a lime-colored head that is reminiscent of cauliflower in its structure, with a floral predisposition like sharp stars. It is sometimes called "Romanesco" or "Coral Cabbage."

Sow and cultivate the broccoli like broccoli, but it is more sensitive to cold when planted outside. Wait until the risk of frost is over and the soil is really warm.

MY FAVORITE

'Romanesco'
This is the traditional, Italian broccolo, and the best, if you ask me.

VEGETABLE TURNIP/RAAB-BROCCOLI

Brassica rapa esculenta

Vegetable turnip is reminiscent of broccoli but it grows fewer bouquets on a longer and thinner stem. Its texture is similar to broccoli, but the flavor is more peppery and gives more of a sense of arugula.

SOW

WHEN? Sow directly in free land, preferably in late summer, as it develops more evenly and better in a fall climate, but you can sow it in pre-summer as well.

HOW? Sow in rows with 8–10 inches (20–25 cm) distance between the plants and 12 inches (30 cm) between the rows. Sow the seeds a small inch deep (a couple of centimeters) and keep the seedlings humid. Each plant may grow unevenly so to ensure that you get to harvest as much as possible at the same time, you need many plants. In other words, don't plant too few. Feel free to cover with fiber cloth to ward off soil fleas and other pests.

PREPARING THE GROWTH SITE, NURTURE AND HARVEST

Vegetable turnips want similar conditions as the rest of the cabbage growths. See white kale.

You can harvest continuously and it continues to give generously until late fall. The plants develop quickly and should be harvested regularly so that they don't blossom and stop giving new shoots.

The Tucan kale 'Nero di Toscana,' a fun feature among the fall vegetables.

CHOY SUM

Brassica rapa var. *parachinensis*

This is an Asian cabbage variety. It has red-violet thin stalks and flower bouquets that looks like small, loose broccoli bouquets. I only grow this in spring and fall because it can blossom a little too fast in midsummer. Long days can stress certain plants. Spring cultivation in a greenhouse or late summer to fall cultivation outside works perfect. There is only one variety on the market. It has the name 'Hon Tsai tai.'

Sow, cultivate, and harvest the choy sum like the vegetable turnip, but decrease the distance between the plants to 2–4 inches (5–10 cm). If you are spring planting in a greenhouse, April is usually a good time, and planting outdoors should start in July. The choy sum grows very quickly and you should harvest while it is still small for the best flavor. Harvest when the flowers are budding. You eat both the stem and flower, raw in salads as well as boiled or woked.

CHINESE BROCCOLI

Brassica oleracea var. *alboglabra*

Another Asian cabbage variety. It grows with lightly swelled short stems with one leaf in the top. Harvest and use whole, leaf, stalk, and flower bud if the latter develops. You can eat the leaves both warm and cold in salads, while the stem should be woked or blanched. It has a mild and good cabbage taste that is very similar to broccoli and it is best with spring or late summer cultivation. Sow and cultivate as described for the choy sum. There is only one variety on the market.

BRUSSELS SPROUTS

Brassica oleracea var. *gemmifera*

Brussels sprouts used to be called Rose Sprouts back in the day. It has a fun and beautiful way of growing as it shoots one stem straight upward that then again grows leaves around the sides.

MY FAVORITES

'Bedford'
A steady variety that gives beautiful small knots. It matures evenly and you can freeze it.

'Rubine'
A purple variety of Brussels sprouts that provide some color and variation in the vegetable garden.

In the leaves are small cabbage heads, Brussels sprouts. We are used to seeing this on our Christmas tables, but it deserves more use. For instance, it is great to boil al dente and serve with olive oil. Boiled Brussels sprouts have a mild taste, but it is even milder if the cabbage gets frostbite out in the vegetable garden.

Basically sow and cultivate like white cabbage, but it is more sensitive to over fertilizing with nitrogen. You should therefore only support fertilize with Algomin or stone meal. The Brussels sprout tolerates a lot of cold and can be harvested in winter.

Harvest gradually as the small cabbage heads ripen. You pick them and at the same time, the leaf will break from its stem. You do this so that the plant can stop using energy on leaf growth in that specific spot. If you want the entire stem to mature at the same time, you have to stop the growth of the plant by cutting the top. Through that, the energy is guided to the already budding small heads, and they ripen more evenly.

GREEN KALE

Brassica oleracea var. *sabellica*

There is an array of green kale varieties with different shapes, color, and sizes. Almost every single one will stand beautifully in the vegetable garden into the winter months and stay light, fresh, and free of attacks. I am sure it is this, combined with its high content of minerals and Vitamin C, that has awarded it such a huge following.

You sow and cultivate green kale like white kale (see p. 174). Do leave a little more room for the plants to grow though, since they have a broader way of growing.

Harvest continuously from the first time the leaf bundles have developed properly. You break the outer leaf downwards and cut them far down with a knife. The green kale will obtain a milder flavor after frost, but it is very good even before that. Since most of the varieties endure winter, it is unnecessary to harvest for storing. But if you want to, blanching and freezing are the best ways.

Brussels sprouts 'Bedford'

Green kale 'Pentland Brig'

Green kale 'Redbor'

MY FAVORITES

GREEN KALE

'Pentland Brig'
A very bushy and lush green kale with lots of good flavor. An absolute favorite for soups.

'Redbor'
Gives high Bordeaux-red plants with large, curly leaves. It is very grand and is of great effect next to green leaves or flowers. It is, of course, a joy to eat as well, but tastes the best if it has experienced frost.

'Red Russian'
A green, curly cabbage with purple stems and leaf nerves. Very good to eat raw!

TUCAN KALE

'Nero di Toscana'
This close relative to the green kale is called Tucan Kale for its growth pattern. A beautiful kale with blue-green narrow leaves in bouquets. It is not as cold-resistant as the green kale varieties, but it is both beautiful and tasty while it lasts in fall.

CHINESE CABBAGE

Brassica rapa var. *pekinensis*

Chinese cabbage is an Asian variety of cabbage that we mostly recognize as the shredded greens on the buffet plate. In my opinion, this is a very boring way to use this soft and mild kale variety. It tastes great roughly chopped and added to various bouillon soups, as a wrap for various dumplings, blanched and later marinated in hot chili dressing make it a great side for grilled meat—yes you can prepare this dish in may ways.

Chinese Cabbage grow in a cylinder shape, as loosely knotted heads. They grow fast, but set high demands to be comfortable: watering, fertilizing, and even temperature.

SOW

WHEN? To achieve as stable conditions as possible, you should preferably sow the Chinese cabbage in the middle of July and after. You sow it directly in the growth site. If you want Chinese cabbage earlier, you have to be prepared to give the seeds and little plants a lot of attention so that they don't blossom or stop developing. In that case, sow like white cabbage, but spend time on slowly making them accustomed for the outdoors and prevent them from blossoming since they are very easily stressed.

HOW? When you sow directly, the seeds are planted an inch (a few centimeters) deep, in rows with 16 inches (40 cm) distance. Leave 12 inches (30 cm) between the plants. If you want, you can cover them with fiber cloth to protect the small plants from attack.

Cultivating and Nurture is the same as for white kale, see page 174.

You harvest when the heads are well packed and large. In fall, you can leave the heads in the vegetable garden and harvest when you need them. To avoid them opening up, you can tie a ribbon around the heads so they keep their shape. They can handle a couple of frosty nights, but if you want to save them for a while you should instead harvest them and store them in a temperature of about 32–33°F (1–2°C).

MY FAVORITES

'Santo'
A favorite with open heads and crisp leaves. The steam is great and can be used as wrapping for small spicy seafood dumplings in chili dip.

'Wong Bok'
A lovely, vigorous salad leaf that provides stable harvesting.

PROBLEMS THAT MAY ARISE

Cabbage has a tendency to attract problems, but as I already mentioned you shouldn't let this scare you off. If you know how to react when a problem occurs, you can most often keep the diseases at bay. The best you can do to prevent problems is to choose an open and airy place for your cabbage and to allocate some of the plant as cover crop. They are called so because they are grown to only attract pests. It is a diversion. For cabbage, arugula, turnips, and radishes, this works well, but it works best of all for Chinese cabbage. You sow an early round of Chinese cabbage before the rest of the plants are ready. The pests will then be pulled towards the tender

Marigolds—a colorful border plant

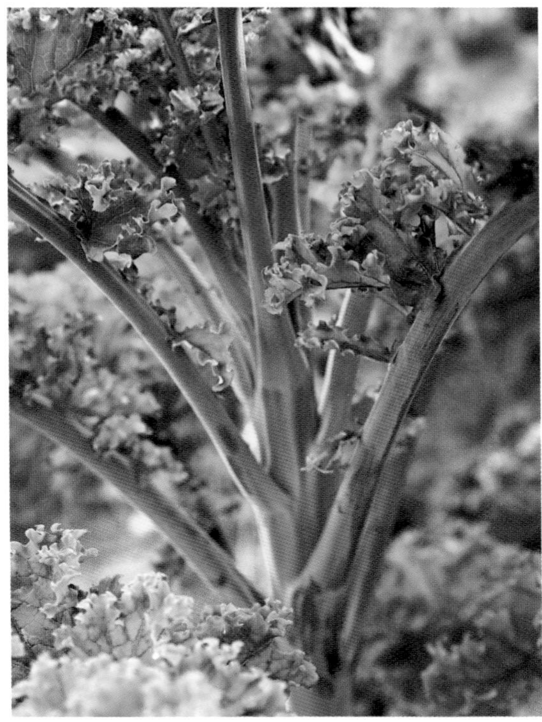

Green cabbages 'Red Russian'

and fine Chinese cabbage and leave the others cabbage varieties in peace. You should continue to remove larvae and keep it as clean as possible around the Chinese cabbage, but these plants are sacrificed purely for the sake of the other plant's health. This method works pretty well.

Clump root disease is a fungal disease that can attack cabbage crops. Infected plants have diffuse symptoms like weak growth, yellowing leaves, and poorly developed roots. If you dig the plant up you will find cysts on the roots. The disease is mostly a result of cold, wet, and low pH. The best way of keeping the disease away is to regularly fertilize with Algomin and optionally lime the ground if needed. Make sure that the growth site is well drained and be extra meticulous about the rotation system so that not a single cabbage growth stands in the same spot more often than every fourth year.

Cabbage plants attract damaging insects, especially the cabbage moth and the kale fly's larvae that damage leaves and roots. Covering the crop with filter cloth will prevent the moth from reaching the plants. To prevent the problem, you can spray small plants with smelly and bad tasting liquids, like wormwood tea, horsetail water, and tansy water (see p.193). You can also powder the plants with lime, ash, or Algomin. If you spray liquids, it is best to do it in late afternoon when the leaves are dry, as the liquid won't stick well to slippery leaves. If you powder the plants, you can do this in the mornings, as the powder will stick better then. Later you need to be on the lookout for egg colonies on the leaves. They turn into larvae in just a few days. The best solution is to remove all the eggs, but if the larvae have time to hatch you need to pick them off as if you're life depended on it. Remember to check underneath the leaves as well.

Another common problem is soil fleas that damage the leaves and can bother small plants until they die. The best way of keeping these at bay is to keep the soil humid. You can also try to cut the leaves of wormwood, lavender, or another strong-scented plant and cover the ground around the plants with them. Covering with fiber cloth is a good idea if you are certain that the attackers are not already in the soil, because in that case you lock them in and the damage on the plants will be even worse.

PROBLEMS THAT MAY ARISE WHEN CULTIVATING

DISEASES, PESTS, AND weeds are a part of the cultivator's everyday, but it still needs to be fought if you want to succeed with your vegetables. The basic rule is to intervene as early as possible against diseases, attacks and weeds. If you succeed then the problems are usually minor. But you'll need to be able to recognize symptoms and know how to attack in the best possible way.

I have already mentioned that we need to be careful with chemical pesticides. These pesticides do not differentiate and kill the useful insects as well. Furthermore, they contain materials that are difficult for nature to break down. Plant care products are usually a little nicer to the environment. They are often based on soap, oils, and bicarbonate and work against soft-bodied insects, like lice. But they don't differentiate between insects either, and will damage useful soft-bodied insects as well, so always use these products as precisely and sparingly as possible. You can also make your own teas and solutions that in various ways will strengthen the plants and protect them against attack. It is cheap and easy.

In addition to the specific measures you can take against various attacks, you can always reduce the problems and the spread of disease by culturing in rotation and by keeping the crop clean. This may sound a bit pedantic, but there are a few simple things to keep in mind: use healthy seeds, bulbs, potatoes and onions, remove diseased plants and leaves, wash tools, pots, and gloves, and use sharp, clean tools when trimming and harvesting.

PLANT DISEASES

Virus

Virus will often give diffuse symptoms like weak growth, deformed leaves, spotted leaves, and poor root development. A virus-infected plant will never be healthy since plants do not have the ability to form antibodies against the virus. On the contrary, the virus will survive on the plant and inhibit seeds or tubers when the plant has died.

A common virus is the mosaic virus that, among others, affects squash and cucumbers. It gives characteristic, irregular, light green to white spots on the leaves.

Virus is spread first and foremost by leaf lice, but also by other sucking insects. The best way to decrease the risk of virus infection is to keep the plants healthy from lice and other pests. The only way to completely protect yourself from viruses is to choose virus-resistant vegetable varieties and to use controlled seeds. Remove sick plants from the garden to keep the virus from spreading.

BACTERIA

If an entire plant or parts of the plant suddenly and quickly dies, this is often caused by bacteria. The bacteria attack will often occur as a result of another problem. If the plant is damaged or has been attacked by fungi, the bacteria can enter that way. Just like we can get bacterial infections in a wound where the infections turn out to be worse than the original wound.

Bacteria doesn't spread easily. The greatest culprits are actually our hands and tools. You don't heal bacterial attacks but rather just remove the dead plants and take extra care when it comes to hygiene.

FUNGAL DISEASES

Various kinds of fungal attacks are the most common disease-problem in the vegetable garden. It emerges as everything from rot on stems and tubers to yellow-brown spots or fuzzy, mealy, membranes on the leaves.

Fungal contagion is spread by wind, animals, soil, hands, pots, plants, and more. Many fungi favor humid cold, which makes the attacks more likely during wet summers. It is impossible to fully protect yourself from fungal attacks and

Picture to the left: Making horsetail tea.

COMMON TYPES OF FUNGAL ATTACKS

Leaf Mold
Often attacks potatoes, tomatoes, lettuce, and onions. The leaves turn golden brown with spots and finally wither and die. Remove infected leaves and burn them. Harvest infected onion right away and eat them fresh; you can't store it. Cut off infected potato tops so that the disease doesn't spread into the tubers and create rot. There is no effective treatment.

Mildew
Often infects squash and cucumbers. It makes a white, powdery membrane on the leaves. Infected leaves are removed and burned. You can later spray the plant with bicarbonate spray or garlic water. There are also ready plant care products based on garlic extract and oils. Water with horsetail tea to strengthen the plant. (see p. 193 for recipe).

Clump Foot
Infects cabbage growths. It gives shrunken roots with blisters and underdeveloped plants. It is a stubborn infection that can live in the soil for a long time. It is not likely that you'll be able to grow healthy cabbage growths on the infected soil within the first five to ten years. There is no treatment, but the disease can be prevented with rotation cultivation, by maintaining high pH levels in the soil, by adding lime or fertilizing with Algomin, and by making sure that the surface is well drained. If you suspect that the crop is infected, remove the entire crop immediately. Burn them and grow something else.

Fungal attack on broad bean

they are difficult to treat once it has settled. The most important effort you could do is to prevent attacks as much as possible and prevent them from spreading.

Make sure that it is airy and clean in the vegetable garden and that leaves always dry properly after watering. Generally, silicone has a nice preventative effect. By strengthening the plants with silicone they can protect themselves better. You can make your own silicone fertilizer out of Field Horsetail, which contains silicone. You fertilize by watering the soil. You can also shower the plants with a mild horsetail tea to give added protection, (see recipe on p. 193).

Certain fungal attacks occur as a natural part of the plant's last phase. For instance, cucumber will be infected by mildew when the growth season is approaching its end. The plants are tired and they've done as well as they could. It can then be very hard to deal with the attack, and it may be best just to remove the plant.

SMALL PESTS AND SMALL DAMAGING INSECTS

Leaf Lice
Leaf lice are softheaded insects that thrive by sucking nurture from growths. In the vegetable garden, they first and foremost choose pea plants. They like small shoots and will therefore often gather at the top or at the edges of the leaves.

The lice damage the plants mechanically. They poke them and suck their juice. The result is rolled leaves and malformations on stalks and leaves. But the lice also spread virus between plants, and they leave a sticky membrane of honeydew that soot fungi can grow in. This gives black spots on leaves and stalks.

Leaf lice is best combatted by simply removing them. If there are a lot, you can use a sheet of kitchen towel so you don't get so sticky. I usually wear disposable plastic gloves. You can also spray the lice with a hard water jet, but there's always the risk that you'll damage the plant while the lice simply roll off to the ground and crawl back up. For lice you'll need ready plant care products against lice or soapy water. No matter the method, the secret is to repeat it for at least a couple of weeks if you want the attackers to retreat.

White Flyers/Flour Mites
This is a different kind of lice that first and foremost attack greenhouses. Tomatoes, cucumbers, bell peppers, and eggplant are among the most vulnerable.

When it is grown, the lice has two pairs of wings and is covered by a membrane that looks like white powder, thus the name. If you carefully shake the plant, they will fly up before they go back to their original "positions," at the front of the leaf's underside. This is also where the lice eggs and larvae sit. White flyers damage the plants the same way as leaf lice, but they are a little tougher to get rid of since they fly and it is harder to pluck them. But you can remove the eggs and the larvae by hand and then you will have to turn to the spray bottle. Soapy water is effective. Spray-treat the growths repeatedly with a few days in between each time. Make sure that you spray the underside of the leaves as well. If you have a greenhouse and large problems, you also use a biologic method with a parasitoid wasp, which is the white flyer's enemy. You can order these online.

Soil Fleas

The soil flea is a small leaf beetle that eats the leaves of plants in the Brassicaceae family, for instance cabbage varieties, radishes, and arugula.

The leaves get small, round holes and if the attacks are large, whole small plants can be consumed.

If you cover your crop with fiber cloth you prevent attacks from the outside, but if the fleas are already in the soil, the fiber cloth will not stop the attacks. By keeping the soil humid you decrease the risk and by changing the growth site every year, you can avoid that wintered fleas attack the plants. If you powder the plants with ashes, lime, or Algomin, you make them unattractive for the fleas.

Nematodes

Tomatoes and potatoes are examples of growths that are vulnerable to nematodes.

This is a sort of roundworm that infests growths. There are many different types of nematodes and they are often species-specific; they only attack a certain variety or a certain plant family. The nematodes can survive the winter in the soil and the attacks can therefore get worse with every year that passes. The one that attacks the potato family is called potato eel or potatocystnematode. The attacks are only apparent through poor growth, and if you look at the roots, you can find small cysts along the root system.

Nematodes are not treatable. If there are nematodes in your soil the only way to get rid of them is to starve them by not planting the plant they like. The best way of preventing nematodes is to rotate the crop so that the same growth family is not planted in the same place more often than every fourth year.

Flies

There is a number of different flies that can cause bothersome attacks on kitchen growths. The most common are the carrot fly, cabbage fly, and onion fly.

They all work the same way. They lay eggs in the soil next to the plants and the larvae that later develops goes down in the soil and ruins the roots or onion. The pupae survive winter in the soil and the attacks can therefore worsen over the years if you don't change the growth site.

Fiber cloth is the absolute best protection against flies, especially in the beginning of the season. The flies are at their most active in May and June and are most damaging to young plants. The flies do not like windy spots, so you can prevent the attacks by choosing a somewhat windy spot to plant.

Leaf lice can be disease carriers and should be fought vigilantly.

Spinning Mites

The spinning mites are small spider animals that suck the juice out of growths. It is most common that growths in greenhouses are attacked by spins, such as cucumber.

The leaves get a dry and dusty look and they wither and ultimately die.

The mite likes warm and dry conditions, while at the same time a little wind. A greenhouse in high summer, where the watering is not as frequent, is a perfect home.

You can prevent the problem by watering regularly so that the soil is always humid. In a greenhouse environment attacks can be fought pretty easily with predatory mites that you order online. You can also use plant care products that contain paraffin oil, growth extract, and starch. You can buy this at trade farms or online.

Larvae

Both Lepidoptera and other insect larvae can severely damage plants. They eat different parts of the plants and leave paths in the vegetable, holes in the leaves, or completely destroyed roots.

The Lepidoptera larvae attack cabbage growths. They are green with black spots and mostly occur in groups. They develop from the eggs that we can find on the underside of the leaves, like yellow spots. If you find eggs or larvae, the idea is to pick them off and kill them as soon as possible. If you cultivate nasturtium next to the cabbage, the insects will first and foremost attack the nasturtium. This will give you time to cover and to remove eggs and larvae while they are still living in the nasturtium. If you don't rinse them off, they will spread to the cabbage quickly. You can also grow Chinese cabbage as a distractor. The larvae can even keep to those plants without spreading, but the Chinese cabbage will, of course, be ruined. To avoid attacks, cover the crop with fiber cloth so that the Lepidoptera don't lay eggs. You can also powder the leaves with lime, wood ash, or Algomin so that they are unattractive.

Wireworms are a small inch long (2–3 cm) and yellow. They make paths in potatoes and carrots. They are most comfortable in lawn soil and meadows. If you break up part of the lawn to cultivate vegetables, you can almost expect an attack from wireworms. Don't cultivate potatoes right away, but choose other plants for the first year. Work the soil deep during the spring and fall to disturb the larvae as much as possible.

The Black Vine Weevil larvae are furry, black brown, and a small inch long (about 2 cm). They chew on roots, root necks, and tubers in the ground. These larvae are hard to defeat, but you can limit them by picking the ones you spot. You can also sprinkle ash or lime around the root necks of the plants to make it less cozy to crawl around there. It is hard to get to them underground, but powerful work on the soil in fall and spring will disturb the larvae and decrease the problem.

I addition to these there is a whole row of small larvae of beetles and Lepidoptera that chew on the leaves in the vegetable garden. If you see fresh bites, you can first find the little criminal if you carefully look through the plant, and remove it. You can also try to shower the leaves with garlic water or sprinkle ashes on them to make them less appetizing.

Snails

Snails have come to be one of the biggest problems in kitchen cultivating. The Spanish forest snail can be up to 6 inches (15 cm) long and has, because of it cannibalistic trait, been named the "killing snail."

The snails are active in nighttime and multiply at crazy speeds. They are most comfortable in humid, tall grass. They hate lime, gravel, eggshells, metal, and sawdust.

The best way to decrease the problem is definitely picking snails. Since they are active in nighttime this has to be done in the evening. Gather the snails and cut them apart or dip them in boiling hot water. Place them in a closed plastic bag and throw it in the garbage or dig them down. This is no fun, but you have to if you want to get rid of them.

To protect the growths against snail attacks, you can draw up rings of lime around the plants, make a barrier out of tape with metal threads, set up low electric fences, build a steel edge around the bed that's bent outwards so that the snails can't get in, use snail poison, or set snail traps that you can buy.

There are certain flowers that scare the snails off. Plant them as border growths and you might keep the snails away.

A snail safe edge around the bed—bent plate.

If you are really struggling with snails it can be a good idea to take away your compost for a couple of years until you have the problem under control. The snails use compost piles to lay eggs and they also stay there during winter.

Other kinds of snails are grey field slug, white-lipped snail, and burgundy snail. They also hate barriers of lime or ashes on leaves.

Ants

You should be careful if you have ants in your vegetable garden. They are not as harmless as they may seem. Ants milk sugar off of the lice, and as a thank you, they protect the lice against enemies. Ants can also gather seeds that you've just planted or sap root systems in the growth bed so that the plants die out. If you see ants, follow them to see what they're up to! Not rarely they will guide you to a small problem you can then take care of.

Ant houses need to be dug up and removed. If there are no plant roots to consider, you can pour boiling hot water in the whole to fully exterminate the rest of the house. If you can't find the house, just the ants, you can repeatedly over a couple of days pour hot water in their path system to make them move. Some people say that ants are scared of tansy. It could be worth watering with tansy water around the plants where the ants seem to hang out.

LARGER PESTS

Voles and Moles

Field Cole, European water vole, and moles are rodents that move by making underground pathway systems. They eat roots, tubers, and onions in the ground and they can be very damaging.

To prevent the problem, it is important to hold the edges around the vegetable garden clean from weeds and tall grass, as this is where the voles are comfortable. You can also blend rough crushed stone in the soil so that it gets harder for the animals to move their way through.

If they have entered your vegetable garden you can use vibration devices that send uncomfortable vibrations into the ground. You can also try digging down empty bottles, with the neck up so that the wind sends wheezing sounds down the bottles—the voles usually doesn't like that either. You can also set traps.

Rats and Mice

The greatest risk of getting mice or rats is if you have compost that's not turned or worked very often. Especially if you put your vegetable leftovers in it. Rats and mice can mess up the vegetable garden, but first and foremost they can move inside your house, and we therefore want to keep them away.

Rats are habitual animals that do not like disturbances in their routines. A compost that you fork now and then, turn, and water is not an ideal home for these animals. This is a reason why you should not have your compost hidden in a corner of the garden but next to the vegetable garden where you see it and remember to poke it, fork it, and turn it often. This way you decrease the risk of a mice and rat invasion.

If you are really bothered by rodents, it is important to get in touch with your municipality or an exterminator to get advice on how to get rid of them.

Roe Deer, Deer, Rabbits and Hares.

We're not the only ones that like vegetables. Wild animals that enter the garden to snack or just make a mess are a problem in almost everywhere. The damage increases with the size of the animal, which makes it crucial to have game protection in the areas where animals frequent.

Roe deer, deer, and moose are best kept away with high fences. They have to be at least 6 feet

(2 m) tall to work. A fence can be combined with plank and dressed in climbing growths to frame the vegetable garden nicely. Roe deer can, to a certain extent, be scared off with smells of blood meal or dog. You can buy liquids and scented pillows or you can make your own blend with ammonia and blood meal that you ball in shearling or similar and place on sticks here and there in the garden.

Movement detectors that are attached to a water pistol can have surprising effects. You just need to remember to turn it off before you go to visit the garden. There are different varieties of this that you can buy.

Hares and rabbits dig underneath fences that are not partly dug in the ground. They can, to a certain extent, be scared off with the help of the same scents as for roe deer.

ABOUT WEEDS

Weeds are basically everything that grows where we don't want it. But the weeds that create the biggest problems are the kind that spread, grow quickly, and will settle in on the expense of other plants. We differentiate between seed weeds and root weeds. Seed weeds spread through seeds and root weeds spread with both seeds and roots.

People say that "You should remove the weed before it shows." I think this is a good idea to keep in mind, but there's not always time. But if you do take the weeds while they are still tiny, you can save yourself a lot of work in the future. A good trick to decrease weeds in the garden is to cover cultivate so that the weeds have trouble breaking though. In areas where you don't cultivate, you can fork the soil often to disturb the roots.

Seed Weeds

Some of the most bothersome seed weeds are thistles, dandelion, pondweed, and wild mustard. The same goes for them as has been previously mentioned about fighting weeds, but if you didn't have time to weed in time and they have blossomed, you can benefit much from plucking the flowers before they start seeding. Later you can take the actual plants when you have more time. You can put the plants on the compost, but the seeds should be in the trash.

Root Weeds

Root weeds are a hassle. But you can fight them with the right method and a good amount of patience. The problem is that the root weeds can survive even if just a tiny piece of the root system is left in the ground, which makes the war against them a lot more difficult than the one against seed weeds. Some common root weeds are, ground elder, creeping buttercup, field bindweed, and couch grass.

AN ELEVATED BED ON TOP OF THE GRASS

The best methods for fighting root weeds are exhaustion and starvation. The easiest way to achieve this is to cover the weed-invaded soil with something that doesn't let daylight through. Without light there is no photosynthesis, and without photosynthesis, the growth will starve and the roots will ultimately die. But it can take a long time and sometimes you want to get the crop started despite the fact that the ground is filled with root weeds. It works just fine to cultivate in heightened beds on top of the cover material. Do the following:

- Remove as much of the weeds as possible.
- Decide where you want the beds and mark the area.
- Cover all the soil between the beds with a black ground cloth that lets water through, but not light.
- Then build edges for the beds, they should be 10 inches (25 cm) tall.
- Cover the bottom of the bed with thick cardboard or a thick layer of newspapers. Water the paper well.
- Fill the beds with new weed-free soil. It can be bought or taken from somewhere else in the garden.
- To make the vegetable garden more beautiful you can cover the ground cloth in the paths with straw, bark, or gravel.

During the first years, you can grow plants that do not need more than 10 (25 cm) inches soil depth so that the roots do not break through the cardboard in the bottom. Lettuce, red beets, small carrots, bush beans, and more, will think that the depth is enough. You can plant the growths that demand more depth in a sack or in a pot for now. Don't dig in the beds for the first couple of years, because that

will break the cardboard barrier in the bottom too soon. If you need to work the soil then do it carefully with a cultivator and a planting shovel.
There is nothing wrong with building planting beds with ground cloth in the bottom, but in that case you need to increase the soil depth a bit so that the roots have more room. The benefit of cardboard is that it decomposes over time and turns into soil. You don't have to have a plastic barrier between the soil layers that a ground cloth will always make.
It is definitely better if you want to have healthy microlife in the planting bed and give the roots access to minerals from deeper layers.

THE SMALL PHARMACY

There is a whole group of plant care products that you can make yourself, and they are cheap and fun to take care of. In my medicine closet for the vegetable garden you can find various flasks and cans with "good-to-have-blends" that I use more or less often. Here are some recipes and directions for a few base products:

Soap Solution
This blend is first and foremost good against leaf lice. I always recommend that you first try to pick as much of the lice as possible by hand and crush them. Afterwards you can spray so that possible lice that are left die. Repeat the treatment multiple times.

5 cups (1 liter) water
1/4 cup (1/2 dl) sap
1 tbsp methylated spirit

Blend everything and pour into a spray bottle. Stir the bottle or shake it before you spray. Always test on one leaf first to make sure that the growth is not damaged by the solution. If spots occur you can dilute the blend with more water.

Horsetail Tea
Field horsetail contains many nutrients and minerals, first and foremost silicone that has an inhibitory effect on fungi diseases. You can spray the horsetail tea over the entire plant as a preventative measure, but also when the plant is already infected with a fungal disease. Remove all of the infected part of the plant and then spray the entire plant; repeat for a couple of weeks. Never spray in direct sunlight, but rather in the morning or on grey days.

2 lbs (1 kg) field horsetail
2 1/2 gallon (10 liters) water

Cut the field horsetail in pieces and place them in a large pot (it is a good idea to do this in two batches). Cover with the water and let it come to a boil. Boil for 20 minutes and then turn the heat off. Let everything sit in the pot for another 24 hours and then sift. Dilute the liquid to a mild tea-color before you use.

Garlic Water
Garlic water is mostly used against mildew attacks, but can also help keep certain insects away, as they simply think that the leaves are disgusting to eat. Remove infected leaves and spray the remaining leaves with the liquid. Repeat the procedure multiple times with a few days break in between. Remember that everything you spray will have a taste and smell of garlic.

5 garlic cloves
9 cups (2 liters water)

Crush three garlic cloves and place them in water, let it come to a boil. Remove the pot from the heat and let it cool completely. Press two fresh garlic cloves and add to the water, let it sit for another few hours. Sift out the garlic and pour the water into a spray bottle. Test on a single leaf before you spray the entire plant. If the leaf gets marks on it, then dilute the liquid with water.

Wood Ashes
This powder is used to sprinkle, first and foremost, cabbage growths to prevent attacks of flies and Lepidoptera larvae. It can also be used against carrot fleas and is then powdered over the carrot top. You can also spread it out as snail barriers. In that case you pour it out as strings around the plants.

I usually save wood ashes from my fireplace in winter time. If you do not have a fireplace you can simply skip the ashes and use only Algomin or lime. You can also use the ashes alone, although I think it sticks better to the leaves if you blend it together.

1 part wood ash
1 part Algomin or garden lime

Blend everything and crush in a mortar so you get a nice even powder. Empty it in an air-tight container so that it doesn't lump together. This disappears quickly, so make a 10 cup (2 liters) batch while you're at it. Sprinkle the powder over the leaves of the plant. Repeat the treatment as often as needed. If it is windy or raining, the ashes will disappear, and also the effect pretty fast, you have to sprinkle the leaves again.

Bicarbonate Spray
Bicarbonate is a wonder material that can be used for everything from polishing silver to cleaning your hair. I use it against mildew in the vegetable garden. It affects the mushrooms chemically so that they can't multiply.

1 tbsp bicarbonate
4 cups (1 liter water)
1 tbsp canola oil or soap

Blend everything so that the bicarbonate dissolves completely. Spray-treat the entire growth, but never spray in direct sunlight. Make sure that the undersides of the leaves are sprayed as well. Repeat the treatment multiple times.

RECOMMENDED READING

Bartley, Jennifer R., *Designing the New Kitchen Garden*. Timber Press Inc. 2006.
Brickell, Christopher m.fl., *Encyclopedia of Gardening,* Dorling Kindersley Limited 2002.
Flinck, Maria, *Tusen år i trädgården*. Tidens förlag 1994.
Fowler, Alys, *Slow Gardening*. Norstedts 2010.
Hansson, Marie och Björn, *Köksträdgårdens historia*. Norstedts 2011.
Israelsson, Lena, *Handbok för köksträdgården*. Bonnier Fakta 2011.
Kvant, Christel och Palmstierna, Inger, *Vår trädgårdsbok*. Norstedts 2009.
Pettersson, Maj-Lis och Åkesson, Ingrid, *Trädgårdens växtskydd*. Natur och Kultur 2011.
Plöninge, Philippe, *Den goda jorden*. Prisma 2003.

MAGAZINES:
Odlingsbeskrivningar för ekologiska grönsaker, Jordbruksverket 2003.
www.sjv.se
Faktablad för trädgård-fritid, Sveriges Lantbruksuniversitet.
www.slu.se

INTERNET:
Franchi fröer, www.gourmetgarage.dk
Kokopelli Seed Foundation, www.kokopelli-seed-foundation.com
Cultivating forum, www.odla.nu
The Swedish Horticultural Society, www.tradgard.org
Runåbergs Fröer, www.runabergsfroer.se
Sarah Ravens Garden, www.sarahraven.com
Örtagården, www.ortagarden.com

Tips for Dark Winter Days

Order new seed catalogues or browse all of the catalogues online.

Tool Day
When the spring comes it will be nice to have clean, freshly oiled, and sharpened tools.

Drawing Day
Half of the fun is planning the kitchen garden—make a plan, dream, fantasize, play.

Build
Nail together cultivation benches and compost sieves.

Rinse and clean
Clean fiber clothes and rinse sowing trays and pots.

Grow indoors
An indoor crop on your kitchen counter that works year-round.

Spice garden in your kitchen window
Buy ready spice plants in the store. Replant them, fertilize with liquid fertilizer, and harvest.

Read
Be inspired by the many different gardening books.

ALSO AVAILABLE

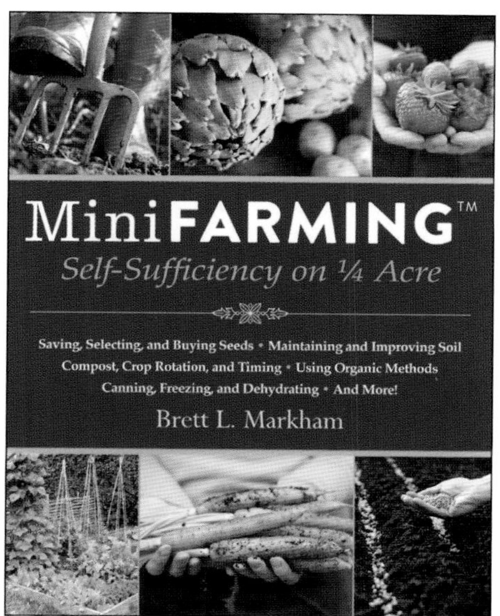

Mini Farming

Self-Sufficiency on 1/4 Acre

by Brett L. Markham

Mini Farming describes a holistic approach to small-area farming that will show you how to produce 85 percent of an average family's food on just a quarter acre—and earn $10,000 in cash annually while spending less than half the time that an ordinary job would require. Even if you have never been a farmer or a gardener, this book covers everything you need to know to get started: buying and saving seeds, starting seedlings, establishing raised beds, soil fertility practices, composting, dealing with pest and disease problems, crop rotation, farm planning, and much more. Because self-sufficiency is the objective, subjects such as raising backyard chickens and home canning are also covered along with numerous methods for keeping costs down and production high. Materials, tools, and techniques are detailed with photographs, tables, diagrams, and illustrations.

$18.95 Paperback • ISBN 978-1-60239-984-6

ALSO AVAILABLE

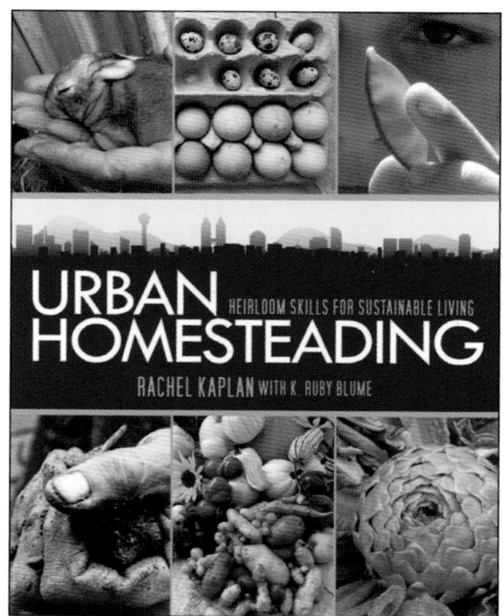

Urban Homesteading

Heirloom Skills for Sustainable Living

by Rachel Kaplan with K. Ruby Blume

The urban homesteading movement is spreading rapidly across the nation. *Urban Homesteading* is the perfect "back-to-the-land" guide for urbanites who want to reduce their impact on the environment. Full of practical information, as well as inspiring stories from people already living the urban homesteading life, this colorful guide is an approachable guide to learning to live more ecologically in the city. The book embraces the core concepts of localization (providing our basic needs close to where we live), self-reliance (re-learning that food comes from the ground, not the grocery store; learning to do things ourselves), and sustainability (giving back at least as much as we take). Readers will find concise how-to information that they can immediately set into practice, from making solar cookers to growing tomatoes in a barrel to raising chickens in small spaces to maintaining mental serenity in the fast-paced city environment. Full of beautiful full-color photographs and illustrations, and plenty of step-by-step instructions, this is a must-have handbook for city folk with a passion for the simple life.

$19.95 Paperback • ISBN 978-1-61608-054-9

ALSO AVAILABLE

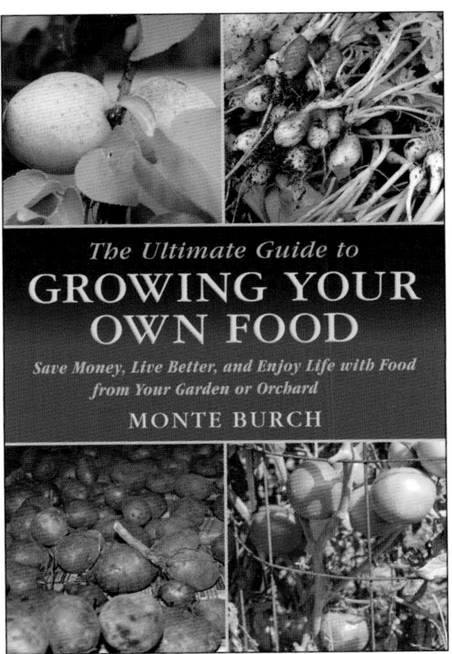

The Ultimate Guide to Growing Your Own Food

Save Money, Live Better, and Enjoy Life with Food from Your Garden or Orchard

by Monte Burch

Growing your own food is a hot topic today because of the high cost of transporting food long distances, the heightened problem of diseases caused by commercially grown foods, and concerns of the overuse of chemicals in mass food production. Many people—from White House executives to inner-city kids—have recently discovered the benefits of homegrown vegetables and fruits. Community gardens, and even community canning centers, are increasingly popular and have turned rooftop gardening into a great and healthy food source. And on a smaller scale, some plants can even be grown in containers for the smallest backyard or patio. The possibilities for growing your own food are endless!

$16.95 Paperback • ISBN 978-1-61608-309-0

ALSO AVAILABLE

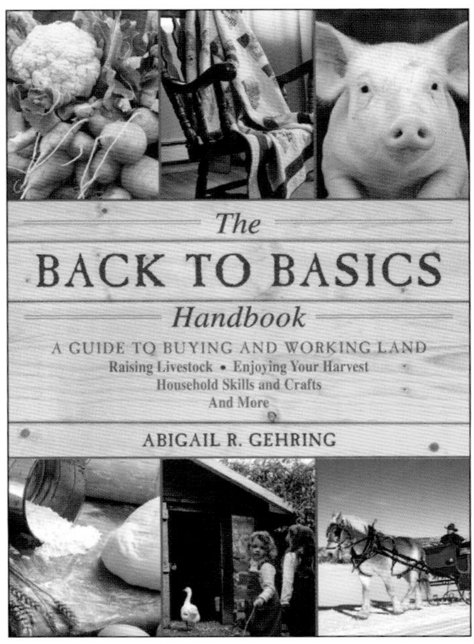

The Back to Basics Handbook

A Guide to Buying and Working Land, Raising Livestock, Enjoying Your Harvest, Household Skills and Crafts, and More

Edited by Abigail R. Gehring

Anyone who wants to learn basic living skills—the kind employed by our forefathers—and adapt them for a better life in the twenty-first century need look no further than this eminently useful, full-color guide. With hundreds of projects, step-by-step sequences, photographs, charts, and illustrations, *The Back to Basics Handbook* will help you dye your own wool with plant pigments, graft trees, raise chickens, craft a hutch table with hand tools, and make treats such as blueberry peach jam and cheddar cheese. The truly ambitious will find instructions on how to build a log cabin or an adobe brick homestead.

$14.95 Paperback • ISBN 978-1-61608-261-1

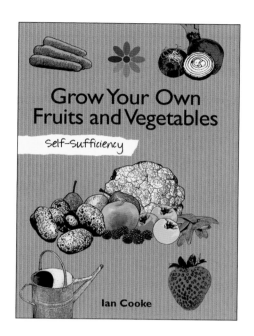